RECIPES *for* LIVING

Sandra Dubs
with Graham Davidson

Mum and Omi are in their happy place, preparing dinner in the kitchen of our Melbourne home. Mum is the main cook with Omi assisting while regaling stories of her youth, intermingled with the latest news of the day. They're speaking mostly in Hungarian, which I don't understand. But I manage to pick up bits of what they're saying when they slip into German, a language my parents and older brother are fluent in.

It's Sunday afternoon and, looking for something to do, I ask Mum to play a board game with me. But she is busy preparing the main ingredient for her delicious family favourite, Vinete (a traditional Romanian eggplant salad), and Hungarian stuffed peppers. Omi is peeling the apples for her compote. All of it made with fresh produce from the weekly shopping trip to the Prahran Market.

"Mum, can I help cook?"

"You can set the table, please," she replies.

I enthusiastically lay out the cutlery, but then I'm still bored and restless.

Mum looks at me and smiles, then hands me a pie dish with a removable base.

I give her a puzzled look, aware that there's no cake mix ready for the dish I'm holding.

In the past I've helped her put it into this same tray, licking the bowl afterwards whenever the mix contains chocolate (my favourite is her chocolate sour cherry cake).

"Go outside," she says. "Take the dish with you… try and find something to do with it."

I hesitate before heading outside, unsure of what she means.

The late afternoon sun is shining as I sit in the yard next to the garden beds, clinging to my dish. What to do?

I take some soil, put it in the dish and make my way to the nearby tap.

I spend the following hour engrossed in making mud pies, using a stick to make various designs in my beautiful mud creations.

Sandra Dubs, aged eight

Also from Sandra Dubs:

My Wholefood Community Plant-Based Cookbook

Special thanks to all those who have contributed to making this book possible through input either in person or via zoom, helping to make sense of the timeline and context of events throughout the years.

Recipes for Living
ISBN 978 1 76109 914 4
Copyright © Sandra Dubs
Edited by Brian Purcell
Cover design by Graham Davidson
Typesetting and book design by Rack and Rune Publishing
rackandrune.com

First published 2025 by
Ginninderra Press
PO Box 2 Bentleigh 3204
ginninderrapress.com.au

*In honour of my parents whose warm hands shared
many ingredients to nourish my life*

*For those with whom I have connected and who have
borne witness to my life
For those I have met briefly on my path
For those who are curious
Here is the pathway into my recipes for living.*

Contents

Part I
Getting Started

It started with a Bang!	9
About Mum	12
The Cover Story	18
About Dad	21
Going to Goa	29
Released	39
Time to Move	42
Heading to Cancun	46
Dubs from Dubs	63
The Sandwich Girl	71
Mullum	75

Part II
Building a Life

Back to Melbourne	83
India, 1982	87
A Bali Holiday	99
Stepping Up	103
Return of the Lump	110
Auction!	115
A New Approach	117
Manna	128

CBD Health Cafe	140
Life in Bali	145
Middle Park	167
Taiwan	171
Sedona Vortex	174
Passion	184
Finding a Voice	187
Bangalore	198
Aloha Hawaii	206
Thailand	211
A Helping Hand	215
Kramer	221
Back to the States	223
Natural Therapies Expo	232
Red String	234

Part III
Staying Alive

Mammogram	241
The Hotel Cabrini	247
For the Love of Music	262
Time to do a Cookbook	272
...and Time to Re-energise	277
Matters of the Heart	284
Living with Grief	286
What about the Lungs?	291
The Fall	295

My Sanctuary	301
Something to Write About	321
It's Back	325
Chemo Conversations	351
Why not take a Holiday?	359
One More Bite of the Big Apple	367
A Last Word	374
Epilogue	378
Acknowledgements	383
A Word From the Scribe	384

Recipes

Sandy's tahini miso sauce	130
Sandy's toasted seed mix	131
Carrot, beetroot arame salad	132
Tofu pouches (inari sushi)	134
Cooking brown rice for sushi	136
Vega morning tea	177
Kale miso soup	249
Broccoli avocado soup	253
Scrambled turmeric tofu	308
My energising alkalizing protein smoothie	310
My raw live food green energising smoothie	310
My favourite drinks	312
Polenta	314
Homemade berry chia jam	335
Soft millet with cauliflower	338
Quick comfort sweet potato mash	340
Green miso pesto	340
Stewed organic fruit with organic coconut yoghurt	342
Cucumber ice cubes	344
Red lentil beetroot soup	346

Part I
Getting Started

"Happiness equals reality minus expectations"
—Lori Gottlieb
2019- Maybe You Should Talk to Someone

Passport photo, aged 17

It started with a Bang!

Ian kissed me before he got out of the car and said, "I'll see you tomorrow." His smile was infectious. I watched him as he walked from my car to the entrance of Melbourne's Trinity College where he had a dorm. It was as if he could feel my eyes boring into him, beckoning, when he looked back over his shoulder and waved calling out, "Thanks for the lift." I blew him a kiss then drove off.

Luxuriating in the warmth of young love, I stopped at the traffic lights on the intersection of Peel Street and Victoria Street. The light changed to green, and I moved through the intersection.

Wham!

A massive jolt to the passenger side of my bright orange Datsun 180B sent it hurtling several metres.

It all became a bit of a blur. So much so that I can't recall much of what happened after that. Someone had come flying through a red light and I hadn't been aware of them until the impact.

My 180B? That was a write off. The police came and contacted my father. I have a vague memory of Dad organising a tow truck and Ian arriving to give me a lift back home. At the time it seemed I was okay, just a bit shaken.

The next morning, I woke up and went out to the kitchen.

"What's that lump on your neck?" asked Mum.

You've got to love my mother. She didn't miss a thing.

I'd gone to bed not thinking much of the sore neck I had after the accident. And now, here I was the following morning in the kitchen, with Mum checking out this mysterious lump that seemed to have manifested itself overnight. I could tell from the expression on her face she was concerned. She showed my grandmother, Omi, then called Dad into the room for his opinion while she continued her own examination. I could feel her fingers pressing into my flesh as they worked their way around the lump, defining its parameters. Dad looked on, concern writ large in his eyes as they followed Mum's probing fingertips.

"We'd better get this looked at." she said.

Dad nodded in agreement then went straight to the phone to call Doctor Goldberg, a friend of the family, who urged him to bring me straight to his practice. Having then had the chance to inspect the mysterious lump for himself, he organised for me to see a specialist to remove it without delay so a biopsy could be performed.

We were soon at St Vincent's Hospital Melbourne. There, we spoke to Professor David Penington, the Dean of Melbourne University Medical School at the time. He organised the surgery without hesitation.

A few days later, the results of the biopsy came through. My concerned parents and I went to see him in his private rooms where we sat down and he asked us, "Have you heard of Hodgkin's disease? It's otherwise known as Hodgkin lymphoma. It's a cancer of the lymph nodes."

Pragmatic as they were my parents asked in unison, "How advanced?"

"It's stage 2A. We've caught it early enough that we should be able to treat it."

It was early July, 1977.

I was just 20 years old.

Up until that moment, everything in my life had been as wonderful as any young woman could hope for. I had job placement at Fell & Starkey (now known as Ernst & Young) as part of the third year of my accountancy degree at Royal Melbourne Institute of Technology, otherwise known as RMIT. I was in my 'sandwich year', where the course required a year of job placement before the final year of study.

Ian and I had met briefly the year before, during the second year of our *Bachelor Of Business (Accountancy)* degrees. Ian, whose older brother had a permanent job at Fell and Starkey, had a placement there as well.

Our relationship had started at a training camp put on by Fell & Starkey each year for newcomers to the business.

RMIT had been a wonderful experience in so many ways, particularly with how it helped develop my network of friends. Among them were Greg and Jennifer, a truly amazing couple who were engaged at the time. Greg was studying medicine while Jennifer was doing fine arts. It seems so ironic. In those days, we'd all hang out at the beach. Jennifer had a tan that was the envy of everyone, while Greg is now one of the nation's leading dermatologists. The idea of spending endless hours lazing in the sun now seems so ridiculous. At the time though, we all loved it.

About Mum

Before getting too much further into the story, I think it's important to tell you a little bit more about my mother. Without Mum having noticed that lump on my neck and showing so much concern, things may have played out very differently. It could have ended up being so much worse.

She was an extraordinary woman who played a huge role in my life.

You may be thinking *there's nothing unusual about that. Doesn't every mother play a hugely significant role in the lives of their children?*

Of course they do!

But, the depth of my relationship with my mother was always special to me.

She was the love of my life, something I became more and more aware of as time has gone by. Even now, years after her passing, I feel her closeness every day.

Born in the Romanian town of Timișoara in 1926, Mum was nineteen when the Russian liberators rode into town sitting on their tanks at the end of World War II.

Timișoara suffered damage from both the Allied and Axis bombing raids, especially during the second half of 1944. On August 23rd of that year, Romania, which until then was a member of the Axis, declared war on Nazi Germany and joined the Allies.

At just nineteen, my mother became an active member of Gordonia Maccabi Hatzair, a Jewish Zionist socialist group. While attending a meeting in Budapest in early 1945 she met my father, Martin, for the first time. She described the encounter as love at first sight, for both of them. My mother told my grandmother about him and a meeting soon followed. My grandparents had divorced when my mother had been quite young. So, she'd been raised by my grandmother as a single parent.

My parents, classified now as displaced refugees, decided they wanted to go to *Eretz Yisrael* (Hebrew for the *Land of Israel*) which was referred to as *British Palestine* while it was under British rule. Their plan to get there entailed volunteering to escort a group of orphaned children. These children had come out of the concentration camps and were therefore also classified as displaced refugees. There were sixteen of them, all aged between nine and nineteen. They spoke Hungarian, a language my mother understood. These children shared tragic stories with my parents about the camps. The tales of what the children had endured shocked my parents to the core. It was the first time they'd heard about the true depth of what had transpired in the concentration camps during the Holocaust.

The journey took them first by train to Austria and on to Italy.

My parents were sad to leave their families in Romania behind. But, as a young couple, they were leaning into their future. They were just two of around fifty-thousand Jewish refugees who passed through Italy between 1944 and 1951, full of hope as they moved towards an unknown future.

Then, Mum fell pregnant. Because of this, they weren't permitted to board the ship that was part of the *Aliyeh Bet* program (the Hebrew term that refers to the clandestine immigration of Jews to Palestine between 1920 and 1948).

Instead, they settled, teenage entourage in tow, in Puglia, a southern region that forms the heel of Italy's boot. It was there, in 1946, that my brother Michael was born.

To be able to work in Italy, they needed documentation that today would seem unacceptable. Presented very much like a passport, it was called a *Certificate of Capacity*, and was issued by the *Society for the Promotion of Handicrafts and of Industrial and Agricultural Work Among the Jews in Italy*.

They were never able to settle in one place for long during their time in Italy. After moving first to Milan for a couple of years, and then Rome for two more, Mum and Dad were unsuccessful in their efforts to obtain the work permits required to remain in Italy. Given the choice between the United States, Argentina or Australia, they came to the conclusion that Australia would be the better fit.

Up to that point, my parents had spent five years in displacement camps run by the *American Jewish Joint Distribution Committee*, an organisation that's spent over a hundred years assisting the Jewish community around the world. To be able to emigrate to Australia they needed additional identity papers to the work permits they'd been issued.

So, identity papers were issued to them, the emigration request was processed and, in the Italian port of Genoa, they boarded the *Continental*, a Panama-flagged ship with an Italian crew.

After a long journey across the Indian Ocean, they disembarked in Fremantle and found themselves confronted by the harsh reality of how different their new home would be to what they'd been accustomed in Europe. Taking in the sight of streets lined with weatherboard houses, they pondered whether they may have made a dreadful mistake.

Their original intention was to move on to Sydney after their arrival in Western Australia. However, while in transit, they met a fellow immigrant on the wharf in Melbourne. My parents knew him from having spent a holiday together while they were still in Italy. He told them, "I like to be here when the boats come in, to see if there's anyone I know on board." This was a common practice among the Jewish people living in Melbourne at the time. He suggested they should consider staying in Melbourne and explained that it would be harder for them to find accommodation in Sydney with a small child. "There's a nice little bungalow that I know is available. You could move in there, it's on Marine Parade."

Emergency Identity Certificates issued by the Liaison and Civil Affairs Branch of Italy's Displaced Persons and Repatriation Division.

COMMONWEALTH OF AUSTRALIA.

Nationality and Citizenship Act 1948-1953.

CERTIFICATE OF NATURALIZATION AS AN AUSTRALIAN CITIZEN.

WHEREAS Eva LUBS has applied for a Certificate of Naturalization as an Australian Citizen, alleging with respect to her self the particulars set out on the reverse side hereof, and has satisfied me that she has fulfilled the conditions laid down in the *Nationality and Citizenship Act* 1948-1953 for the grant of such a Certificate:

NOW THEREFORE I, the Minister of State for Immigration, hereby grant, in pursuance of the *Nationality and Citizenship Act* 1948-1953 this Certificate of Naturalization, whereby, subject to the provisions of the said Act and of any other law affecting the rights of naturalized persons, the said

Eva LUBS

shall, as from the date upon which she swears or affirms allegiance to Her Majesty Queen Elizabeth the Second, her heirs and successors, and swears to, or affirms that she will, observe faithfully the laws of Australia and fulfil her duties as an Australian citizen, become entitled to all political and other rights, powers and privileges, and become subject to all obligations, duties and liabilities to which an Australian citizen or a British subject is entitled or subject, and have to all intents and purposes the status of an Australian citizen and British subject.

Dated this tenth day of March One thousand nine hundred and fifty-five.

Issued by authority of the Minister of State for Immigration

Authorized Officer.

Minister of State for Immigration.

CERTIFICATE BY JUDGE, MAGISTRATE OR PERSON APPROVED BY THE MINISTER.

I, Edward C. MITTY do hereby certify that on the Eighteenth day of July 19 55. the grantee of this Certificate

Eva LUBS

appeared before me at St. Kilda swore allegiance to Her Majesty Queen Elizabeth the Second, her heirs and successors, and swore to observe faithfully the laws of Australia and fulfil her duties as an Australian citizen.

Signature J.P.

Title Mayor, City of St. Kilda.

[OVER.

Mum's naturalization certificate

When Mum and Dad met the owners of the bungalow they got into conversation.

"What did you do for work in Europe?"

"I'm an optician," said Dad.

"I worked as a seamstress," replied Mum.

"Oh?" the owners gave a smile of reassurance. "We know a man who owns a factory in Russell Street. They make Ladies suits there. We'll introduce you and see if he might have a job for you."

They employed Mum straight away. After so many years as displaced refugees, they had found the city that would remain their home for the rest of their lives.

A Tradition of Heroic Actions

The Suppression of the Hungarian revolution of 1888 created a massive refugee crisis when thousands of Jews were forced to flee the country by boat. With neither Rumania nor Hungary being willing to accept them, they found themselves stranded in what were effectively floating prisons on the Danube.

With the refugees facing potential starvation and disease, one man, a rabbi named Rabbi Jacob Prerau (my mother's grandfather) stepped forward. He established a kitchen on the river to prepare food that could be taken out to the refugees on small boats and then met with Baron Rothschild in Vienna to plead asylum on behalf of those stuck in limbo. Baron Rothschild took on the task of helping them. For his efforts, Rabbi Jacob Prerau was recommended for a medal of honour.

The Cover Story

"It was the car accident." What a great cover story that guy who crashed into my car had so unwittingly handed me.

Can you blame me for wanting privacy and avoiding the risk of ending up trapped in an endless maze of people's curiosity? Did I really want to face their well-intentioned questions about the real reason behind my spleen's removal?

Yes, that's right... my spleen was going to be removed.

My parents were adamant. There was little to be gained from the barrage of inevitable questions that would follow if all our friends and our broader community knew the truth.

It was confronting enough just knowing my life would now be forever impacted by the big 'C' word. That on its own was more than enough for a twenty-year-old to deal with.

Aside from my boyfriend Ian, there were just two of my friends my parents *did* feel comfortable sharing the diagnosis with. They were Greg and Jennifer. Being unsure how I would feel about keeping the news of my condition private, Mum actually asked them what their thoughts were about letting others know. They both agreed that it would be better to exercise discretion. Mum was greatly relieved to know that I had friends who would back her up, and whose opinions I would be likely to respect with regard to keeping the situation within the family.

It was during this time that I came to realise I prefer privacy. I didn't want to have this news spread either. I wanted to walk into my future without the stigma of having my cancer as everyone's talking point. I know it's a bit of a cliché now, but I didn't want to be 'defined by my cancer'.

It might sound counter-intuitive that a lump on the neck should lead to having your spleen removed. But Professor Penington had explained it in a way that left my parents and I in no doubt that there was little choice other than to proceed as soon as possible.

To be honest, prior to my diagnosis I'd never given much thought to what a spleen is and what it does for you. Typically, the spleen is about the size of your fist. Purple in colour, it's located in the upper left area of the abdomen. If you're trying to poke around to find where it is as you read this, don't bother. It's one of the organs protected by your rib cage. An important part of the immune system, the spleen doesn't only filter the blood, it also acts as a warehouse for your body's red blood cells, white blood cells and platelets.

No doubt you're likely still curious though as to why such an important component of the immune system needed to be removed.

Professor Penington explained how the thinking at the time was that, when Hodgkin lymphoma starts to metastasize, the first place it spreads to is the spleen. So, the wisest course of action was to remove the spleen as a precautionary measure. This would happen before commencing the intense localised ionising radiation therapy, attacking the cancer cells already detected in my lymph nodes. Your lymph nodes are a network of bean-shaped structures constituting another crucial part of the immune system's arsenal. He went on to tell us the body was good at compensating, that I would be able to live a normal and full life without my spleen. But it wouldn't be without its challenges, as my immune system would still be compromised. I'd have to be wary of any sort of infection, scratch or cut.

There was more to it than that though. They didn't want to operate just to remove the spleen. Since I was about to receive trailblazing cancer treatment, there were precautions they wanted to take to reduce the risk of the radiation impacting other parts of my body. They made a much larger incision than required to remove the spleen, as they wanted to push the other organs as far away from the mantle, or upper torso, as possible.

It was only one week earlier that I'd been involved in the car accident that led to that little lump on my neck revealing itself. The trauma to my neck from the accident must have pushed something forward that had already been lingering in the background, exposing it so it could be seen. Now, here I was in St Vincent's Private Hospital in Melbourne, about to have one of my body's organs removed.

I was so fortunate and blessed to have Ian's support. This boy I'd become so close to made a massive difference when he chose to lie next to me on my hospital bed, just to be close and help me feel I wasn't having to face this on my own.

There were also friends who came to visit. But none of them would ever know the truth that I'd shared with so few. Instead, they all heard the concocted cover story—"The car accident... it caused a rupture in my spleen... it had to be removed. There was no other choice."

When I look back on it now, there's not a great deal beyond that I can recall about my stay in hospital for the splenectomy, but I still carry that scar. It runs from my rib-cage down past my belly button. To this day, it's a constant reminder of how they removed my spleen and moved inner organs in preparation for the radiation treatment that was to follow.

About Dad

When diagnosed with cancer, you discover just how quickly the hospital system rolls into gear as your treatment gets underway. I was about to benefit from what was seen at the time as significant strides forward in the use of Mantle Radiation Therapy (MRT). It was the cutting-edge technique used to treat Hodgkin lymphoma from the mid-seventies through until the nineties.

Having wasted no time in being operated on to remove the spleen, I was booked in to commence a series of forty daily radiation treatments, as soon as it was deemed that I'd recovered enough from the splenectomy. The first session at the Peter MacCallum Cancer Centre in Melbourne was a mere three or four weeks after the surgery.

The target lines were drawn on my chest with thick felt tip pens. Protective lead-lined sheets were laid around the borders of the radiation target area, which was the bulk of my chest, armpits, and neck. My arms were raised during each session, so the armpits were more exposed to the therapy. Each treatment took around two hours. And each of the treatments left my tongue and the back of my neck burning, making eating, or swallowing anything at all quite difficult. I also felt hot all the time. Then, after the first few treatments, the hair on the back of my neck fell out, as did the hair in my armpits. Fortunately, I had long hair then so the bald area underneath could be covered by the remaining longer hair from above. Interestingly, my armpit hair has never grown back (I guess that's at least something to be grateful for).

Mum and Dad drove me the fifteen kilometres to the first session to offer support and observe the process. After that we decided it would be best if I drove myself to each of my subsequent appointments. I was fine with that. I'd somehow already developed an inner strength thanks to the rational conversations and support from my parents and trusty medical team. I decided it was best to surrender fully to the process, a strategy I would continue to employ when faced with adversity and challenges into the future. It was an important lesson learned early, and a central ingredient in my *recipes for living*.

After the third round of treatment, I made my way to Ian's room at Trinity College. I just wanted the comfort and warmth of feeling his arms around me; to have his gentle reassurance that everything was going to be alright. It was almost Friday night, a time when I usually had dinner with my family. We had traditionally observed the sabbath ritual of lighting candles for Friday night dinners, something that was particularly important to Omi.

I called home to let my parents know where I was but it was my brother, Michael, who answered the phone. Two words are all I've ever been able to remember from that brief conversation.

"Come home."

It was obviously something serious.

At the time, Ian and I assumed it must have been something related to Omi. Ian called his sister as she was close by. Then he drove me home in my car, his sister following behind in his car. I sat silent throughout the journey. The previous three sessions of radiation had left me feeling wiped out and I couldn't make sense of why Michael had answered the phone or his lack of explanation for the urgent need to return home.

We arrived and drove into our driveway. Despite having moved out years earlier, it was Michael who opened the big front door.

Mum stepped forward from behind him to stand by his side. Her big watery eyes told me what was wrong before Michael had the chance to say, "it's Dad."

Sometimes, it's those two-word sentences that have the biggest impact. Maybe he actually said more than that. Maybe everything else just disappeared into a hazy fog. But those were the only words he said that night that I remember, the only ones that seemed to matter. In among the blurred reality and shock of hearing this revelation my mother said something to me that cut through the fogginess of the moment and is burned into my memory even more than Michael's two-word statements. "Sandra, on Monday, you continue your treatment."

Looking back, I see what an extraordinary woman she was. Her ability to rise above the immediate emotional trauma of her grief and reaffirm the importance of maintaining my treatment regime astounds me to this day.

As it turns out, Dad had taken the day off work. In the morning he'd put on his favourite blue Adidas tracksuit with white strips... the tracksuit that he always wore when he wanted to be comfortable around the house. He went to do some errands and when he came home, he'd commented to Omi that he'd started to feel a slight pain in his chest. Concerned about what it may be, he decided to drive down the road to the doctor. As he lay down to be examined, he suffered a massive heart attack, right there at the doctor's surgery. This was a time before doctors had defibrillators on hand. So, the doctor had to call an ambulance. It was while the doctor was calling that ambulance that Dad passed.

It was Friday 26th of August 1977.

The funeral took place on Sunday.

On Monday I drove myself back to the Peter MacCallum Centre for the next round of treatment.

I can't begin to tell you just how much more difficult it was to raise my arms for that treatment than in the previous sessions. Tears streamed down my cheeks as I silently cried my way through the entire session.

I see when I look back that Mum was right. The treatment needed to proceed regardless. Fortunately, there was support on hand from the nursing staff.

It was only later that I would learn from my mother just how much my father had put in place to help while I was undergoing the radiation therapy.

My father had talked to my managers at Fell and Starkey after my diagnosis and offered to cover my wages during the treatment so they could keep me on. Whether or not they agreed to take dad's money, I don't know for sure. But thanks to him there was an arrangement of some type that was put in place to ensure I was kept on. This allowed me to complete the hours I needed working with them to attain my degree.

My father's death was a huge shock to our tight-knit Melbourne Jewish community.

His was a life that had been filled with purpose, commitment and hard work in many fields. As a young man, he had studied optometry in Romania. This helped him land his first job in Australia at Coles and Garrard, a major Melbourne optical firm in the 1950s. He later studied work safety at RMIT, which led to a job at General Motors Holden. There, he initiated an eye safety program and introduced the use of safety glasses within the workplace. He'd worked other jobs as well, even being employed at the popular Melbourne restaurant, Mario's, as a singing waiter. I cherish my memories of him walking around our home singing the Italian song, Volare. He did whatever was necessary to provide for his family.

With my father in front of the Olympic Tower in Munich, 1973

When Mum and Dad arrived in Australia with four-year-old Michael, they had little more than a couple of suitcases and a few pounds.

Dad adored my mother and had a deep love and affection for his mother-in-law and our extended family.

He was a charismatic man, and our home was regularly hosting parties where the music and dancing went on late into the night. While supposedly asleep, I would sneak out to spy on what was going on. I bore witness to many a conga line drifting through the house with rhythmic music playing and cocktails flowing. Perhaps that in some way inspired my love of throwing parties and organising gatherings.

Dad also possessed an admirable work ethic, a trait he likely picked up from his hard-working mother who'd been left to raise three boys on her own in Romania, her husband having left while their family was still young. She loved to cook and ran a home based restaurant for travelling salesman.

But there was so much more to the man than just his career and his love of family.

Throughout his life he extended himself to help others, always involved in charitable causes for the Jewish Community and Israel.

In 1973, he arranged passage for my Uncle Armin and his family out of the USSR and into Germany; being well over a decade before the collapse of the Soviet Union, this was an extraordinarily difficult process at the time. I was seventeen, and had the good fortune to accompany Dad when he flew to Rome to meet them. My uncle, his wife and their son were all doctors. As such, they were able to relocate and use their skills practising medicine in Germany. I met my uncle and his family in a small hotel room where they laid out plates of continental sausage, bread and vodka - on the bed! They'd brought the treats with them on the train from Moscow to celebrate their new life.

My father and I spent six weeks overseas together on that trip. We travelled through Israel and Europe, visiting relatives in Switzerland, Germany and even communist Romania.

It was a time when travel to places like Romania was well outside the normal travel plans for most people going through Europe.

Bucharest and Timişoara impressed me as being dull and drab. The people seemed oppressed and lacking in vitality. There was a sadness that first became apparent at the airport. But it was also permeating everyone we encountered in the streets, and everywhere else for that matter. This was Ceausescu's Romania, one of the most closed of the Soviet states. Wherever we went, the people seemed to be lacking that spark that we can so easily take for granted. People who recognised us as tourists weren't shy in asking if we had any Levi's Jeans or western cigarettes to give them.

There was one incident in particular though that will always stand out for me: the laughter when a hotel concierge in Bucharest, Romania's capital city, mistook me for being my father's partner rather than his daughter. Dad thought it was hilarious. While checking into the hotel, the concierge offered us the option of a queen-size bed, leaving Dad having to explain that I was his daughter. The concierge was hard to convince so we showed him my passport. When you consider that I was seventeen and Dad was fifty-three it's a sad reflection on social standards in Romania during that time.

Our time together on that trip was precious in a way I could never fully appreciate at the time. There were plenty of times on the trip when we clashed. The thing was, we hadn't had that much time together before, at least, not just the two of us. But we certainly learnt a lot about each other in those weeks spent abroad. Now, when I look back, I think those clashes were inevitable. The thing is, we were both quite similar in our sensitivities and both had forthright natures. Perhaps it was something to do with us both being Scorpios? My mother used to say that she was living with three Scorpios (Omi was one too) and that we were all just as passionate as each other about issues. There was never a dull moment when the three of us were around.

During my final year in high school, 1974, our family moved into what was my parents' dream home in the Melbourne suburb of Hawthorn East. It was extraordinary considering it was only two and a half decades earlier that they'd arrived in the country with so little.

Up to the end of his life, Dad continued giving to the community while he worked in property development. His passing left a huge hole in the community. He was only fifty-six, and I was twenty at the time of his passing.

For many years after he passed, I encountered people who knew and praised him. It was a tragedy to have lost him so early in life, but I am so proud to be able to say I'm his daughter.

Going to Goa

My brother, Michael, is ten years my senior. In 1972, when I was fifteen, he and his lovely girlfriend. Lilli, got married

They were important role models who inspired me with their lifestyle choices – choices that were so different to those of my friends and their siblings. The age difference opened my mind to attitudes and ideals that were outside the bubble of the Melbourne Jewish community and the Mount Scopus College scene that I was familiar with.

While I was at high school, Michael and Lilli travelled extensively around the hippie trail through Nepal, India, Morocco, South America and other countries. On their return to Australia they moved to Eltham, about thirty kilometres from their respective families. Eltham is located in an area often referred to as a "green wedge" or "Melbourne's lungs", a suburb with abundant natural bushland and green spaces, art communities and a high regard for environmental and sustainable practices.

Their move led to some concerned reactions from their holocaust-survivor parents. It was so new and unusual for them that their children would want to move away from the radius of the family community. Michael and Lilli's motivation to have more space and a more rustic environment surrounded by like-minded, nature loving people was initially difficult for all the parents concerned to comprehend. Eventually though, our whole family embraced it, enjoying good times in the warmth of Michael and Lilli's Eltham home. I loved hanging out

Michael and Lilli with their sons, Marlon and Joel and myself in Goa

there on weekends, listening to their travel stories. My nephews, Marlon and Joel, were born in Eltham and I also relished the opportunity to spend time with them.

Michael and Lilli grew their own vegetables, using them to prepare the most delicious vegetarian meals. With the help of friends, they'd hand-built a mud brick studio where Lilli spent time creating elaborate weavings. Michael developed his woodworking skills and was making furniture with a close friend. As a result, my parents reaped the benefits with a handmade teak wood dining suite along with jarrah wood coffee and side tables and a kauri pine blanket box. They're beautiful and, since my parents passing, these same furniture pieces adorn my own home. They're precious to me, a reminder of the many weekends I'd joined them, and their friends, in their Eltham home during my teenage years. Playing music, cooking, wandering through the gardens, picking fresh produce, and swimming in the pool. It exposed me, both as observer and participant, to artists, music, cooking food and creativity. I enjoyed it... and I wanted more.

To put this in context, my food choices had been quite simple before then.

Like so many Australian kids, I'd enjoyed my fair share of Vegemite and Kraft cheese, on both crackers and sandwiches. Although my parents were health and diet conscious most of the time, I was a chubby kid as a teenager. Poor Mum had some challenging times going shopping with me to buy clothes or swimming costumes, only to have me complaining that I was fat in them. Perhaps it was too much bread and cheese? In my early twenties, I'd discover I had a dairy and egg allergy as well as a gluten intolerance.

This was a time when it was considered healthy to eat barbequed meat and fish with salads, often followed by a walk after dinner.

The family would sometimes go to a restaurant in Acland Street, the Vineyard, for Sunday lunches where Dad loved ordering the small European grilled sausages with coleslaw and thin fries. We rarely indulged in takeaway food, except for the odd occasion when Mum and Dad would bring home KFC.

In those days I had a sneaky supply of coins that I 'collected' from my mother's purse.

"I might just go for a ride on my bike," I'd tell my parents.

"Good," they'd say, "Get some exercise. It's good for you."

But of course, armed with a handful of coins, I'd often end up at the corner shop, our local milk bar where they sold lollies.

This was back in the days when lollies would be four for one cent and kids would stand at the counter going, "I'll have one of those, and two of those... No, make that two of those..."

Mum was a great cook though and Omi made the best apple compote. Throughout my childhood there were always wonderful aromas from their food preparation wafting through the house. Every night we enjoyed homecooked meals celebrating the cuisines of Romania, Hungary, Italy and of course Jewish culture.

But then Michael and Lilli introduced me to eating more vegetarian foods. Many of them from other cultures. Indian, Chinese, Thai. These plant-based foods appealed to me and opened my mind to healthier choices and different flavours. I often felt better after eating these foods, less heavy... I was losing some of my chubbiness. It was the beginning of my path to healthy eating. A path that would ultimately have a profound impact on my life.

In 1978 Michael and Lilli decided to travel to Goa with their two young children: Marlon, who was five, and their one-year-old, Joel. As they talked about their plans I thought of how exciting and exotic it sounded. Full of enthusiasm I blurted out, "Can I come too?"

I was twenty-two.

Although my father had recently passed away and I would be leaving Mum and Omi for the first time since then, I'd largely recovered from the radiation treatment and felt ready to travel again.

Michael and Lilli were happy to have me tag along. However, my doctors were very much against the idea, concerned that my compromised immune system would leave me vulnerable in a country like India.

I had no intention of listening to them.

Aside from my trip to Israel and Europe with Dad in 1973, I'd also been there a few years earlier with both my parents.

And the trip with Dad had given me the confidence to travel to Bali with a friend in the same year.

Two seventeen-year-olds alone in Bali. What could go wrong?

We had memorable adventures, not all of them comfortable and some quite bizarre. When I look back I see it was an important part of my development, a crucial ingredient in my *recipe for living* at the time. Bali was a completely new cultural experience and after I surrendered to the more rustic style accommodations, rough roads, Balinese rituals and food, I loved it. And, I learned a great deal on that journey about my capacity to handle myself and deal with life's challenges.

Back then the island of Bali was still a secret from the hordes of tourists who go there now. Surfing was already a big thing and young people were drawn to the magical island for the beaches, rice fields, the people and their Hindu culture with its daily ceremonies. It attracted loads of artists, spiritual seekers and free spirits. There was the traditional accommodation (losmans), the small warungs (roadside stalls) that fed us and the sandy pathways where we rode our bicycles.

It was also the first time I encountered the experience of smoking 'buddha sticks'... potent heads of the cannabis plant, oozing with cannabis resin, that were compressed and tied onto thin, skewer-like sticks. That experience in itself opened my mind. It broadened my horizons and allowed me to get to know aspects of myself I'd previously had little awareness of. And it led to some funny and weird experiences. The first time I tried it was my girlfriend's first stone as well. She didn't handle it quite as well as I did. Her voice was trembling as she said, "Sandy…"

"Yeah?"

"Do you see the geckos?"

"The ones on the wall?"

"Why are they on the walls? Why are there so many of them?" I still so clearly remember her scream… "ARRGH!" … and me trying to stay calm while helping her hold it together. "They're so big," she said. "They're going to get us."

"It's okay."

"I can't handle it! Make them go away! SANDY! YOU'VE GOT TO MAKE THEM GO AWAY!"

It took time, but in the end, I managed to help her calm down and settle in to what was an incredible stone that lasted for two days. From that time on, my friends and I have generally had a preference for cannabis over alcohol when partying and having a good time.

I met new people there, including a Balinese prince who said that I'd be his girlfriend (apparently there were quite a few guys in Bali at the time who claimed to be princes). He drove us around in his Toyota Corolla, a big deal for someone in Bali to own in those days. My friends and I were treated as princesses in the best sense of the word.

"Meet my girlfriend, Sandy," he'd proudly declare to all and sundry as he drove us from place to place. "She's from Australia." It was all terribly innocent and certainly a lot of fun.

I took in the new aromas and sounds, the heat and the beach, the food (favourites included tempeh, nasi campur, gado gado). I especially revelled in our travels around the island in open air mini-vans, or Bemos. It was a rough ride on hard benches, sometimes getting drenched in sudden tropical downpours.

Based on my previous travel experiences, I saw travel as a wonderful recipe for opening up to new adventures, a powerful assistance on my pathway to full recovery. After all, what point is there to life if you're not *living* it? That question becomes particularly pertinent when you're a young person who's been through what I had in the preceding two years. And I wanted to experience more, to burst out of the constriction of my regular environment's bubble. I felt like a big sponge, yearning to learn about faraway places and the people who lived in them. I was curious, how would I handle the various situations I'd find myself in, situations I'd never encountered before?

With those marvellous memories of adventure into different cultures in my mind, and knowing that Michael, Lilli and the kids would be renting a small house on the beach, I enthusiastically embraced my plan of joining them in their travels to an even more exotic destination than Bali had been.

Of course, there was also the question of Ian and whether or not he'd be able to join us. I felt enormous love for him. He was what my parents called a 'mensch' a Yiddish word for someone of integrity and honour. "Do you want to come?" I asked him.

He thought long and hard about it before finally telling me, "I'd like to, but it's just that I'd really like to focus on work for now. But you go. Go and have a good time. I'll be here when you get back."

And so, I headed off, comfortable in the knowledge that this wonderful man, who'd been there for me and done so much during my cancer treatment would be waiting for me.

What can you say about Goa in the seventies? As much as I'd already experienced travels that had taken me to several continents, it was this trip that really opened my eyes to different cultures. Far more than even my trip to Bali.

There was an incredible sense of freedom. We had a small, white house on the beach and met people from all over the world. Interestingly, some of them were from Melbourne. Goa was a popular destination for 'alternative' travellers. I hadn't been aware of that beforehand, so it was an unexpected treat to meet new people from my hometown, developing lifelong friendships with some of them.

I loved dressing in colourful lungi (a type of sarong), particularly when there were beach parties to attend. Wrapping oneself in flimsy, loose material with sequins and colourful fabric was a fun way to develop a creative sense of fashion.

On the beaches it turned out clothing was regarded as an optional choice. This became a gateway for me to just let go... to not care what others thought of my body... scars included. By that time I'd already had a breast reduction when I was seventeen after my mother saw how much I struggled with heavy boobs. They'd caused back aches and I'd found it difficult to run and play sports. Most of all though, I had a scar running almost the length of my abdomen from the operation to remove my spleen. I'd been quite shy about my body even before then. The scars just added to my reluctance to show my body. But, at that time, in that place, I felt all that shyness disappear (not to say that it never returned later on). I experienced a sense of freedom... and I liked it. I was learning to let go and embrace my experiences and accept the tragic and traumatic phase of my life during the previous two years.

It was also on that trip that I first met natural medicine practitioners. I stopped eating meat and, for the first time, started to learn about the nutritional side of a vegetarian diet. Those six weeks in Goa introduced me to the idea that the food I chose to eat could make a significant difference to my health outcomes.

And what of my doctor's fears about the risk to my health?

As it turned out, they were right. My comprised immune system *did* end up succumbing to illness while we were there.

I was sick, really sick. I hadn't experienced a sickness even remotely like it before.

I was told it's called *amoebic dysentery*!

If those two words aren't enough to make you appreciate just how truly awful it was, consider this: the toilet was a hole in the floor. The waste would flow down to the other end of an underfloor area where pigs would feast on all the crap. Being sick meant frequent trips to this somewhat confronting toilet.

Fortunately, a new friend I'd made while there cared for me while I was battling the illness, constantly bringing wet towels to help soothe the fever. I was too weak and unwell to spend time with my family and it was a slow week of lying low, sleeping as much as I could between rushing to the hole in the floor that was the toilet. I only drank liquids and after recovering I *felt* lighter. I ended up considering it a worthwhile detox cleanse.

Despite the bout of illness, the overall experience of the trip was wonderful and indeed life-changing. I also realised that, even though I didn't have a spleen and my doctors had rightly warned me that I would be at risk, I *could* deal with that risk and travel on.

I enjoyed eating more vegetables while still enjoying a bit of fish. I had firmed up and my skin glowed. I swam and slept and rested my way back to health. Ultimately, I'd never felt better.

I also met some incredibly cool people... and some not so incredible people who were affected by a history of bad drugs and having no place they could now call home. Encountering these lost souls really affected me. It opened my eyes and helped me realise my life was too precious to waste.

Towards the end of my six weeks in Goa I was sitting around with some of the guys from Melbourne I'd met there when one of them said, "We're looking to head off to Israel from here."

Without hesitation I asked, "Can I come too?"

Released

I looked out the window of the plane and reflected on how I was just fourteen when on my first trip to Israel with Mum and Dad, then seventeen on my second visit there with Dad. Now, I was embarking on a third trip and, for the first time, I was doing it unaccompanied by any family members.

The trip to Goa had boosted my confidence in travelling, to the point where I then felt comfortable tackling this trip on my own. Michael and Lilli had headed back to Australia with their kids. But I was discovering more about myself than I possibly could've at home. It felt like the travel was bringing out the best in me, like I was *really* living. It made me feel more grateful than ever before to be alive.

But what about home? I had Ian back there, my wonderfully supportive and loving boyfriend who was waiting for me. Somehow, it didn't feel fair to me that he should be putting an important part of his life on hold while I continued on my great adventure. I resolved that I'd get in touch, that it was time to set us both free. It's not that I didn't love and care about him anymore. We were on opposite sides of the globe. I wasn't even sure when I'd come home. I was revelling in my new-found freedom. A freedom to be open to the unknowns of travel. It was a precious experience that I knew was right for me, it was what I needed then. It felt so unfair to continue holding Ian to the promise he'd made. We were young and, to be perfectly honest, I was unsure that I was ready for commitment, especially after facing cancer and the loss of my father. The first chance that came up, I called him. "Don't wait for me." That was all I remember from the call.

I had no idea at the time just how much more profound the impact of this journey to Israel would be than the earlier ones. Before arriving, I vowed to develop a greater understanding of the country's history and culture than on my previous visits.

I'd just been through the transition from being someone who ate meat regularly to becoming a vegetarian and was now going to a country where the healthy Mediterranean selection of foods made a vegetarian lifestyle easy. Salads, fruits, tabouli, falafels, and hummus were more than enough to satisfy my taste buds and appetite.

And while on that trip, I had the privilege to meet people who would go on to teach me a great deal about herbal medicine and natural therapies. Among these were a couple, Suzette and Shulka. Originally from Melbourne, Suzette was a professional photographer and Shulka, who grew up on a kibbutz in Israel, was involved in film and television production. They lived in Ein Kerem, a charming hillside village famed for its centuries-old holy sites, that was now a neighbourhood in Jerusalem. They introduced me to a variety of herbal teas with specific health properties: my first encounter with any form of herbal medicine. The two of them would later have a profound impact when I embarked on a venture I couldn't possibly have dreamed of at the time.

I also had my first real introduction to yoga while there. I'd seen people doing yoga on the beach in Goa and had tried it out with a friend who had already been practising. But this was different. I liked how the movements made my body feel, the breathing effect and the idea that the mind can become more peaceful through awareness and letting go. While still emerging from the major challenges of the previous two years, I now felt that I was blossoming into a more conscious and capable, resilient woman.

I hung out with new friends who were mostly older. Some had been to Goa as well. Others were expats from Melbourne who knew Michael and Lilli and were now living in Israel.

I also spent time with relatives. My late father had an identical twin brother, Seppi, living there. I met his wife, Bertha (my aunt), and my cousins, Ari and Rina. These older cousins told me how they'd dealt with going into the army for their obligatory national service, and about all that Israel represented for them.

In my quest to explore the country's cultural heritage, I travelled through it extensively, visiting Haifa, the Dead Sea, and the Sinai Desert. It opened my eyes to how the people there lived in an environment of constant self-defence and how they dealt with being a rare and small democratic country in that part of the world.

I experimented with hashish, allowing myself to feel free about losing control (I did, however, get to know my limits). My new friends recommended books to me on Buddhism and other practices that were spiritual in nature. Reading them filled my life with interest and a sense of meaning I'd never experienced before.

Ever since my diagnosis and the ongoing implications of the treatment on my immune system, I'd been focused on the need to be health conscious. But now, for the first time, I realised that maintaining my health would require a more holistic approach. I needed to find an all-encompassing set of *recipes for living* a healthy life. And this overseas trip, through Goa and then Israel, had revealed some of the necessary ingredients for those recipes.

It left me hungry to learn more.

Time to Move

As much as I'd loved my travels, it was time to head home. I'd been away for three months and had experienced so much. My eyes had been opened to whole new perspectives on living and I had a sense my stamina had improved.

My idea though – that I'd be going straight back to my regular life at home with Mum and Omi – was about to be shattered.

While I was away overseas, Mum had been spending time with a man who'd been introduced to her by her best friend. Ted had also lost his partner and was now a widower. Mum would later tell me she was initially reluctant to date so soon after Dad had passed away as she was still greatly mourning his loss. Her own mother, and her best friend, (both of whom my mother trusted) encouraged and ultimately convinced her to meet this man, despite her misgivings. Being wise and philosophical (the result of her own experiences in life), Mum eventually opened herself up and accepted the date.

She explained to me how Ted had met her several times and gently helped her relax into being in this new relationship. It was hard for me to accept that Ted had become more than a friend. It was also hard for me to appreciate at the time that, at fifty-one, Mum was still so young and vibrant with so much of her life ahead of her. They dated for several months then married in May 1979.

Mum wanted Ted to move in and Ted wanted to move in with Mum... but not until *after* Omi and I had moved out.

It was all a bit hard to comprehend at the time. Everyone seemed to be across what was going on but me. Ted had bought Omi an apartment across the road from our family home, and she was thrilled. Who could blame her for feeling that way? For the first time in her life, at eighty-one, she had a home that she could call her own.

For me though, it came as a shock. It was less than two years after my father's death… a death that had happened during my treatment for Hodgkin lymphoma. Even though I had grown in so many ways during my travels and felt healthy again, I still found this change in our family confronting.

"It's okay," Jenny said to me, "Greg and I have plenty of room, you can move in with us until you find somewhere else." It seemed as though she and Mum had already had discussions about it while I was overseas. But, regardless of that, I was grateful for the offer. At the end of the day, I had no choice but to move, and spending a couple of months living at Greg and Jenny's home seemed the perfect way to soften the blow. It was indeed a generous offer, particularly given that they'd only recently moved into the home themselves as a pair of newlyweds. I waved goodbye to the mid-century modern home that held so many memories. It also meant a great deal to Mum, who had no intention of leaving there.

Fortunately, it didn't take long after moving into their place before I found an apartment I could move into on my own.

"It's in Warra Street, Toorak," I excitedly told Jenny, "right across the road from the railway line."

"That's wonderful," came Jenny's reply. "We'll help you move."

I know how that may sound, but really, it wasn't that they were trying to get rid of me. It was a genuine offer of kindness. And being across from the railway line? It's not like it was particularly noisy or anything. It was actually really handy for getting to and from work at Fell and Starkey (yes, they'd kept me on after I'd finished my degree).

On the day of the move Greg, Jenny and a few other friends pitched in to lend a hand. Despite the mattress not wanting to co-operate with finding a way up the stairs leading to the mezzanine bedroom level, ingenuity and determination won out in the end.

I was about to spend my first night in my first home that was all to myself!

As the sun went down, I decided it would be an ideal time to run a hot bath, to get warm and luxuriate in my good fortune. I turned on the light switch in the bathroom. Nothing! *Oh well*, I thought, *tomorrow I'll have to get a new light bulb.* I turned on the hot water tap and ran my hand under it waiting for it to get warm. I waited, and I waited some more. Stone cold after several minutes. I ran through the rest of the apartment, testing one light switch after another. None of them worked. It was getting dark and I was starting to panic. I had to call Mum. She'd know what to do. She always knew what to do. My heart was thumping as I grabbed the phone, hoping against all hope there'd be a dial tone.

Brrr...

I was in luck! The phone at least was working. I dialled Mum's number, anxiously waiting as the dial slowly wound its way back after each number.

"Hello?" she said as she answered in her still-thick European accent.

"Mum, it's me. There's something wrong. None of the lights are working, and there's no hot water!"

"Hmmm... did you arrange for the electricity and gas to be turned on before moving in?"

A few seconds of silence followed as reality sank in. It had never even occurred to me that I'd need to do that. Hearing my mother's question, it suddenly made sense. As strange as it may seem now, I simply had no idea at the time. Had I moved directly from Mum's to my new place I've no doubt that she would have run through a kind of checklist with me of the various things I needed to attend to. It's easy to look back on it now and laugh, but at the time it wasn't so funny.

Once I'd settled in, that little apartment served me well. I had my own home and a job at Fell and Starkey where I'd been officially employed as an auditor. But the routine and strict working guidelines were destined to create a conflict in the way I wanted to live. Within a year my desire to travel and open up to new adventures would push me to question whether it was a lifestyle that really suited my developing personality.

Heading to Cancun

When it comes to good quality ingredients in a *recipe for living*, I'd have to say that travelling is right up there, near the top of my list.

I'm not so much talking about the structured tours. You know, the ones where everyone gets herded from one tourist attraction to another. I was already aware by then that I enjoyed travelling far more as a 'free spirit'. It's about experiencing other cultures, immersing yourself in them and discovering how other people live. Or even just travelling to a great location, making new friends and relaxing in a resort or spa (as I would discover in the ensuing years).

By the age of twenty-four, I'd already experienced Israel, parts of Eastern Europe, Bali, and India. My earlier journeys had been with my father, my brother and his family, and a friend from school. But when I travelled to Israel from Goa, I'd taken the initiative on my own. Sure, I'd gone to Israel with people I'd met up with while in India, but I'd done so with a sense of total independence. And that experience had filled me with the confidence to take on the world.

Mum had been helping me with the funds to travel, adding to what I'd put aside from my income. I was incredibly lucky that she was always so supportive of this travel impulse, regardless of how nervous she was about me going into the unknown. She had confidence in my abilities to make good decisions. After all, she'd seen me deal with so many challenges already from a young age. "Your tenacity and your resourcefulness amaze me," she would often say. While she was a shy person, I was becoming more outgoing, enthusiastic and 'out there' as she saw it.

It was 1980, and I had the United States of America in my sights. I formulated my plans and purchased my ticket to the USA. In those days there was no internet for research and bookings. So, I went through multitudes of brochures in the travel agency and asked questions of friends who had travelled whenever I had the chance.

In the end, I decided to spend time in California before making my way to New Orleans and then down to Club Med at Cancun in Mexico.

On the 27th of February, 1980, my flight touched down at Los Angeles International Airport. For some reason, perhaps from seeing so many American movies and television programs, being at this airport felt more like a movie than real life. The hustle, bustle and intensity of the place was exciting. I recognised so many famous faces, right there, at the airport. *Wow!* I thought to myself, *I'm in Hollywood Land!*

After a few days spent recovering from the flight and getting the feel of Los Angeles, I went to see the famous Capital Records Tower in Hollywood. Since I was a teenager, I'd had an avid interest in music and building up my LP collection. As it turned out, there was a record market happening at the time. I mixed with the public and as I mingled had the good fortune to meet and hang out with a host of singer/songwriters. One particularly memorable one was a guy called Rob Laufer. The experience left me dreaming of how wonderful it would be to work in the music industry one day. I was enjoying the more confident version of myself that my travelling was able to coax out... a version that was able to chat so easily with people I'd never met before.

Family and friends had provided me with some contacts in LA. So, whatever happened, there would at least be some friendly faces I could visit. One such friendly face was a friend from Melbourne who was living in LA at the time. I slept on the couch of his small Hollywood apartment for a while... and we certainly had some fun! All I'll say here about that is that there was a lot of partying going on. I was opening up more and more while also having a great time (he also connected me to a guy from Hawaii who lived on the island of Kauai so that later on in my travels I could take the opportunity to stay there and meet up with him and his friends).

Having no intention of letting the inadequate American public transport system restrict my movements, I hired a car and, on the 6th of March, headed north to Sausalito, on the Northern side of San Francisco's Golden Gate Bridge. To my surprise, it only took a few miles to get the hang of driving on the right-side of the road in a left-hand-drive vehicle.

There was *so* much to see in that near four-hundred-mile stretch from L.A. up to San Jose and San Francisco. When I think of that trip it's a reminder that one of the great joys of travelling on your own is the freedom to go exploring. Like being able to stop off and check out some of the great beaches along the way; Stinson Beach, north of San Francisco, being just one example of a beautiful pause in my journey that I could take thanks to that freedom. I drove as far north as Mendicino and Fort Bragg.

One of the highlights of my little self-drive tour was doing the seventeen-mile drive through Del Monte Forest, south of San Jose, through to Carmel-By-The-Sea in Monterey, a beautiful beach location. It's also home to the Carmel Mission Basilica, established in 1770. Teeming with birdlife at its southern end, the beach is also popular with surfers.

The river feeding into the Pacific at Monterey is watched over by the Santa Lucia Mountain Range. These mountains are famous for the stretch that hugs the California Coast just to the South of Monterey. It's an area known as *Big Sur* and is considered one of the most rugged stretches of coast in the United States. The drive to get there took me through the stunningly beautiful state forests along Skyline Boulevard.

I then spent a few weeks in Sausalito with Diane, a friend of Michael and Lilli. She and a few of her friends took me on my first *ever* camping trip. I look at photos from that time and smile, reminded of how much fun we had. Discovering how to be comfortable while camping was a whole new skill... but can I tell you something? After that experience, camping was not something I planned to do again.

My network was growing though. Being on my own made it possible to take advantage of opportunities that may have been problematic with a companion. It enabled me to discover an eclectic variety of places, people, adventures and nourishing experiences along the way, both for the body *and* for the mind.

Despite all the fun times, I was very much aware that moderation was essential for me. Seeing and talking to so many of the 'lost drugged out souls' in India and Bali had been a profound lesson. I had too much to live for to risk joining their ranks.

How could I be any other way, given the extra time I had to devote to self-care because of having had cancer?

Having spent a month in California, I wanted to move on to the next stage of my journey, a stopover in New Orleans before moving on to Mexico. And I knew I'd have to leave the USA as my tourist visa was coming to an end. By leaving and then re-entering, I could get a fresh visa and continue my travels through the country.

You may be wondering why I chose Club Med as my ultimate destination?. Well, I just didn't have any contacts in Mexico and in those days Club Med was the latest thing in travel options. My investigations suggested it would be a great destination, that I could arrive at Club Med on my own and meet people from other places while adventuring in a country I'd never been to. Mexico sounded like one of the more interesting Club Med locations. The Club Med Resorts prided themselves (and still do) on providing all-inclusive holiday experiences in magical locations. I even wondered whether it might be fun to try working at a Club Med resort for a while? This meant I'd need to go there and check it out for myself!

On the 10th of April, I landed in New Orleans for a two-day stopover before flying out again to Cancun in Mexico. As soon as I got off the plane, the humidity hit me. And there was something about the vibe that just didn't feel right... a vibe that was confirmed when I got ripped off by the cab driver who took me from the airport to my hotel. Fortunately, it didn't take long before I met someone at a local café who I felt I could talk to. More importantly, she was someone I sensed I could trust.

The moment I met Teresa it seemed obvious we'd be friends. One of the first things I'd learned about travelling is that you have little choice but to trust your gut feelings, and I certainly wasn't wrong this time. I felt comfortable enough to accept her invitation to stay with her in her lovely home. Her husband lived in the duplex next door. They had a unique arrangement with a door through the central wall so they each had their own space. If they wanted to be together, they could do that too. I so liked this idea that, from then on, I decided that if I was to be in a serious long-term relationship, this concept might work for me as well (not that I was really looking for 'the one' at the time as I was more interested then in 'the many').

The next few days flew by! I loved the houses and style of New Orleans. There were wide streets and big creole-style houses, melding the French, Spanish and Caribbean architectural influences, tree-lined streets and trams. Of course there was also the music that New Orleans is so famous for and, while there, I enjoyed different jazz styles: Zydeco and, for the first time, Cajun. I ate red beans and rice, and cornbread, new flavours for me at the time that seemed the perfect accompaniment to the music.

One night we went down to the French Quarter, a particularly rough part of New Orleans. As we were walking along, this big black guy, black as black can be and bombed out of his brain, started walking alongside us.

"I'm not prejudiced!" he declared, as though that would somehow make us feel more comfortable that he was, "just happening to be going our way."

Two white girls walking around New Orleans with this stoned black guy wanting us to feel secure in the knowledge that he was not prejudiced about us? Yeah, right!

He continued walking with us until we turned into a street full of other people. I didn't know what to do or think, but Teresa was used to homeless people in New Orleans and more able to take it in her stride. As for me? Well, I hadn't really experienced anything like that before in my travels. It was a whole new experience.

The Mississippi River was just as rough as the neighbourhood that day. We found a comfy spot by the river where we sat and watched a ferry cross the river's murky turbulence as we passed a joint between us, a kind of ritual bonding. Despite having been a little scared and confronted by the stoned homeless black guy, I soon found myself pleasantly stoned and feeling relaxed. Feeling like we needed something to eat after our little smoke, we stopped by a place called Houlihans, an American food restaurant where Teresa feasted on oysters. "Aren't you going to have some?" she asked.

"No, thank you. I don't eat them."

"What? You're kidding me."

"No, really. I've never liked them."

"Well," she said, "you're the one missing out."

I should mention at this stage that I felt somewhat overwhelmed by the big portions of food I saw people eating around me. I'd never seen such large people before either. It was a good thing I liked rice, beans and corn chips. Otherwise, I might have struggled.

When travelling alone, the cinema becomes a great way to fill in what would otherwise be empty nights with little to do. I'd already been to see a few movies since arriving in the States. But now I had a companion to join me. Teresa and I went and watched the *Coal Miner's Daughter* that night. The movie introduced me to the life of American singer/songwriter, Loretta Lynn and the country music genre, one that I hadn't really paid much attention to prior to that night. I was expanding my musical experiences as they became more varied and interesting. It got me thinking again about how much I'd like to work in the music industry, something I was really starting to aspire to.

The next day I was booked on a flight to Miami, with a connecting flight from there down to Cancun. Teresa and I spent the last night we thought we'd be able spend together laughing and carrying on until two-thirty in the morning. It was bucketing down outside when I called to book the cab at 6am. Not needing to be picked up for another hour, I figured there was plenty of time and no cause to worry. I waited… and I waited some more. And the rain… it just kept bucketing down. Little did I know the suburbs between where I was staying and the airport were by now under three feet of water. In all, eight inches of rain fell on New Orleans that day. Needless to say, the cab never arrived. And, amid a flurry of panicked phone calls, I missed my flight.

It was nobody's fault, but still stressful and frustrating. I made phone call after phone call, about forty US dollars worth in total, a lot of money to be spending on calls. In those days, long distance phone calls weren't cheap at the best of times. Finally, I managed to get a different flight, but was going to have to wait three days and shell out an extra ninety US dollars! Poor Teresa ended up feeling almost as stressed and bamboozled as I did. I'd never been caught in a flood before and learned through the experience that New Orleans has a low elevation in relation to sea level, making it vulnerable to storm surges that can breach levees and floodwalls. The heavy rains there often outpace both the ground's ability to absorb water and the drainage system's capacity to disperse it.

It was an eye-opening experience.

With the rescheduled flights in place and Teresa having loaned me her wet weather boots and raincoat, I decided to go for a walk around the neighbourhood between the ongoing showers. It was an opportunity to check out some of the grand old mansions around New Orleans and the magnificent Tulane University downtown campus that specialises in the health sciences.

I found it hard to relax though, and I was still upset that I'd be getting to Club Med late. That feeling persisted until I was in the air and on my way to Cancun, Mexico on Tuesday, April 15th.

Arriving at Club Med late became an exercise in going from one weird experience to another. It was dark, making me feel particularly conscious of being on my own. As I wandered around, I came across no one who spoke English. That is, until I met a guy who called himself Gypsy (his real name was Joseph). He took it upon himself to be my unofficial guide. When I eventually made it to my room, I felt relieved to finally put my stuff down and get some sleep. At first light, I was up and had a shower, put on my bathers and wrapped myself in a sarong I'd bought in Bali. It was time for a holiday resort experience! Having already missed two days of my one week booking, I had much holidaying to do in the remaining time.

Gypsy continued to show me around, introducing me to one person after another. "This is Sandy. She's the Australian contingent."

The Australian contingent? That was a new one. Being the only Australian there at the time, I guess I had a bit of a novelty value to them.

I probably should explain a little bit about the Club Med philosophy for those who have never experienced one of their resorts. Club Med, a French company, have established resorts all around the world. They aim to provide a full holiday experience within the resort, one where you don't feel the need to leave the resort for anything. It's almost like they're little holiday villages, and the management actually refers to them that way. They even refer to the resort managers as village chiefs.

Guests arriving at Club Med were originally known as *GMs*, or *Genteel Members*. Although that nowadays translates to *Great Members*. The staff are referred to as *GOs*, or *Gracious Organisers*. The GOs are encouraged to socialise with the GMs (including the Australian contingent).

So Gypsy, who was one of the GOs, worked hard at his job of making me feel relaxed and special. I have to admit that, at the time, I was feeling disorientated. It was such a huge change from the previous few days trying to depart from New Orleans. That's one of the things about travelling. It picks you up out of one world and drops you into another. You've got little choice but to adapt to each new situation as it comes along and to expect the unexpected.

Determined to ensure I settled in though, Gypsy took me out for a sail to see a wreck that was four miles out. I'd never been sailing before. Despite the seas being rough, I soon discovered there's nothing like the exhilaration of being on a yacht with nothing but the sound of the wind in the sails and the water rushing against the side of the boat.

It was an all-new experience and I loved it!

The first night had merged into the second day. More names. More faces. It was too many too quickly to have any chance of remembering more than a few of the standouts.

There I was, a single, young woman, the only Australian in a magical resort, teeming with good looking male GOs who all seemed determined to ensure my holiday was one to remember. As you might expect, most of the guys were super confident and flirty. Then it happened that I met David, a May 7th Taurus. I had a keen interest in astrology in those days and had started to think there was a pattern of vibes for each sign. Unlike most of the other guys there, David appeared to me as a wise and sensitive man. I fell blissfully into a holiday romance. Everything in David's world was, in his words, "great". And it was feeling that way for me too. Oh, and did I mention he was a sailing instructor? Could that be what led me into becoming a bit of a sailing groupie? He serenaded me with his guitar and even gave me a cassette tape of some of his songs. But alas, the bliss was soon undermined somewhat by an underlying sense of insecurity and jealousy, a sense that I was just another GM and that he was merely fulfilling his duty as a GO. I felt like

Hanging out amongst the Mayan ruins near Club Med,

he'd no doubt do all the same things with the next guest once I was safely on the plane back to Australia. These were new emotions for me. Jealousy? I'd certainly never experienced *that one* before.

One night, while enjoying a ritual joint with one of the other GOs, a lovely guy called Tim showed me some photo albums. Page after page fed my anxiety that I was just another face—that I wasn't as 'special' to David as I'd believed myself to be when our holiday romance started. It was indicative of a young girl who was new to holiday romances and how to handle them.

Regardless, David *did* offer me a job. He managed to organise an offer for me from Club Med management, working as an au pair in New Caledonia. As an added bonus, he was going there too as his next posting.

It was tempting, and I gave the offer serious consideration.

After just five days, it was time to leave. I'd fitted so much into the few days I was there that it was a truly amazing experience. Despite the fact that I'd known David, Gypsy and Tim for less than a week, I was overwhelmed with emotion as I prepared to leave. Memories of the preceding days and nights rolled over in my head as the bus left the resort enroute to the airport.

I was snapped out of my emotionally-tinged daydreams by another of the GOs who sat next to me. "I remember you," he said. "I saw you hanging out with David. Nicest guy you could ever hope to meet. You certainly seemed to make an impact on him." For the rest of the journey to the airport I found myself comforted by the thought that our brief romance really *was* special after all.

Those thoughts stayed with me till my flight touched down in Miami. Also on my flight was Rhonda, a Jewish girl I'd met during the week at Club Med. We'd clicked immediately and got to talking while waiting at the airport.

"Have you got somewhere to stay in Miami?" asked Rhonda.

"Not yet," I replied.

"Well, you're welcome to stay at my place if you want."

"Oh, thank you. That would be wonderful."

While I'd hooked up with David at Cancun, Rhonda had hooked up with Tim. And when she sang? David and I had agreed that her voice was reminiscent of Joni Mitchell. She played me all the songs she was preparing to record for a demo tape, and I have to say that I enjoyed every one of them. So much so that I followed along when she went to record them at her friend, Neil's, recording studio. He's one of those all-rounders who's a muso-come-producer-come-engineer… and a great guy to top it off.

Personally, I've never been able to sing or play a musical instrument. But loved being around musos.

Rhonda and I were still on a high from our trip to Cancun when we went out to dinner at a Chinese restaurant on our first night back.

While sitting there ordering dishes to share, this really attractive guy walks in… on his own, and sits at the next table.

"He's *so* good looking... and on his own," Rhonda whispered to me. "Go on," she was prompting me, "ask him to join us."

"I can't do that," I protested.

"Of course you can... go on."

Before I knew it, Rhonda convinced me to be the ice-breaker. "I hate to see you eating alone," I said. "You know what? I'm not even from this country and *I'm* not eating alone. Would you like to join us?"

He seemed just as stunned as I was with what I'd just blurted out. Despite that, he *did* end up joining us. He ordered more food, transforming our meal into a veritable feast. He turned out to be a really nice guy. A surreal conversation ensued where we hit him with all sorts of questions.

"My name's Arthur—"

Before he had a chance to continue, Rhonda started asking a barrage of questions. I didn't get a word in after my initial ice-breaker. There was no reason to be upset about it though. It was Rhonda after all who had shown an immediate interest in him. Besides, I was her guest, and she was the one who lived in Miami. Anyway, she was the one asking all the questions.

"...what do I do for a living? I'm an orthodontist."

"...my car? Which one? The Mazda sports or the Mercedes?"

"...my age? Thirty-five. Why?"

"...my home? That's at Fort Lauderdale."

"Yeah, well I am Jewish..."

Jewish! There you go. It's pretty amazing that with just fifteen million people worldwide who primarily identify as Jewish we're so damned good at finding each other.

Arthur came back with us to Rhonda's place. Unfortunately for Rhonda though, it didn't take long before he propositioned *me* while she was out of the room. I swear, I had done nothing, other than the initial invitation to join us, to suggest I may have had any interest in him.

It was just so weird. Here I was, just back from an amazing and very emotional time in Cancun and I meet this lovely Jewish guy who wants to hook up with me. It was something I certainly did *not* want to tell Rhonda about – and I felt a sense of relief when Arthur eventually left.

The following night Rhonda, her friend Barbie and I went to a cocktail party thrown by a local radio station at *Beau Arts*. There were a lot of pompous men there and I really didn't like their energy. Yet, somehow, I managed to have a good time anyway. I guess largely because I was there with Rhonda. She had a heart of gold and a beautiful sensitivity that made me feel privileged to be able to call her a friend.

The next morning, I spoke to Mum for the first time since leaving Australia. It was so comforting to hear her voice, then she yelled "Jenny's pregnant!" I remember her excitement as she told me, her voice filled with so much joy.

"That's great, Mum. I'm really happy for her." Was that a touch of envy in my voice? Was I perhaps a little bit envious of their loving relationship?

Having always felt that motherhood was *not* something I yearned for in my future, these questions came as a bit of a surprise. Don't get me wrong, I'm not suggesting that I was somehow wishing to have a baby myself. I *do* get why people want to have children... and I *do* love them. But it was just not something I yearned for in my own life and never have to this day. On the flipside of that, I know a lot of people who have expressed wonder at my ability to live my life as a free spirit, a lifestyle that wouldn't have been possible while raising children. I'd become an aunt when I was seventeen and I loved spending time with my nephews. But Jenny and Greg were my first friends to conceive a child. It made me reflect more on what I wanted for myself.

Talking to Mum that day though and hearing that Jenny and Greg were going to become parents lifted my spirits. It helped prepare me for yet another rigorous day of lazing on the beach sunbaking.

After just three days in Miami, it was on to Washington DC. Once there I stayed with yet another friend I'd made at Club Med, Susan. We had wonderful long discussions about our magical five days at Cancun. She'd hooked up with Steve, who was a guest while we were there.

It was refreshing after my stay with Rhonda. As nice as she'd been, I was still floating in the aftermath of my holiday romance with David while staying with her. But she had refused to entertain any discussion about there being a special connection between David and myself. "It was about the sex, that's all," is what she'd say. Maybe that had been the case for her and Tim. They were both thirty-something singles... and obviously a bit more cynical than me.

Susan saw it differently. "You and David? You guys had something special going. I could see it. Everyone could." It was reaffirming to hear her say that. After all, I've always been a believer that every relationship, even a short one, can be something special and meaningful. They can all create memories worth treasuring when the right people come together. Listening to Susan's words made me glad that I hadn't allowed myself to fall into a cynical attitude towards love like Rhonda and so many others had.

Anyhow, the next morning was an opportunity to explore DC, the heart of American democracy. Walking from the Washington Monument through the park, and then along the reflective pool toward the Lincoln Memorial, I marvelled at the scale of it all. It's one thing to see these places in pictures, but you can't truly appreciate them until you're there.

From the Lincoln Memorial I headed north, up 23rd Street and through the Washington University campus to Pennsylvania Avenue, then on to Georgetown. By that stage I was getting hungry, so stopped to get some lunch. Thankfully I found a vegetarian café. By then I was into eating far more plant-based foods for my health. My feet were already telling me that I'd covered a lot of distance. However, what bothered me more was what I noticed in the faces of the people who were passing by. Or, maybe it's more apt to say it's what I *didn't* notice that bothered me. There was something missing. Perhaps it was something that I was more sensitive to after my recent time in Cancun where everyone was so full of life and vitality. What I was seeing here was such a stark contrast, in that all these multitude of faces looked stressed. No one was smiling. This was the harsh reality in the heartland of American politics and serious business.

I decided it was not for me.

Having eaten, I headed up Wisconsin Avenue and indulged my fashion sense with some shopping. But it was hard to really get in the groove as, by this stage, my feet were *really* starting to ache. Ah well, no new clothes for me that day. I found the bus that would take me back to Susan's and, as it weaved its way through the tree-lined streets with so many picture-perfect houses, I found myself appreciating what a lovely area she was living in. There was an abundance of cherry blossoms and the abundance of trees in general made it feel like a forest.

On Friday, I'd decided to go to the Smithsonian. It doesn't take long before you realise the Smithsonian can't possibly be done in one day. To really appreciate this collection of museums it would take weeks. Each one is truly amazing in its own right. I managed to skim the surface of the History Museum, the National Art Gallery, and the Space and Aircraft Museum.

In the middle of all these buildings is a park that's buzzing with carnival acts, merry-go-rounds, and food vendors. Walking into this throng of activity left me feeling conscious of experiencing it on my own. This was an unusual realisation for me—the person who was so quick to point out how much I loved travelling on my own. Perhaps I might have enjoyed sharing that particular experience. I got a sense that DC was the type of city that requires company. Perhaps because it wasn't particularly easy to talk with strangers in all that hustle and bustle?

Could it be that if I'd been going through these amazing museums with someone else, I'd be stopping to really take everything in?

In a way it felt like I was just moving through it all with little more than a casual glance at these incredible exhibits that scream for your attention.

I managed to find my way to the underground and headed up to the historic and cosmopolitan DuPont Circle. By this time there was little more that I could take in, so I caught the bus and took my overloaded self back to Susan's place. It's funny, even though I'd had that moment of wishing to share the day with someone, I think I'd absorbed as much as I possibly could've in a single day anyway.

That night Susan and I went to a Thai Restaurant. The food was great and we followed it up with a trip to the famous *Kramers and Afterwords* in Dupont Circle for some ice-cream. It's a bit of a DC cultural institution... a bookstore, bar and cafe all rolled into one. It's still there today, albeit with rebranding as just *Kramers*.

We were so exhausted by the time we got back to Susan's that we flaked out for the night.

On the Saturday, I went along with Susan to her ballet class. While I love contemporary dance music and theatre, I realised while watching the class that, although I appreciated Susan's interest, I was not at all into traditional ballet. As the class went on I took the opportunity to bring my journal up to date.

I cooked vegetables that night for the two of us before we went out to visit a couple of Susan's friends, Marlene and Dick. Their house was extraordinary. Marlene was studying to be a landscape architect, which I found fascinating, as I was starting to appreciate gardens and landscapes so much more, courtesy of my travels.

I wanted to know more about what they were doing, but they just kept bringing the conversation back to questions about Australia. It was just so foreign and exotic to them. And, like so many Americans at the time, they believed all the cliches, like the idea that we were living among kangaroos.

It didn't change the fact that I was meeting new people, learning, wising up, leading me to see the world through fresh eyes.

So much was happening that I would have loved to share with a companion. But I was on my own, and that's the thing. There was also a great many experiences I was having purely because I *was* travelling on my own. The whole Club Med experience and the people I met through going there on my own became such an important part of the whole experience.

Dubs from Dubs

It was towards the end of 1980. I hadn't been back from the States for long when I visited Debbie, one of my old school friends.

"Guess what," she said. "Richard's got a job at a Sydney radio station."

"Wow, that's pretty cool. So, you're both going to move up there?"

"Yep, in a couple of weeks. We've found a three-bedroom house in Balmain."

"How amazing. Can I come too?" There it was again, my enthusiasm getting ahead of me and the question just popping out. Debbie didn't seem to mind.

"Yeah, come on up!" Richard was going to be throwing himself straight into work and Debbie didn't have a job to go straight into when they got there. "We'll have a ball."

And have a ball we did. I packed up what I could fit in my car and drove up to Sydney, then had the furniture moved up by a removalist. Balmain and another new life awaited!

For those of you who don't know Balmain, its network of narrow streets and terrace houses sits on a peninsula on the southern side of the harbour, just west of the Sydney Harbour Bridge.

We settled into the gorgeous cottage... and what joy I had helping to set it up. Once Richard had gone off to work, we'd smoke a joint, spend an hour or so discussing the meaning of life and what we needed for food, then we'd go for a wander through the streets of our new home turf. It was 1981 and Balmain was alive with a vibrant bohemian vibe that blended with its working-class roots. It had its fair share of 'yuppies' and artists as well, and that all combined to create an incredible atmosphere that seemed insulated from the rest of Sydney. But you can't get by living in the city without a job. Debbie had just found a job with a real estate agent and I was coming to Sydney armed with my Bachelor of Accounting. I was determined to put it to good use. I looked through the job classifieds and found something that looked interesting. After going for just the one interview, I found myself landing a fantastic position: *Financial Assistant to the Financial Director at Reader's Digest.*

The ad in the paper stipulated the need for proficiency with personal computers, something that wasn't part of my bachelor of accountancy course.

Hell, I couldn't even type at that stage in my life. Although my mother encouraged me to do a short typing course when I was still living at home. I hadn't practised for years.

But hey, this was 1981 and personal computers themselves were still quite new. Not many others had those skills either. What I *did* have though was my Bachelor's degree and a two-year job placement at a distinguished Melbourne firm under my belt. I'm quite sure my new boss was aware that he'd end up having to give a bit of help and guidance to whoever ended up with the job. He was kind and he was patient. But he also recognised that I was a good worker. It was amazing. I'd managed to walk straight into a job that had me on one of the upper floors of the company headquarters in Surry Hills. I was joining the company executives for lunch in the rooftop garden and enjoying all the trappings of a great opportunity. And those computer skills? I picked them up quickly, my confidence improving every day.

Here I was, living in a trendy part of Sydney and having this great job. Melbourne was still within easy reach and I had just become involved with a guy down there, Sam. I'd actually met him at my going away pyjama party. The first weekend after I'd moved to Sydney, I flew down to join him at a party where I met a friend of his, Fay. "You're living in Sydney?" she asked.

"Yes, in Balmain."

"How cool. I've got to move up there shortly too. I just got a job with a new publishing company. They're putting together a book called *A Day in the Life of Australia*."

"Have you found a place yet?"

"No," she replied. "I was going to try and find something when I get there."

"I'll introduce you to my housemate, Debbie. She's working in real estate."

So, Fay rocked up in Sydney with a carload of her possessions and spent a day driving around with Debbie checking out apartments.

"They're all a bit pokey," said Fay.

Debbie nodded in agreement. She'd been a bit disappointed in what was on offer at the time as well. "I'll tell you what," she said, "we've got a spare room at our place in Balmain. Why not just move in with us?"

One of the great things about that household was that we were all vegans, something that wasn't overly common in Sydney during the eighties. It's not that we had consciously sought each other out for that reason, it was just a happy coincidence. I guess you could also say that like-minded people tend to be drawn to each other.

Fay and I hit it off immediately. The girl liked to party… and so did I. With Debbie and Richard also enjoying a good time, the house was party central. We laughed all the time and the four of us got on so well that, when the Balmain house was starting to feel a bit small, the whole household moved together to a bigger house in Lilyfield, just a couple of suburbs to the west. The handy part of having a housemate working in real estate is getting first dibs on the best properties when they come up.

Meanwhile, I was continuing with the job in Surry Hills. The only trouble was, the longer I worked there, the more I became conscious of the work culture. I came to realise that it was one that didn't sit well with me. The company relied on the top-down approach, with nothing allowed to flow the other way; and there was an overwhelming focus on profits. It went even deeper than that though. I found that I couldn't really connect with the ethics driving their whole business model and the push marketing methods they'd use to help drive subscriptions. The more I watched everyone arrive at work and sit down at their desks with their little desktop calculators, the more I realised the truth. It just wasn't me. I'd spent about a year working there by then. Throughout that time, although I knew what an extraordinary opportunity the job had been, it wasn't going to be where my future lay. It was time to move on.

I'd been wrestling with my reservations about the Reader's Digest job when, through my contacts, an opportunity came up to work at Polygram Records, home of two of my favourite record labels, Astor and Motown.

Perhaps I should explain a bit about how absorbed I was in my love of records and music before I go on.

For years I'd been an avid collector of vinyl records. I used to buy 45s when I was a teenager which led to buying LPs as they were referred to back then. The album covers and inserts provided hours of pleasure while I played the albums over and over. Whenever my parents or I travelled via Hong Kong, where everything was cheaper in those days, I'd add at least a dozen albums to my collection. In 1974, while studying for my last exams at high school, I entered a competition on my favourite radio station, to win 100 top albums. I won! I was studying for my economics exam when I'd heard my name read out as the winner. As soon as I started to earn money at Fell and Starkey, I purchased a top-class record player, amp and speakers (I still have the JBL speakers I bought in 1978 and the sound is just as good as it was then). I loved dancing around the house to the music that I was now going to have a hand in bringing to the public.

I was given the job of running the dubs library in the Motown arm of the company, 'dubs' being copies made from the master recordings that would then need to be sent out to radio stations and the like. Needless to say, it wasn't long before everyone was commenting on 'Dubs from dubs.'

By this stage, Debbie and Richard had decided to start a family. So, Fay and I moved into an apartment in Rose Bay that Debbie kindly found for us. We needed a third flatmate to make it work. So I contacted my friend Suzi, who was looking to move up from Melbourne anyway. She had a fantastic voice and, once settled into Sydney, became a backing singer for one of the country's most successful performers.

And that led to many nights spent going to hear Suzi and this megastar of the Australian music scene as they performed in venues across Sydney.

Music! Oh, how I love the way it makes me feel. And thanks to my work and the exposure to the live music scene from watching Suzi, I was developing more interest in a broader range of genres.

Let's face it: listening to music, both live and in the home, just has to be recognised as a fundamental ingredient when it comes to *recipes for living*. And at that time, more than ever before, my life seemed to be filled with it. It wasn't just the gigs we'd go to see where Suzi was up on stage. Fay just happened to be going out with the tour manager of *Dragon* at the time. They were regulars at the Manzil Room which was just up the road in Kings Cross. A night going to see them play there typically led to leaving the venue in the early hours and looking for somewhere to get some breakfast or a slice of chocolate cake from Dean's (who happened to make what we considered the best chocolate cake in Sydney at the time). The Cross was such a happening place in those days, always with something open.

It wasn't always going to listen to Suzi or bands like Dragon when I went out though.

There was a little venue hidden away in a back laneway called the *Comedy Store*.

Comedy? Yeah, that's another important ingredient in some of the best *recipes for living*.

I ended up becoming a regular at the Comedy Store, particularly going to see George Smilovici and Sandy Gutman, who later became known as Austen Tayshus.

It was an easy place for me to go to by myself and it was great to meet new people now that I was living in Sydney.

I still remember so clearly the first time I went to see George performing there. He became famous for a routine that he built around his claim of, *I'm tuff* (which peaked at number ten on the Australian singles charts). During part of his show, he blurted out to everyone that he was Jewish. *Oh,* I thought to myself, *that's interesting*. I was sitting at the bar after his performance and he came up and joined me. "Hi, I couldn't help but notice you seemed to be enjoying the show," he said.

"Well, yeah. It was hilarious, and I kinda like that you're Jewish."

"Oh. So would that mean that you're Jewish too?"

"It might," I replied.

"I'll take that as a yes then."

I smiled. "You can take it however you want."

"There wouldn't be any chance of getting your phone number, would there?"

I blushed as I took a sip from my glass of water then dutifully wrote down my number on a coaster.

Didn't I say it before? How amazing it is the way people in the Jewish community are so good at finding each other? It's almost like we've got some kind of radar. I felt like I needed to pinch myself. Could this be really happening? This wonderful, funny, hunk of a guy, who just happened to be Jewish, wants to take me out. What good Jewish girl wouldn't feel swept off her feet?

The next day, I could hardly wait to get on the phone to tell Mum. "I met this really nice guy. He's so funny, and good looking, and such a gentleman."

"Oh, this is good."

"And get this, Mum. He's originally from Melbourne, and he's Jewish."

"Oh, this is wonderful. What's his name?"

"It's George, George Smilovici."

Mum laughed. "George? I remember him so well. When you were little, you and George played together all the time. His younger brother, Alexander, used to join in too. You were around five years old. The three of you were so cute."

As it turned out, the Smilovici family were old friends of my parents and they had been very close.

My dreams fell away like they'd suddenly been turned to dust. When George called, I didn't quite know how to break the news to him. "I called my mother this morning and told her about meeting you."

"Okay." I could tell by his tone of voice in that one word reply that he knew something wasn't quite right.

"It seems we've met before, a long time ago."

"Go on..."

"Our parents, they knew each other, when we were kids."

The silence on the other end of line told me he was listening intently.

"Apparently we played together... all the time. We were only like, five years old."

More silence.

"I'd been so hoping we'd be able to..."

"Yeah, me too. But hearing what you're telling me now. I don't know... it'd just feel wrong."

"I know, now that we know... it's like we're brother and sister."

It might seem to you as you read this that it shouldn't have been such a big deal. After all, it's not like we were officially family. But to us, it felt like we really might as well have been blood relatives. At least in each other we'd managed to find friendship, a friendship I still cherish.

Trying to put the lost dream of romance behind me, I headed back into work the next day at Polygram Records, resuming my role as 'Dubs from Dubs'.

Pretty cool life I had, huh? Despite my disappointment about having to settle for a platonic relationship with George. Hanging out with musos and comedians at night then working in a recording company through the day. That's how I'd wanted to perceive it – but the day job was not quite as glamorous as it looked from the outside. In reality, the recording industry seemed to be overrun by people who behaved like overgrown adolescents. The 'sex and drugs and rock and roll' vibe was just ridiculously over the top. I really didn't like it, particularly the misogynistic attitudes of just about every male working there. That was like nothing I'd ever experienced before.

I'd been there six months when my boss came up to me one day. "Hey Dubs, we need to talk."

"Okay," I replied, with just a touch of trepidation.

"I don't think you're cut out for this," he said.

I quietly nodded in agreement then went through the motions of handing in my resignation. This was a guy who'd made a couple of tokenistic efforts to flirt with me—to include me in the music scene with guys hitting on me while the drugs and alcohol flowed. But you know what? I had no intention of allowing myself to fall into their 'rock and roll' lifestyle, where I was expected to be charmed into doing things I didn't want to.

Walking away from that job was a huge relief.

The Sandwich Girl

Walking away from Polygram left me with a slight problem. I really wanted to enjoy the Sydney outdoors and beachy lifestyle, but the sad reality was that I needed to earn money to do so. It was time to tap into my inner entrepreneurial spirit. I came up with a novel idea that also suited my developing interest in healthy cooking. Having visited the 2MMM radio station while working at Polygram, I knew the station was close to where I lived. It seemed they might appreciate if someone were to visit their office around lunchtime with pre-made sandwiches, saving them the need to go out and get it themselves. Although I was a vegetarian, I recognised that my potential market for the most part wasn't. So, I made a range of sandwiches featuring chicken and salad, as well as vegetarian ones with avocado, tofu and salad. I then took them through the offices to the staff. My trial run proved successful.

In fact, it was more than successful... it was great! I was my own boss and, for the first time, I'd found myself working with food to make a living.

The people at 2MMM were nice to deal with and it meant that I still felt a connection with the music industry. I even got to hear the inside story about what was set to become popular by joining in conversations with the 2MMM staff.

Every day they greeted me with a smile and compliments.

"Loving these sandwiches, Sandy," said one.

"...delicious!" said another.

And then, "How good is this, the best sandwiches, and you're bringing them to our desk. Love the service you're providing."

As well as providing healthy food to the staff, a welcome byproduct was that my record collection kept expanding, courtesy of hot tips from the staff about new releases as I did my rounds.

"Hi Sandy. Hey, did you know the Stones have a new album about to come out?"

"Really?"

"Yeah, it's called Tattoo You. There's a single from it that I reckon will be a bit of hit for them: it's called *Waiting on a Friend*."

"Cool, thanks. I'll watch out for it."

This was the dream, playing out just as I had imagined it would. It worked so well in fact that I only needed to work three days a week. How did I spend the rest of my time? At the beach!

And what about that whole 'moving to Sydney' thing? It finally felt like it was working out and, with the extra time I had on my days off, I started thinking about what else I might like to try my hand at. What other entrepreneurial activities would suit a young woman's lifestyle?

I thought about all the places I enjoyed going to during my spare time: vegetarian restaurants, nightclubs, music venues and especially the Comedy Store.

I'd met a lot of people in Sydney by that stage, and there were also plenty of people living in Sydney by then who I'd known in Melbourne. They were all so interesting that I thought about how much fun it could be to create a big event where I could bring them all together. This was in the back of my mind when I paid a visit to the Natural History Museum in College Street, one of my favourite cultural haunts. Across the road from Hyde Park in Sydney, it's a grand old building with a magnificent sandstone facade.

While there, I discovered the museum's top floor, complete with balcony, was available to hire out for events.

You've no doubt already guessed that I enjoy a party. Now I had the opportunity to throw a party in real style, and potentially generate income at the same time.

I asked a few friends what they thought.

"Love it!" said one.

"Great idea Sandy," said another.

I was excited. Everyone I spoke with was excited by the idea too.

I spoke to Fay and asked if she'd like to help out organising it.

She nodded as she replied, "Yeah, I'd love to."

"We can do this, I know we can," I said. "I'll get my friend, George, from the Comedy Store. He can do a stand-up routine. Then we just need to organise a band."

I called the museum and met with the manager to finalise the deposit and set the date. Can you believe it? I had actually booked the top floor of the museum to throw a party. It was going to be a night to remember! Catering for two hundred people, music, dancing and whatever else goes along with partying. While it may have been a lot to pull together, I was up to the challenge. I had a postcard invitation designed and printed which friends helped distribute as the word spread through my extended social network.

It was very much a closed network though. I wanted to ensure the party was an exclusive private affair for invited guests who had booked and paid in advance. This also meant that I knew how many people to cater for and that there'd be little wastage.

It was amazing! The tickets all sold. George put on a great performance and the band had everyone up and dancing.

Life was rolling on quite nicely. I'd found a *recipe for living* in Sydney that was filled with friendship, music, laughter, fun, and a work/life balance that gave me ample time to enjoy life.

Then one day, something totally unexpected happened. I arrived at the 2MMM building's carpark and unloaded the sandwiches I'd prepared to sell that day. I approached the lift as was my usual routine. Then, I came to an abrupt halt. My path to the lift was blocked by a group of people who looked angry... angry with me.

"Where do you think you're taking those?"

"I've made sandwiches..."

No response.

"They're to take upstairs..."

The biggest one spoke up. "You're not taking them up there. Not anymore, you're not."

"But... I..."

Yeah, that's right, I was a little lost for words. They weren't though. As it turned out they had pretty good reason to be angry with me. They owned a sandwich shop on the building's ground floor, and apparently a part of their lease arrangement was that no one from outside was allowed to bring in sandwiches to sell upstairs.

Oops!

It honestly hadn't occurred to me that would have been an issue, but when confronted by those angry shop owners, it was hard to make a case to defend myself.

These days, with all the regulations around food preparation, I wouldn't have been able to do it anyway. The good thing though was that I'd finally found my calling. Food preparation. I loved it and I was determined to create a future for myself revolving around healthy food.

Mullum

During the few years I'd been in Sydney, there was a steady flow of new people who'd found out I was there through other connections, both from Sydney and Melbourne. Naturally, as I was single, I was open to expanding my social scene and open to new adventures!

One of the guys who rocked up one day from Melbourne with a couple of his mates was connected via Annie, a friend I'd met in Goa. His name was Geoff, and he seemed like a cool guy. "I've got a property up in Mullumbimby," he said.

"Oh? I've never been there," I replied.

"It's magical. There's rainforest everywhere you look. Heaps of people are moving up there to live an alternative lifestyle, growing their own food and building their own homes from local materials. A lot of them are living in communes, it's just great."

"That sounds interesting. What's your property like?"

"It's on a few acres about an hour out of town. There's a permanent creek running through. It's really private and just so peaceful. I'm heading up there next week... I just need to organise the transport."

Can you guess how I responded?

"Can I come too?"

What else would I say? That line was already one of my most common ingredients in my *recipes for living*. I did follow it up with an offer though.

"I've got a car. I can drive us up there." He was thrilled, and a few days later, I was off on a new adventure.

My car at the time was a Datsun 180Y. Anyone who was around in Australia during the eighties will know the car I mean. One of the original two-door hatchbacks. Of course, having always been a city girl, I had no idea what sort of car you needed if you were headed to a property outside Mullum. The 'road' was more of a four-wheel drive track. Of course, Geoff hadn't mentioned this to me beforehand. It was like he'd just assumed I would've known the roads up there are more suitable for goats than Datsuns. Somehow though, my little car made it to his property, albeit with the suspension completely shot afterwards. Oh, and did I mention that my memory of the drive up there is somewhat hazy? Geoff loves to drive. So, I was happy to be in the passenger seat and act as the designated DJ for the trip, playing my favourite music in my up-to-date sound system. To be honest though, I can't quite remember which way we went or where we stopped on the way. One thing I do remember is that we had a lot of fun… I'll leave it to your imagination to work out why that might be.

Once we'd worked our way up the mountain to where his house stood, I was in for yet another surprise.

I looked at what appeared to be an outdoor entertaining area, with a floor and some posts supporting a simple roof and some furniture scattered about. "So, where's the house?"

He took a deep breath and smiled as he stretched his arms out. "You're looking at it." There was no power, no plumbing, and everything was made with materials sourced from his property.

"Okay…" I was somewhat taken aback. In reality, I had only two options, to turn around and head back on a road that had just killed my little car's suspension, or I could stick it out and try at least a night of getting a bit closer to nature than I was used to. Considering that the light was already fading, it was a bit of a no-brainer. "…I'll get my things out of the car."

You know what? I ended up having a great time while I was there. Although our relationship was totally platonic, it was a two-week period that had a profound impact, particularly after a trip to a commune just out of Bangalow. I loved the freedom at Geoff's property, showering with buckets of cool water in an open paddock and crashing out in a sleeping bag on the floor in the open with just a roof for protection from any rain.

Geoff showed me around, driving my Datsun with the not-so-stable-now suspension up and around the hills. We visited people who lived in Main Arm and then spent some time visiting a Commune that was reminiscent of a kibbutz I'd been to in Israel—a community living off the grid and sharing facilities while growing their own food and living with nature. We arrived when they were just about to start their weekly meeting and were invited to join them. They offered us some delicious vegan food and the people were all warm and friendly. Some of them were into natural therapies as well, an area I was becoming more interested in as time went on. I paid attention to everything and loved what I'd seen, so much so that I began to wonder if *this* was actually the lifestyle that suited me.

But as this meeting of the commune inhabitants continued, it opened my eyes to one of the more prevalent problems within alternate lifestyle communities. The discussion swung around to being all about how they were going to make money. These people had chosen to drop out of society without having given much thought to income. No matter how idealistic the alternate lifestyle may have appeared, money is still an essential element to being able to live. It seemed so clear to me that, if you want to drop out from a structured life, you really need to have some sort of income-generating projects in place to support your lifestyle. I'd come from a background where my parents worked hard to provide. I'd studied and worked in finance, and this commune lifestyle was new to me. I suggested they do things like take photographs of nature, or make postcards, or collect pots of the herbs they grew on the land – all things they could sell at the local markets. Although they made notes about what I was suggesting, I never found out whether or not they followed through on any of it.

Of course, there were those who moved up there who came from wealthier families. I met at least one person who fitted this category and was able to support himself that way. Nevertheless, there was still much to admire. I looked at the focus and joy that these people were putting in to living healthier lifestyles, not just growing their own food but also avoiding the use of chemicals. They tried to do everything as sustainably as they could, and had created their own family of people they chose to live with in a community.

But was it the lifestyle for me? Was this potentially a healthy *recipe for living* that would make a good fit for my needs?

Geoff ended up asking. "Do you think you could handle this lifestyle?"

I shook my head. "To be honest, I don't really think it's me."

"You're not happy where you are though, are you?"

I dwelt on that thought for a moment. There was a guy in Melbourne that I'd hooked up with when he was in Sydney for a record fair. His name was Peter, and I *really* liked him. "I kind of miss Melbourne," I replied, "but then, I was really enjoying the little sandwich business I had going in Sydney."

"So, you enjoy working with food? We established that when I first met you."

"I know, but I want to learn more about it. I really love the idea of food as being the foundation of good health. I want to focus on *healthy* food."

After a couple of weeks in Mullum' and Byron Bay it was time to return to Sydney. Geoff's friend Henry was still staying in Sydney as well and we spent time together forging lifelong friendships. But my thoughts had become occupied with what I wanted to do next, how I wanted to live, and where. And there was Peter, who I really liked and wanted to spend more time with.

"You're someone who seems like you need to keep yourself busy with new things," said Henry one day. "Do you know what you want to do now?"

"I had a couple of good conversations with Geoff about that... I enjoyed doing the sandwich thing so much that I really want to learn more about good, healthy food and how best to prepare it. I want to somehow make that into my work."

"You know what?" said Henry. "I know a woman in Melbourne... you need to talk to her. She's got a health food shop in Balaclava. I know her from when my parents had the fruit shop next door."

"I know that area, I grew up around there. My family were living near there when I was born."

"Well, she told me she's looking for someone to help pack the shelves and help serving customers. I'll give her a call if you want."

"Really?"

"Really."

It was time to go home to Melbourne.

Part II
Building a Life

"Accept this moment as if you have chosen it"
—Eckhart Tolle

Back to Melbourne

"Hi, I'm looking for Margaret Barrett?"

"You've found her."

I extended my hand. "My name's Sandra, Sandra Dubs. My friend, Henry... he told me you're looking for someone to help out."

Her grip was warm and reassuring as we shook hands. "Ah, yes. I got a phone call about you the other day."

That was my first conversation with the woman who was destined to become such an important mentor to me. A nurse by trade, Margaret was probably the most knowledgeable person I'd met by that stage regarding health and nutrition. Plus, she owned her own health food store, something I'd started to imagine myself doing in the future. I'd become more interested in healthy eating, vegetarian cooking and natural therapies. I wanted to learn how to cook and learn about the nature of foods as medicine for a compromised immune system like mine.

Margaret and her husband, Don, had opened *Bango Health Foods* in 1979. Two years later they changed the name to *The Muesli Specialist* in 1981, but were known to everyone as *Barrett's Health Food* until selling the business in 2007. They were true pioneers of the health food industry in Melbourne.

I was destined to learn so much about health and nutrition from Margaret over the ensuing years of working there. But it was about more than that. There were also important lessons from her on *other* aspects of life.

"If a customer asks you about something and you don't know the answer, don't try and bluff your way through. Just tell them. Say, 'Sorry, I don't know.' They'll be grateful for your honesty," was one such pearl of wisdom. Another was, "It's important to listen. Listen to everything a customer tells you. Don't assume that you know what they're talking about. *Listen* to them." Those two pieces of advice seem so simple, and yet they were a revelation to me at the time.

"What led you to buy the store?" I asked her one day.

She paused and looked reflective before responding, "my son, he's got some mental health issues. It's made me so aware of how important diet is – it makes a huge difference for him. But good, healthy food can actually be hard to find in the supermarkets. So, I decided that owning my own health food store would be the best way to ensure I always had good food choices and good quality nutritional supplements available."

My imagination roamed and ideas started forming into a plan. Could I perhaps follow the same pathway? What better way could there be to access the healthiest foods than to own a health food store? Could I build a career around healthy food? It was a lifestyle that I wanted to embrace. It resonated. I was drawn to the philosophy that I'd first encountered in Israel, of enjoying healthier options by using nutritious foods as medicine.

Margaret had taught me the importance of listening, and I took that lesson on board with enthusiasm. More importantly though, she inspired me to study and learn more about health. I embraced it all. She was my first *real* mentor.

Fuelled by this new-found motivation, I attended courses on nutrition at the *Southern School of Natural Therapies,* wanting to learn more about how the body works, what it needs and where to get it from. Looking through old notebooks from that time is a potent reminder of the lessons learned about all the minerals our bodies need. One such mineral being selenium which, following cancer, radiation therapy and a splenectomy, was extremely important for me personally. In fact, selenium is still a daily add-on in my health support routine. It's a mineral that's important for reproduction, thyroid gland function, and protecting the body from damage caused by free radicals and infection. Selenium is also an essential component of various enzymes and proteins, called selenoproteins. These help the body manufacture DNA and protect against cell damage and infections. And do you know what? It's not hard to find where to get it from – you can find it in Brazil nuts for example.

I discovered there was a cornucopia of foods that supported health in myriad ways. Like the compounds in shiitake mushrooms that may help fight cancer, boost immunity, and support heart health, I was becoming a fan of eating sea vegetables (or seaweed). They contain a wide range of vitamins and minerals, including iodine, iron, and calcium. Some variations can even contain high amounts of vitamin B12. They're also a valuable source of Omega-3 fats.

I learned that weakness and muscular pain can be linked to low Potassium, an essential mineral needed by *all* tissues throughout the body. It's sometimes referred to as an electrolyte because it carries a small electrical charge that activates various cell and nerve functions. Potassium is found naturally in many fruits and vegetables and is available as a supplement. Its main function in the body is to help maintain normal levels of fluid inside our cells. And sodium, its counterpart, helps maintain normal fluid levels outside of cells. Potassium also helps muscles to contract and supports normal blood pressure.

I was becoming a sponge for nutritional knowledge and applying health-supportive foods in my own daily selections.

My return to Melbourne, after living in Sydney for two years, couldn't have been better. I was working for a woman who inspired me like no one had before. The fact that her health food store was just around the corner from where my family had lived when I was born seemed almost prophetic.

I was back in a familiar neighbourhood and, the more time I spent working with Margaret, the more I found myself daydreaming about owning my own health food store.

I reflected on my reasons for returning to Melbourne: that my flatmates were moving out and moving on, that my main entrepreneurial project had been brought to an abrupt halt. Also, I had met Peter. Returning to Melbourne hadn't just meant getting a job, it also meant finding somewhere to live. I'd made enquiries with Melbourne friends prior to leaving Sydney. Someone knew a woman, Ruth, who had a room in a flat in Prahran. We spoke and decided I could move in with her. My relationship with Peter was still new and, as much as I was totally smitten, I hadn't lived with a guy before. So I felt more comfortable about sharing a home with Ruth. We had a lot of fun as we got to know each other and she remains a special friend to this day.

Although Mum and Omi were thrilled that I was returning, they weren't so sure of my decision to give up being an accountant and embrace the world of health food. With time, they'd come around to realising what a good fit the change was and how beneficial it was destined to be.

All in all, being back in Melbourne was the right move in so many ways.

My future looked bright.

India, 1982

As I said before, I felt like I had found someone really special in Peter. I also felt like it was time to travel again. Could it be that this time I'd found someone I could travel with?

"Have you thought of going to India?" I asked Peter one day.

"India? Yeah, that'd be great. I haven't been there yet and it's right up there on my 'must go to' list."

Being a seasoned solo traveller by that stage, I was keen to see how it would go travelling with someone I was in love with. Could love be another ingredient that, combined with travel, would add a spicy flavour to the recipes for living I was formulating?

I was about to find out as our plane touched down in Delhi at 5am on Christmas Day, 1982. We checked into the Imperial New Delhi. Peter had a keen interest in historic hotels, and staying in such a plush hotel was certainly an upgrade for me after more modest accommodation during my previous trip to Goa four years earlier.

Built on an eight-acre estate and set in magnificent gardens, it was a safe haven and refuge in the heart of India's bustling capital. The hotel is home to a priceless collection of over five thousand original artworks from the seventeenth and eighteenth centuries, spread throughout the common areas and individual rooms.

It's reminiscent of a nineteenth century Indian Palace, in the land of Maharajas and Maharanis. Opening in 1936, it was the first hotel to open its doors in New Delhi.

Peter and I excitedly settled in before indulging in a midday breakfast, set in the Imperial Gardens. The day ended up being a bit of a blur as we rode around on a scooter provided by the hotel, finishing our day with a midnight dinner at another luxury hotel that Peter had heard about, the Siddarth Hotel. Peter was making the discovery of new foods and places to dine a pleasure. What a dream start to our Indian adventure!

The next morning, it felt a bit easier to take things in. "It's so different to what I was expecting," I said to Peter.

"Oh? How so?"

"Well, I was expecting more poverty. It's more of a bustling metropolis than I thought it would be. Quite a pleasant surprise." We did a tour that took in some of the big tourist attractions. Ghandhi's Tomb, the Red Fort and the largest mosque in India: the Jama Masjid of Delhi, Then we immersed ourselves in the hustle and bustle of the Sunday Markets. The smells, sights, feel and taste of local living were all a pleasure to soak up. I absolutely loved it!

The frantic pace of our sightseeing continued the next day, starting with a four-hour bus ride to Agra, home of the Taj Mahal. There wasn't any time to chill out on the way though. Unlike me, I could tell that Peter was keen to maximise what we could fit into each day. This conflict of priorities was quickly creating tension between us, Peter letting fly with a series of criticisms that I wasn't sure how to take.

I sat in the coffee lounge the next morning gazing in awe at the poetic beauty of one of the world's most famous buildings – one of the seven wonders of the world. It was just after sunrise. The rain and grey clouds hanging over Agra that morning did nothing to dampen its ability to impress itself into my soul. It seemed an incredible contrast to the thoughts and feelings racing around inside my head in that moment. More than anything, I felt confused.

Left: standing in front of the Taj Mahal, a monument to love

What sort of person am I? These things that Peter's saying about me, is there truth in them, are they faults in my personality? If they are, then I'm a mess. I felt inadequate. Was I being too sensitive to criticism? It was such a cruel irony to have these thoughts while basking in the glowing aura of this monument to love.

But Rajasthan awaited. "Come on, we need to get the bus to Jaipur," Peter was anxious about our agenda and wanted to get on the road again, to tear me away from this indulgence of one man's love for his wife that's mesmerised so many throughout the centuries. We'd already discussed the travel plans for the next stage of our holiday… he wanted to catch the same bus as the locals so we could experience the journey as they did.

"Deluxe! Deluxe!" they kept chanting at us. After a good deal of frustration, we convinced them to let us board the same bus as the locals. When the bus finally arrived, my jaw dropped. Had we made a mistake to forgo the deluxe model intended for foreign tourists? It wasn't so bad once we were on board. Yet, no matter how much we wanted to experience the journey as they did, as Westerners we stood out, and passengers who'd already been seated insisted we take their place. Was it something to do with caste? I don't know for sure, but with the bus ride lasting six hours (including several stops along the way and a change of bus after the first one broke down), we kind of felt glad to have a seat by the time we reached Jaipur at 9pm that night. Even though it was hard to see the pink city in the dark, the vibe was wondrous.

I pulled my jacket tight around me as the bus drove through the city to yet another luxury hotel, the Rambagh Palace, Jaipur. where we intended staying.

"I am very sorry to inform you, Sir," the manager said to Peter, "we unfortunately only have one hundred and five rooms and they are all booked this evening."

"Do you know anywhere else we might be able to get a room for tonight?" asked Peter.

"If you and your lady friend would like to have some dinner in the restaurant, I will phone around and see if I can organise something for you."

No sooner had we sat down than I heard a voice call out.

"Sandy? Peter?"

I turned around. "You've got to be kidding me! What are you two doing here?"

"Small world, huh?"

"Too right it is." I shook my head in disbelief.

It's one of the amazing things about travelling. The world is such a huge place. Yet, so often, you'll find yourself running into people you know in the most unexpected places. When you're travelling you really do learn to expect the unexpected. Meeting these two out of the blue was certainly that... and quite welcome. I was so tired and Peter was getting somewhat grumpy. So chatting to these two friends from Melbourne over dinner, while the manager sought alternative accommodation for us, was a welcome distraction.

"Excuse me." It was the manager. "I have found you a room, it's at the York, just down the road from here."

Hooray! At long last we had a room for the night. At least, that's how I felt when the manager first told us he'd found us a place. When we got there though, it would be fair to say my enthusiasm waned somewhat.

It was noisy.

The room was damp.

It was the pits.

To make it worse, we had nowhere else to go.

You know those times when you're dead tired, totally exhausted, but you still can't get to sleep? Think about that and multiple it by five. That's how bad it was. Even trying to wipe ourselves out by smoking hashish didn't help (the hashish had been given to us by a guy at The Imperial New Delhi). We just couldn't get to sleep in this room that would have to be a candidate in a competition for the world's worst hotel room... ever!

The next morning, we moved into a suite at the Hotel Mansingh. What a relief after the nightmare of the previous night. But the sleepless night hadn't been good for someone with a compromised immune system. I was starting to feel a bit feverish.

Regardless, we headed off to the markets, which probably wasn't such a good idea. Jaipur at the time had a population of 700,000. And it seemed like every one of them, plus their relatives and friends from out of town, had decided to descend on the markets that day.

To make it worse, as I looked around, I commented to Peter, "I can't believe how polluted it is here."

"Lighten up will you," he replied. "We're not here to pass judgement."

Really? It was just an observation. Was it absolutely necessary to bite my head off over such a simple comment? By this stage it was like we were constantly at loggerheads with each other. It was getting really hard.

Waking up on New Year's Eve, it was Peter this time who was feeling unwell – in fact, really quite crook. The sad part was that I kind of relished the opportunity to spend a bit of time on my own. On this last day of 1982 I could spend a bit of time alone with my thoughts... an opportunity for some reflection.

Why must emotions sometimes be so confusing? I loved Peter dearly. When he wasn't there, I missed him. It was such a contradiction; when I was alone, I felt more together, even though it felt like part of me was missing. But when he was around, we seemed to bring out the worst in each other. I was still quite young and just learning about being in a relationship, while he'd already been through a marriage and divorce. I didn't know how to deal with the constant criticisms. Was it my fault? Did I expect too much of him? I found myself wishing so much that I could understand the *recipe for living* in a happy relationship. What are the ideal ingredients for that? Did I use too much of one ingredient and not enough of the other? And what of his contribution? Is that where my problem was? Is it that I couldn't control his input? He kept telling me that I made it too hard, too much of a struggle. Did Peter have any idea just how unusual it was for me to be able to imagine spending my life committed to someone? These questions kept racing through my head when I joined up with three young Italians ready to celebrate the New Year.

"Happy New Year!" Every Indian was crying out in the street, dancing with an intoxicating vigour, their faces radiating joy. . The occasion seemed to mean more to them than to all the western tourists. And the dancing? I let myself go and flowed with the music.

"How are you feeling?" I asked Peter the next morning.

"Much better, thank you," he replied. "I needed to just sleep and not eat."

An Indian, Kiky, came to collect us from our room. He'd promised to take us to visit his father, a seller of precious and semi-stones.

"You like that?" Peter asked as I held a necklace up and spent longer than usual inspecting it.

"It's beautiful." I was entranced as the light danced on the cut surface of the stones.

"Consider it yours then."

I could almost feel my heart flutter with joy. It seemed the charming and caring Peter I'd fallen for was back.

After lunch we visited the Amber Palace, aka Amber Fort. It was constructed in 1592 by Raja Man Singh, the Rajput commander of Akbar's army. It was later expanded and renovated by Raja Jai Sigh I. Set among the hills overlooking Maota Lake and located eleven kilometres from the city, the palace is a fine example of Indo-Islamic architecture that carries the pride of Jaipur on its shoulders. I thought of how extraordinary it was to have been built over four hundred years ago, and what a rich life those who served in the army in those times lived.

The next day, it was a 5am flight to Jodhpur. Once again, Peter had done his homework evaluating the options regarding where we should stay. I'd also spent considerable time poring over my Lonely Planet book and its recommendations of what to see and where to eat. Our research had left us hoping to stay at the amazing Umaid Bhawan Palace, one of the world's largest private residences. Construction took from 1929-1943 and it was named after Maharaja Umaid Singh, grandfather of the present owner, Gaj Singh. The palace is the principal residence of the former Jodhpur royal family and has three hundred and forty-nine rooms, part of it now hosting a museum as well. But had we learned from our previous experience and booked in advance? Of course its forty-five hotel rooms were fully booked. Oh well, all we could do was go with the flow (something I was starting to learn to accept on this trip). India has many palaces that now act as hotels. At the recommendation of our driver, Dax, we booked ourselves a room at the Ajit Singh Palace.

"Wow!" It was the only word that came to mind as we approached.

"Yes Madam," said Dax, "indeed you may find this building impressive. The palace was built by the Maharajah for his brother, Ajit."

"It's just amazing."

Peter nodded in agreement. "Yeah, it looks pretty special alright."

The Ajit Bhawan Palace was built in 1927 as a residence for the family of Maharaj Ajit Singh, younger brother of the late Maharaja of Jodhpur, Umed Singh Sahib. In the nineteen seventies it was converted into India's first heritage hotel, taking advantage of the building's old-world charm.

While smaller than the Maharajah's own Umaid Bhawan Palace, it was a palace nevertheless. It's hard not to feel a bit like a princess when you stay in a place like that. They treated us like royalty from the moment we checked in. We were taken to a gorgeous free-standing room built with the traditional adobe rammed earth method. It had been inspired by a book the Maharajah had read about a woman travelling through the Australian desert. Elegantly appointed, the room featured a host of traditional artworks and a luxuriously comfortable bed.

The sense of luxury continued as we headed back to the Umaid Palace for dinner. When our meal came, Peter exclaimed, "This food is just amazing!" He was in a special quarter of heaven that's put aside for those who enjoy Indian cuisine. And his day was about to get even better.

A man seated at a table near us asked Peter, "Do you play squash?" The question came from none other than the Maharajah's grandson. Peter couldn't resist the opportunity to play a game of squash with true royalty, an invitation match on the Maharajah's own private squash court. He was absolutely thrashed, but it didn't matter, even though his opponent was glowing with pride after the win. The thrill for Peter was embedded in the opportunity itself.

Back at the Ajit, we were joined by a French couple for a dinner that featured good conversations and laughter. As I glanced across at Peter's expression, I could see that he was enjoying himself as much as I was. Everything felt as perfect as it could be.

The next morning we dragged ourselves out of our comfortable palace bed to board a train for a trip to see the fort at Jaisalmer.

As our train rattled along, I said to Peter between coughs, "It's so dusty."

He looked out the window at the landscape rushing by then nodded. "Yeah, but it could be worse. We're travelling first class, remember?"

And he was right, it really could have been so much worse. It was small comfort when I was struggling to breathe.

An Indian man joined us in our compartment. He had a transistor radio going so he could listen to the cricket. "...*caught by Chappell after a splendid ball from Hogg. Gavaskar is out for just nine runs.*"

Peter's ears pricked up. "What's the score?"

"It's one for twenty-seven. The Australians sent India in to bat after winning the toss."

Great! I thought. *Dust and a cricket broadcast.* Not a great recipe (at least, not from my point of view) for an enjoyable day rattling across the sub-continent.

Our companion looked at us. "You're from Australia?"

"Yes," I replied, "from Melbourne."

"Ah, yes. Home of the MCG. I'm from the Punjab. I'm on my way to a new posting."

"What do you do?" I asked, hoping to move the conversation away from what was happening in the cricket.

"I'm a captain, in the army."

"...and he's out! Shrikanth has been caught by Border after another short ball from Thomson."

"Yes!" cried out Peter, before he and the captain fell into a conversation about bouncers and fine edges and a host of other cricket terminologies that were all but meaningless to me. Peter hardly spoke with me on that long trip, lost in cricket banter with the army captain.

Hours later, the dust seemed to be swirling around in my head. By the time we arrived at Jaisalmer Station it was 8.30pm. I was really tired and run down as we checked into Jaisal Castle.

"I feel sick," I told Peter the next morning, "really sick." I felt like I couldn't get out of bed... until I needed the toilet that is. And when I needed to go, I really needed to. I spent the next day alternating between being unable to get up and having to rush to the toilet. I'd almost forgotten about my compromised immune system, but when I got sick, my vulnerability was laid bare in front of me.

To his great credit, Peter fussed over me during the time I was stuck in bed. He even went out and bought a mini-portable stove, saucepans and vegetables so he could cook for me, right there in our room. It made me feel loved and cared for in a way that washed away much of the angst I'd felt at times throughout our trip.

I don't even remember the train journey back to Jodhpur, but we made it in time for our flight to Bombay where we stopped for lunch. We had a good meal, at a recommended restaurant, before flying on to Goa later in the afternoon.

Even though it was only a few years since I'd last lazed on the beach there, I felt like a different person now. Memories of the impact my first trip to Goa came flooding back as I watched Indian tourists rush excitedly into an ocean they'd perhaps never seen before.

Our final days there were spent browsing through markets and mingling with the flowing tide of humanity that is India..

As someone who was seasoned as a solo traveller, this was the first time I'd travelled with a partner, with someone I loved more than I'd ever loved anyone before. But it somehow just wasn't the same. Travelling with Peter had highlighted the cracks in our relationship. As we flew home, I felt unsure whether or not we had a future after all, despite the depth of my feelings for him.

We returned to Australia ready to see what 1983 would have in store for us.

Relaxing on the beach in carefree Bali

A Bali Holiday

I'd been back in Melbourne for a while when a friend walked into the store.

"Hey Sandy, how you doing?" asked Benny. "How was India?"

"Great." I could tell by his expression. He could see I was hiding something. "Well, mostly it was good."

Benny had picked up on the fact that Peter and I had a few issues before the trip, so I wasn't surprised when he asked, "How's things going with Peter?"

"We've broken up." I shook my head. "It just wasn't working." In hindsight I now understand that he'd been recently separated when we'd first got together and wasn't comfortable at that stage committing to our relationship. I also had a good deal to learn about compromise, a concept I wasn't accustomed to. "I still love him," I sighed, "but sometimes I just wonder whether we're good for each other. And you know what? I think he's already seeing someone else."

"I get it." I could always rely on Benny to understand. "Maybe you need to get away again, put a bit of space between the two of you?"

I shrugged my shoulders. I knew he was right. But it didn't change the fact that I felt torn over what to do. I changed the subject. "So, what about you? Anything interesting happening in your life?"

"Funny you should ask about that. I'm planning on going to Bali for a couple of weeks and was hoping to ask you about it, seeing you've been there before."

My face lit up. "Bali?" What a great time I'd had there as a teenager ten years before. Benny was right. I did need to get away. And I couldn't think of anywhere better than Bali to go and clear my head. Somewhere that'd be far away from Peter and with a plethora of adventures in a tropical paradise to look forward to. "Can I come to?"

Benny's eyes betrayed his surprise. He'd been hoping to pick my brains before finalising his holiday plans, and now it looked like he might have a travel companion. "Well, I guess so. I can't see why not."

A few weeks later, we were landing in Denpasar. It seemed to me like this was just what I needed. I'd let Peter know what our plans were, as I had nothing to hide. My friendship with Benny was purely platonic, the kind of friendship that I needed.

It felt so wonderful to be back in Bali. By this stage, there were plenty of expats living there, from a variety of western countries. Benny introduced me to a Dutch woman who was making hand painted clothing there, taking advantage of the incredibly cheap prices of the materials. Despite this, she was struggling.

"This butterfly dress," I said, "I've got a friend back in Melbourne who'd love it."

"Thank you."

"How much?"

"Because you're a friend of Benny's, you can have it for fifteen dollars Australian."

"Oh, okay. What about this one?"

"That one's lovely, isn't it? You can have that one for thirty."

They were bargains, and I had a couple of hundred dollars that I could afford to spend on gifts for friends back in Australia. I decided that I'd spend it all here and now, so I could give Benny's friend a bit of help. All up I spent A$205 on buying three t-shirts, three dresses, a couple of skirts and a really cute butterfly-patterned top. It was a little more than I'd been intending to spend, but I knew how much it would help her.

"Are there many people doing what she's doing up here?" I asked Benny after we'd left.

"Oh yeah. There's so much opportunity here."

Ideas began ticking over in my head. I loved my job working for Margaret in the Health Food store, but hey, this was Bali. I looked at how relaxed most of the expats were and it certainly looked appealing. The people, the creativity, the food, the lifestyle and natural beauty all resonated with me.

It was such a relief to be thousands of miles away from the problems I'd been having with Peter. I could let my mind roam and explore ideas without having him swoop in and cut them down or takeover with his strong-minded personality.

So you can imagine my surprise when, early in the morning on my third day in paradise, there was a knock on the door of the bungalow we were renting.

"Surprise!"

"Peter? What are you doing here?"

"I missed you."

"I've been missing you too. But…" I was dumbfounded. This wasn't what I'd planned.

"I've organised a room for us."

I turned to Benny as he approached through the lush garden, my eyes expressing my total surprise at our unexpected guest's arrival. "Hi Peter. What a surprise." He extended his hand, the vibe being decidedly uncomfortable as they gripped each other's hands and attempted to wear sincerity in their smiles.

"Good to see you, Benny. I was just saying to Sandy that I've organised a room for us."

"You're quite welcome to stay here with me and Sandy if you want."

"Thanks, but I think Sandy and I will be more comfortable if we've got a place of our own."

I felt so embarrassed... and annoyed! But at the same time, here was a man who'd travelled across an ocean to be with me. Shouldn't I be happy that he'd obviously realised just how important our relationship was to him? Wasn't this a display of the kind of commitment to our relationship I'd been wanting from him all along? Dutifully, I packed my bag.

Despite Peter's incredible effort to display his love by following me across the sea, the next couple of weeks were emotionally challenging. While there were some fun times, there were plenty of difficult ones too. I was torn and definitely *not* as relaxed as I'd been before Peter's arrival.

It felt awkward whenever I caught up with Benny during the rest of that trip, with Peter constantly ensuring he was the focus.

I'd actually been hoping that having a break from him by going to Bali might end up being a catalyst for rebooting our relationship – but his unannounced appearance had blown that idea away.

The up-and-down nature of our relationship seemed sadly stuck in its dark mode for the duration of the trip. And Peter's presence made the flight back even worse. I remember crying a lot. Poor Benny was stuck having to endure this tension as well for the duration of the six-hour flight.

Stepping Up

Not long after returning from Bali, I came across a job advertisement in the local newspaper. It was for a full-time manager at Soulfoods, a health food store in South Yarra (they also owned another store in Fitzroy of the same name). I'd loved working with Margaret, but was only working part-time there. This was a full-time position. Plus, I'd be the *manager*. It'd be a step up for me both in responsibility and pay.

I spoke to Margaret and she recognised what an important opportunity it was. "You'll do well," she said. "I'm very happy for you."

I went for the interview and talked about my passion for healthy wholefoods, my employment history with Fell and Starkey, Readers Digest, Polygram, the discovery of my entrepreneurial capacity (establishing the homemade, healthy sandwich business) and my time working with Margaret since returning to Melbourne.

And you know what? I got the job! It was just what I needed after what I'd been through with Peter in Bali.

My understanding of healthy foods and its preparation was developing further as I began to explore the benefits of macrobiotics, a philosophy on nutrition with its origins in Japan. Interestingly, back in the eighties, health food stores were still largely seen as part of the counterculture, essentially part of an 'alternative' lifestyle philosophy.

Having grown up in the surrounding suburbs, managing Soulfood's South Yarra store was perfect. It brought back memories of shopping trips with my mother to the nearby Prahran Market, a haven in those days for consumers

seeking quality fresh fruit and vegetables. It was all about developing relationships with the sellers and having the best quality ingredients. Soulfoods brought that quality into a store in the main street, a store I had already frequented myself on many occasions to enjoy the fresh juices they had available.

When I got to appreciate the location more fully, I couldn't believe my luck. It was virtually right across the road from the Como Hotel where many Australian and overseas stars of film, television and music stayed. People like Telly Savalas, Peter Graves, Jane Badler, Joe Creighton and others came for fresh green juices and snacks. They enjoyed its organic and natural foods, or smoothies, salads and vegan snacks from the store's small takeaway café. There were also international tennis stars competing at the Australian Open. Jim Courier and Martina Navratilova became regular drop-ins while the tournament was on.

Organic foods were generally hard to come by in Australia at that time and my elite, tennis-playing clientèle were all accustomed to having ready access to quality organic produce in their home countries. I worked hard at stocking the best possible produce and artisan breads, even if it meant being my own produce courier.

The store attracted people I knew from my social circle as well. People who were just starting to become interested in wholefoods, organics and natural products.

One product range I was particularly fond of was the offerings from Spiral Foods, an importer of traditional and macrobiotic food products from Japan. It was owned by a guy called Jim who I'd met when he delivered stock from time to time at Margaret's health food store. It turned out he was a regular shopper at Soulfoods, so it gave me the chance to get to know him a little bit better.

Left: Nursing a more unusual visitor to Soulfoods

"So, how did you come to own a company like Spiral Foods?" I asked one day.

"Oh, that's a bit of a long story. An old friend owned it originally," replied Jim. "He died in a car accident." He paused for a moment and took a breath. "So, rather than see it fall away, I took it over."

I nodded solemnly then asked, "What did you do before that?"

"What, when I wasn't surfing? I worked for Juke. You know, the music rag?" Juke was a weekly music magazine based in Melbourne that ran from 1975 to 1991. It grew to become Australia's leading music magazine of the time, featuring work from some of the country's top music photographers. It was mostly popular though for its definitive gig guide. "I was doing marketing and all sorts of stuff for them."

"That's a bit of a change... going from a music magazine to importing macrobiotic products."

"Yeah, it might seem that way. But it was working for Juke that led me to get into macrobiotics in the first place." It turned out that Jim had developed that interest when he'd been involved in an article Juke ran on some of the big names in macrobiotics who'd come to Australia.

The managerial role at Soulfood was going well, and meeting people like Jim was an added bonus as I was keen to learn as much as I could about the zen macrobiotics philosophy of nutrition and lifestyle.

I devoured books and journals about herbal medicine, natural therapies, macrobiotics and using foods as medicine. My bookshelf was soon overflowing (I still have many of these books at home today).

Soulfood's owners Warren and Sharon were wonderful people to work for. Even though their main store was the one in Fitzroy, the South Yarra store was a thriving business in its own right.

On top of the job change, it was time to move on from the apartment I'd shared with Ruth since returning from Sydney. And you might be surprised to discover I'd ended up moving in temporarily with Peter while looking.

I wasn't sure about this, but I had nowhere else to go. Even though neither of us was feeling particularly committed to the relationship at the time, it seemed a touch ironic that he was the first partner I'd travelled overseas with and now, the first partner I'd lived with.

One night he asked me, "Are you going to have a party?"

"A party? What for?"

"Well, you're turning thirty this year."

"Do you have to remind me?"

"That's a pretty big deal. It's worth celebrating!"

"Yeah, I know." I thought about it for a moment before replying more fully, "I'd love to have a party, but I'm still trying to sort out somewhere to move to."

"We can have the party here, at my place."

Spontaneously, I threw my arms around him. For all the difficulties we'd been through, he was still capable of a thoughtfulness that warmed my heart and made me appreciate why I loved him. Again, I found myself lost in wondering whether the problems we'd experienced throughout our relationship had come from him or from me. I'd felt like I was being tested and criticised so much of the time. But perhaps that wasn't it all. Could it have been that I was just being insecure?

The party was wonderful!

Peter's house was the absolute perfect location and he loved to host a party almost as much as I did. There was the most amazing spread of food and drink laid on and everyone had a great time hanging out in his magnificent garden. It was the perfect way to celebrate thirty trips around the sun.

However, living together wasn't easy.

My heart wanted to be with him, but there was so much that I was trying to deal with and, in that regard, Peter wasn't much help. I needed either to live on my own or be with someone who knew how to build me up when I was at a low point. Someone who could support me with empathy and an understanding of my health problems. He was so much more confident and gregarious than I was at the time; I felt like he was hindering my potential to develop my own career.

I was having a coffee with Michael and Lilli a few days after the party and explained the difficulty I was having with Peter and how little success I was having in my search for alternative accommodation. Without hesitation Michael said, "You can move in with us until you find somewhere."

"Really?" I turned to Lilli. "Is that okay with you?"

"Of course it is, we've got plenty of room."

When I told Peter, he accepted my decision. "I still love you," he said. "You do know that, don't you?"

As it turned out, moving in with Michael and Lilli was just what I'd needed at the time. It allowed me to spend quality time with my young nephews, as well as considering my feelings toward Peter. It also allowed me to refocus on my health issues.

I went over to Mum's after settling in. She wanted to have a serious word with me about what I should do next.

"Sandra, you should use this as an opportunity to buy yourself a house. Renting is just not a good idea. All this money going on rent, it's not giving you security and financial independence. You've got a good, full-time job now. It's time you buy a place for yourself."

I nodded. "I know, but the deposit—"

"Don't you worry about that. I'll help you out with the deposit."

"But, Mum—"

She took my hands in hers and said, "I give with a warm hand. I want you to have some security. It's important."

There were many ingredients in my *recipes for living* that I learnt from my mother. And this was one of the most potent ingredients of all. *Give with a warm hand*, it was something she would say often. Her attitude was that there's no point in giving to someone if you're going to make them feel some sort of guilt for receiving your generosity. You give because you want to see them succeed, or because you can see they need a hand, and you celebrate that you've been able to help them. I could feel within her generosity that she acted on behalf of my late father as well, seeing he had left her with the security of a house and other investments they'd built up together through decades of hard work after their arrival in Australia.

Return of the Lump

As the end of 1986 approached, I was struggling to understand why there was still so much tension in my relationship with Peter. I loved him, and he professed to love me. I was confused and unsure of what was real and what wasn't. My heart was being broken. It seemed the only way forward was for us to have a break. To me, that's all it was, a little break. Was that naïve on my part? Was it realistic to think we could have a break and then maybe pick up later from where we'd left off?

Just to make my anxiety worse, I got up one morning and noticed a small lump on my neck.

And where was it? The same spot where I'd had one before.

Memories from ten years prior, when that first lump appeared, came flooding back. The biopsy, surgery, the intense radiation and my father's passing all raced around my head in a frenetic haze. I ran my hands along the scars on my neck and belly, potent reminders of the consequences of that first lump's discovery.

I called Mum. "Call Professor Penington, right now!" she said.

"Hello, Sandra?" he said when the receptionist had put me through to him.

"You remember me?"

"Oh, yes. Very much so." I guess it sticks in a doctor's memory when someone as young as I was required urgent treatment for cancer. "I'll send you a referral to a specialist. That'll need to be looked at very soon." He was running the medical school at the university full-time by then, so wasn't able to see me himself.

I dutifully made the appointment and went to see the doctor he'd recommended. It all happened so quickly that I don't recall the specialist's name, or even which hospital he was attached to.

His prognosis? "We'll need to remove that."

"Could it be related to the radiation treatment I had before?"

He shrugged his shoulders. "I can't really say, but I doubt it."

"Is it likely to be a problem?"

"I'm not really sure, but we should remove it anyway. Then we can find out whether or not it's cancerous." There it was, that word, 'cancer'. Nothing can prepare you adequately for hearing that from a doctor, even when you've been through it before. "We'll perform a thyroidectomy just to be safe."

"What does that mean?" I had a pretty fair idea what it meant, but still felt the need to ask the question.

"We'll be removing half your thyroid gland and the nodules where the lumps are." Well, at least this time it was only half of something getting cut out of me.

In case you don't already know, the thyroid is a butterfly shaped gland located in the front of the throat. It produces hormones that it sends throughout the body that are stored in nodules, some of which are located in the side of the throat. The thyroid gland and the body's immune system have an interactive relationship. My immune system had already been compromised with the removal of my spleen. Now, I had a doctor casually telling me he was going to perform surgery that would further compromise my body's defence system.

"Are you *sure* it's not related to the mantle radiation from before? I mean, it's in the same spot."

"I really can't see any reason why it should be. You were lucky to be able to get that treatment when you did. Radiation therapy wasn't readily available back then. You do realise that, don't you?"

I was swept up again in the whirlwind of the health system kicking into action. Despite the doctor's scepticism, it just seemed like too much of a coincidence that this new lump was in the same spot as the one I'd had when I was twenty. I felt all the angst from my treatment come flooding back.

The despair that I felt walking out of the specialist's office and making the journey home is something I'll never forget.

The first time round I'd had Ian to support me, to follow the whole process through and encourage me to believe it would be okay. Now I was also dealing with the break in my relationship with Peter. So I had no boyfriend there to reassure and comfort me. There was only Mum.

I jumped in my car feeling torn apart by emotion. *Breathe Sandy,* I thought to myself. *You need to get a grip. Breathe in, three, four. Hold, two, three, four. Breathe out, three, four.* I repeated the exercise four times before feeling in control enough to start the car and drive home.

Rather than taking my car back to Michael and Lilli's, where I was still staying, my car seemingly guided me to Peter's. I thought, *yes, this is where I need to be.*

Pulse racing, I knocked at the door.

I needed him... now more than ever before.

I knew I'd made a mistake the moment Peter opened the door only partially, like he was avoiding the possibility that I might walk in. "Sandy?"

"Hi, I... I needed to see you."

"What's up?" I could see his eyes glancing down toward the prominent bandage on my neck.

"The cancer—"

A woman's voice called out from the distance. "Peter? What are you doing?"

Peter's expression betrayed conflicting emotions.. Was I wrong to think we were just having a little break? Had we actually broken up? In hindsight, I should have known better than to turn up unannounced. It had simply never occurred to me that he might have someone else with him. "I'm really sorry Sandy—"

My voice was choking on tears as I responded. "No... it's okay." I'd already started backing away from the door.

I heard the voice in the distance again. "Don't let her in."

Peter appeared lost for words.

"Don't worry..." I was struggling to get the words out. "I shouldn't have stopped by unannounced." I turned and walked away.

Could it have been any worse? As I walked back to my car, head spinning wildly, I heard Peter call after me. "Sandy, wait—"

I got in the car, ran through my breathing exercises again and drove off.

"Sandy!"

I glanced up at the rearview mirror. He was running after me.

Should I stop? Give him a chance to explain? So many questions raced through my mind. I opted to keep driving.

I looked in the mirror again and there he was, still chasing my car.

I put my foot down on the accelerator, tears blurring my vision. Peter must have run a good few hundred metres by the time he disappeared from view.

A few days later I was on the operating table for what I'd been told was considered a straightforward procedure. The surgeon made an incision in the side of neck, pushed the muscle aside, then cut away and removed half my thyroid, along with the nodules that were attached to it in my neck.

A week or so into my recovery from the surgery, I heard a knock at the door to my room.

"Hey, Sandy." It was Peter, standing in the doorway with a friend of his, there no doubt for moral support. "I just wanted to apologise for the other day and check in on you, see how you're doing."

The voice of the woman who'd been at his place when I'd stopped by was still echoing through my head. Was I right to feel let down? Rightly or wrongly, in my vulnerable state I still felt anger toward this man whom I had loved so much, and who had gone to such great lengths to express his love for me.

I didn't respond. He hadn't been there when I needed him. As far as I was concerned, he might as well have not been there in my room either.

When I next looked up, Peter and his friend had gone.

Auction!

"Have you seen this one?" asked Mum. "Oh, that looks interesting."

There was an auction coming up for a house in Malvern East, a quaint little cottage. I'd been staying with Michael, Lilli and the boys for over four months, far longer than I'd expected to be there. The thyroidectomy had been a distraction to finding a new home.

I walked through the house with the real estate agent and could see myself living there. It was reasonably close to where both Mum and Michael's houses were, and it was a good fit for my budget.

Have you ever bid at a real estate auction? It becomes stressful and quite the game. Everything happens so quickly. The bidding starts. Someone else makes a bid. You make your bid. Someone else makes another bid. Then you realise you've made another bid that may have reached the edge of what you'd decided beforehand was going to be your limit. Then you notice everyone else has stopped as the auctioneer calls out, "Do I hear any more bids?" He followed up a few seconds later with, "Going once!"

My heart was racing as the auctioneer looked at the last person who'd put in a bid before mine. They didn't blink.

"Going twice!" The auctioneer fixed his attention on the first bidder, a husband and wife. They turned to each other. She said something in her husband's ear, and he shrugged in response. Her expression told me she wanted to put in another bid, but he didn't. Perhaps my bid had exceeded the limit they'd agreed on before the auction? The excitement built as I wondered if it was real or just a dream.

"Going three times!"

I just wanted him to finish before someone else threw their hat in the ring and made a bid. I fiddled nervously with my scarf; the garment so carefully positioned to hide any physical evidence of my recent operation. The auctioneer again turned his attention to the person who'd made the last bid against me.

"This is the last and final chance..."

No! I thought, *please, don't invite them to make a bid!*

The person shook their head, and the auctioneer turned his attention to me. He stared directly at me and extended an arm in my direction.

"SOLD!"

Yes! It was mine!

All of a sudden, I became a homeowner. For the first time I had a place that I could *really* call my own. That I could decorate the way I wanted to. I had a place for the art, fabrics and mementos I'd been collecting on my travels. Michael and Lilli gifted me my favourite art deco couch and some wooden tables Michael had made. I spread plants throughout my new home, inside and out, and revelled in listening to music as I set up my belongings in the house. More than anything, I was excited to finally have fun creating healthy vegetarian foods in my kitchen... a kitchen that I could truly make my own.

A New Approach

The first customer of the day dropped into Soulfood. They picked up a few groceries then approached the counter. "Nice scarf, Sandy."

"Thank you," I replied with my broadest smile. It's an involuntary thing, that smile. I just can't help it. When someone says something nice to me, my face lights up. And this customer's comment had made me particularly happy, because I wanted to control who did and who didn't know about my thyroidectomy. I was so lucky to have the job at Soulfood, a constant reminder that food itself is the most important medicine. But that lump in my thyroid had needed more than just good nutrition to deal with it: it had needed to be removed. And if I got into a conversation with someone about that, it would ultimately mean having to talk to them about my previous brush with cancer. The accompanying explanation would've just been too long and I didn't want to find myself having those conversations with customers. The scarf seemed like the best solution.

The day went on with customers coming and going.

Then Jim walked in. "Nice Scarf, Sandy."

"Thank you." There weren't many other customers in the shop at the time so I decided to put aside my to-do list and engage in a bit of banter. As we talked, I steered the conversation toward nutrition and health. I wanted to know more about his business and how he got into macrobiotics. "I'm keen to learn more about it, about Spiral Foods and macrobiotics. It just seems to make so much sense."

"I admire your enthusiasm," he said. "It's because the Japanese eat these foods that they're among the longest-lived people in the world." Jim was just as enthusiastic talking about macrobiotics as I was listening to what he had to say.

And there was something special about this guy. You know those people who have the ability to talk with ease to absolutely anyone? I'm always in awe of people with that ability, and he was clearly one them. I'd watched him casually engage with other customers from time to time. He'd speak to people he was meeting for the first time as though they were old friends. Being a bit of a surfer, he was fit too. Having just recently seen a definite end to my relationship with Peter, Jim was looking like he'd be good to get to know better... if not for the fact that he was in a relationship already and had two children with his partner.

The job at Soulfood South Yarra was going really well, but I always felt the need to further my education. Although I continued to attend courses and seminars, I found it difficult to find courses in Australia that were focused on my main areas of interest, particularly regarding macrobiotics. Jim explained to me how the understanding of this approach to nutrition in the United States was way ahead of Australia at that time.

A company called 'Eden Foods' had been importing traditional Japanese food into the United States for many years, much longer than Spiral had been importing them to Australia. Having been to plenty of trade shows in the States, Jim was well aware of what was going on over there and was happy to share his knowledge. My interest piqued; I wanted to go there myself to expand my knowledge. I started to investigate where the best centres were to learn from the top teachers of natural food, macrobiotics and wholefood nutrition. I wrote letters to the authors of books I was studying asking where they recommended I should go.

In the middle of 1997, I decided to take the plunge. I took leave from Soulfoods and booked a trip to the USA to spend time in California before heading to New York to learn from one of the western world's most knowledgeable people about nutrition and using food as medicine.

On arriving in California, I got in touch with the daughter of one of Ted's friends, who was living in an outer suburb of San Francisco. I stayed with her for a few days before catching up with Ginger, my friend from Bali days who had recently moved to San Francisco. She was getting involved in the digital world by then, building websites and all things tech-based. San Francisco was a bit of a hub for that back then and Ginger was an early adopter. Daniel, a good friend of my nephew, Marlon, was in San Francisco at the same time and was looking for work. I took the opportunity to introduce him to Ginger and she ended up giving him a job!

But I had only four months in the USA so it was time to move on and make the most productive use of my time there.

There was a highly respected expert in New York I was enthusiastic about learning from. Annemarie Colbin was the founder of the Natural Gourmet Institute, an educational organisation that's taught thousands of wholefood and plant-based chefs and cooks. Established in 1977, it was the longest running health-based culinary school in the United States.

Annemarie had an impressive range of book titles to her credit such as, *The Wholefood Guide to Strong Bones*, *The Natural Gourmet* and *Food and Healing*. Born in Holland in 1941, Annemarie's family moved to Argentina after the World War II. When her father fell ill, Annemarie's mother sought help from a Seventh Day Adventist group who put him on a twenty-one-day vegetarian cleansing diet. After following the diet for the first eleven days, Annemarie's attitude to health and nutrition went through a profound change.

Through her ongoing studies and experiences, she developed her own philosophy on nutrition and of how food should be prepared. This philosophy included many macrobiotic principles and was based on seven basic and deceptively simple principles: that food should be seasonal, local, whole, traditional, balanced, fresh, and delicious. Everything within her philosophy seems obvious once you've looked into it. Attending her classes in New York over the years and learning from her had a major impact on me in the years to come, and her cooking videos continued to inspire me in the ensuing years.

My time in New York wasn't just spent in cooking classes though. During the nights I enjoyed the music, comedy, poetry and the nightclub scene. Ruth and Valery, who I'd met in Bali a few years earlier, lived in the Lower East Side. We'd always stayed in touch so I reconnected with them and established other friendships that would endure the test of time. I was enjoying one of the most important ingredients I'd found in my *Recipes for Living*, that of being a free spirit in my travels.

I arrived back in Australia invigorated by the wealth of knowledge gained and feeling culturally fulfilled. I returned to work at Soulfood, but something was about to happen that would have a huge impact on me. Jim walked into the office one day not long after I'd returned. "Did you hear the news?" he asked.

"What news?"

"Michio's coming. Michio Kushi. He's coming to Melbourne to promote his new book. You'll really like him."

"You know him?"

"Well, yeah." He said it as though it should have been obvious. And I guess it was a given considering how much time Jim had spent in Japan with Spiral Foods. I was excited. Did this mean I'd be able to meet Michio in person? It seemed I was at the right place at the right time.

Jim explained that Spiral Foods was going to be a sponsor for his trip and he invited me to join the committee organising his tour!.

Michio Kushi opened my mind even more than I had expected.

By that time, the reason why many Japanese people were known to be living longer, healthier lives than the typical westerner (eating the standard American/Australian diet, otherwise known as *SAD*) was becoming clear to me. It's to do with their approach to food: a balance of simplicity, nutrition and flavour. Their consumption of seasonal local foods including vegetables, seaweeds, tofu, using nutritious mushrooms, fermented foods (such as miso paste), as well as other lifestyle choices, has led to Okinawa having a high proportion of centenarians. In recent years there has been more mainstream information being shared via media about Okinawa as being a part of what is called 'The Blue Zone'. Netflix has even streamed a series *Live to 100: Secrets of the Blue Zone*. The people of that region have a low stress, community orientated mindset. (I loved learning about *nankuru nai so* for example, which means *'things will work out somehow'*).

Listening to Michio inspired me to explore a broader range of plant-based foods than I had before, sea vegetables and fermented foods among them. He spoke about how macrobiotics and plant-based diets could help to prevent the onset of a range of health challenges. It all reinforced and strengthened the knowledge base I'd established in my travels to California and New York.

Among the wisdom and insights he shared with me was his emphasis on the importance of chewing, reinforcing what I'd been taught in the United States. It's not just what you eat, it's also *how* you eat. Michio reminded me how chewing your food properly is crucial to good digestive health. As small an issue as that may seem, it makes a significant difference.

These truly brilliant people that I'd had the privilege to learn from were the rockstars of the health and nutrition world. My own health issues were being better managed with the enhanced understanding of living a health-supportive lifestyle learnt from these icons. And I was keen to share this knowledge with others.

But there was more that had changed in my life by then. Jim and I had become firm friends as well as business associates. More important than that, he and his partner had broken up while I was away in the States. It seemed so natural that it was just a matter of time before we fell into a relationship. For me, it felt like a match made in heaven. We both had our little bits of history of working in the music industry and we were both passionate about our love for music, food and nutrition.

It was such a special time in my life. My career had developed in ways I couldn't have imagined a few years earlier, I was settled in my little cottage in East Malvern and I'd never felt so connected to someone as I was with Jim.

Jim also had big plans going forward for Spiral Foods, and started expanding the range. He loved saying it was important to *Keep the bastards honest and sell, sell, sell*. But his philosophy ran much deeper than that.

"I like how you do this," he said to me one day when he'd stopped by for his weekly shop.

"What's that?"

He gestured toward the Spiral product displays I'd set up. "This, the product placement and displays. You seem to have a natural flair for marketing."

"Well, I did do marketing at CIT and accounting at RMIT. I've told you that before."

"Yeah, but not everyone who's done a marketing course is actually *good* at it. You seem to have a certain flair."

A broad grin exploded across my face.

"I need someone to help deal with the marketing side of things... and a lot of the other stuff too," he continued. "Why not come and work for me?"

It was an offer to good to pass by. I'd been managing Soulfood for quite a while by then and relished the idea of a new challenge. This was an opportunity to be a part of a company that was bringing good quality food products into Australia, and I'd just been offered a position where I could help spread the message throughout the country.

Spiral Foods was a small team. There were less than half a dozen of us, with everyone doing whatever was needed most at the time in addition to their main responsibilities. We were located in a Richmond warehouse; it was basically a big tin shed. Hot in summer, freezing cold in winter. Jim had a great head for business but wasn't particularly interested in worrying about the creature comforts at his workplace. But the rest of us? We wanted to be a bit more comfortable during weather extremes. In the end, we found a rather creative solution, setting up a couple of parachutes under the roof to act as a simple kind of insulation.

Jim was well connected and pulled together some amazingly talented people. All the packaging and logo work was designed by a woman who was one of the top contemporary artists in Victoria at the time. He regularly travelled to Japan and worked with the suppliers over there to develop new product ranges targeting the Australian market.

I immersed myself in the business. There was so much to do. From marketing and ordering to the more mundane task of packing. It was a whole new education for me too. Although I'd done a marketing course, I had to learn so much more, like the intricate details of branding. It's far more complicated than you can appreciate! You need to market a range of products in such a way that they feel as if they belong to the same family. Trust me, it's not as easy as many people think.

I was learning a great deal from Jim about how to run a business. From the creation of products, to labels, to distribution. I visited the stores who stocked the products, established new outlets and set up events to educate shoppers.

Then one day a whole new world of opportunities opened up.

"Hey, do you know about Daylesford?" asked Jim.

"Where they have the spas?" I replied

"Yeah, that's the one."

Daylesford is a town that's a little slice of paradise about an hour and a half's drive north-west of Melbourne's CBD. The town was home at the time to a few basic health and spa resorts that had been established to take advantage of the abundance of mineral-rich springs in the area.

"There's going to be a festival up there." Jim said. "It'll be all about health and nutrition… all vegan and vegetarian."

"That sounds interesting."

"The organisers called earlier today to have a chat about sponsoring it."

"Are you going to go with it?"

"Yeah, it's probably worth having a crack at it. We'll set up a big marquee and hand out some product samples." He hesitated for a moment, as though making sure he had my attention. "They asked if I knew anyone who might be able to help them organise the food stalls. You know, co-ordinate them all and make sure their food is in line with the festival's ethos."

I gave him a look that indicated I was still listening, feeling sure that he wasn't quite finished.

"I gave them your name. I figured you'd enjoy doing something like that. You won't be doing it as an employee of Spiral. It'll be your own gig."

The festival would be the first of its kind in Australia. A celebration of healthy living and good nutrition. The inaugural Daylesford Spa Festival. They needed someone to co-ordinate the food and cooking aspects of the festival. And here I was, having spent the preceding years totally immersed in learning about plant-based and macrobiotic approaches to cooking, something still quite uncommon in Australia at that time. Food vans selling purely vegan and vegetarian food were virtually non-existent, making for a more challenging job of curating the food for the festival than you might expect. I worked closely with the food van owners and stall holders, helping to ensure their menus were in line with the festival guidelines. No dairy or animal proteins being a critical one. I also wanted to have some gluten-free items, as that was starting to get more attention by then in the United States.

In the end, Daylesford was a huge success. Spiral Foods and Bonsoy (a soya milk product that Jim owned as well) were the main sponsors and had a huge presence. Meanwhile, I felt in my element curating the food and ensuring there was a good choice for festival-goers to choose from. Working at Margaret's health food shop and then Soulfood had given me so many contacts. It gave me the confidence to put together an array of food stalls that would inspire the attendees to the festival.

And the response from the festival organisers?

"Hey, Sandy. Great job! Are you coming back next year?"

"I'd love to." How fantastic! The organisers had invited me back to do it all again. They'd set up the festival with the hope of attracting more government investment in the region's tourism industry.

How my world had changed in just a couple of years! Going from making sandwiches in my apartment in Sydney to sell to the staff at Triple M, then onto managing a health food shop, getting equipped with a knowledge and understanding of nutrition. An understanding that I'd absorbed from true titans in the field. And now, I was looking after the marketing for a supplier who specialised in macrobiotic and organic, natural foods, and even curating the food at a festival celebrating health and nutrition. It felt as though I'd been surrounded and then guided by wisdom that naturally led me to achieve success in areas I'd never dreamed of delving into just ten years earlier. Enjoying a relationship with Jim was a bonus.

One of Jim's promotional strategies involved flying a couple of Japanese chefs down from Sydney to do public cooking demonstrations using the Spiral product range.

"This is great." I said to Jim after the first demonstration. "But how come you've got to get these guys down from Sydney? Isn't there someone local who could do it?"

He shrugged his shoulders. "I know these guys and I know they're good."

"We need to be doing more of this. Maybe we should try approaching a Japanese chef in Melbourne and see if they're interested."

"Yeah, you could probably even do it yourself, you know... the demonstrations. I reckon you'd be pretty good at it. There aren't many Japanese chefs around down here. But we can have a look around." As we discussed it more, Jim suggested that, seeing it was essentially my idea, it should be done as a separate company. "I'll give you a bit of a hand if you need it. You'll need Spiral's stock, but I reckon you'll probably manage alright on your own with it for the most part."

At that time, there were only half a dozen or so Japanese restaurants in the whole of Melbourne. Jim and I had dined out at all of them, so we knew where to find the best chefs. We approached Osamu Ito (Itosan), the master chef behind one of our favourites.

"We want to educate the population about how food really should be prepared, the way the Japanese have understood for centuries," I explained. "We have the traditional, natural and organic products that people need to prepare these meals at home. I also want to share nutritional information and explain how these traditional ingredients were made."

Osamu Ito nodded in agreement. He had limited English but he shared our desire to teach Japanese cooking and had some experience doing cooking demonstrations from when he lived in Korea. "It's a good idea," he said. "What would you call it?"

"We'd keep it simple," I said, "the Japanese Cuisine Company."

He nodded again. "I like it."

The demonstrations evolved into classes and proved to be a hit. They were popular and helped to sell more of Spiral's products. It also fitted neatly with Jim's overall philosophy. As time went on, I invited other macrobiotic and vegetarian chefs I'd met when Michio was in town to teach classes and give demonstrations.

Eventually, I developed the confidence to do these classes myself. With the support of Spiral Foods, I'd started Melbourne's first traditional Japanese cooking school. The student had finally come of age and become the teacher! It was an important turning point in my life. All these incredible influences of the previous few years had become potent ingredients in what was to become the most important *recipe for living* my life: teaching people about cooking and nutrition.

There was also a call for cooking classes that were focused just on vegetarian cooking that wasn't necessarily Japanese. So the *Vegetarian Cooking School* was formed shortly afterwards as well.

Manna

Everything was moving in a positive direction, or so it seemed.

As special as my relationship with Jim had been, it was becoming a little strained. It's hard at the best of times to have a good, healthy relationship when you both work and play together. But in this case (as happens for so many couples) there were other complications on top of that. Jim was recently separated and his children from that marriage required much of his attention, as they should have. He's a great guy; in fact we're still friends. But he wasn't able to be completely available to me. This was particularly apparent in times when I was unwell. As time went on, it began to feel as though we'd somehow mistimed our coming together. It wasn't obvious initially, and we didn't really talk about it, but the drift had started.

Then, an opportunity presented itself. The Soulfood South Yarra health food store that I'd managed before taking on my role at Spiral Foods was on the market. I'd first found myself dreaming of owning a health food store back when I'd been dabbling in food preparation in Sydney. A dream that grew as I travelled the world and learned about nutrition. Now, I had the opportunity to realise that dream.

I jumped at the chance. My mother and brother were sceptical, but again my mother put forward the ten thousand dollars I needed to buy the business. And she gave it to me with a warm hand.

Soulfood South Yarra became the *Manna Natural Food Store*. The name was inspired by a favourite health food store in Amsterdam called *Manna*.

And in the book of Exodus, manna was a food miraculously supplied to the Israelites in the wilderness. It has always been spoken of as a spiritual and nourishing food.

All the amazing people I'd met and learned from in the preceding years, all the experiences I'd been through, all of it was coming together now in the guise of my very own health food store. I intended to make sure this new venture became a reflection of all I had learned about health and nutrition.

Talk about a great *recipe for living!*

I worked my way through the stock lists, making valuable decisions about which products to keep and which to let go. This store would be a reflection of my values. So, I wanted nothing but the best organic produce and the most ethical product range available.

Most of the old regulars from when I'd managed Soulfood a few years earlier, were still customers and excited to see me return.

Soulfood had featured a juice bar with snacks available in the back area; but from the day I walked in, I reimagined the space, and transformed it into a little cafe area. Rules and regulation then did not allow an area to sit down to eat, so the emphasis was on takeaway.

Now that I owned the store, I could serve the foods I most enjoyed. There was no official kitchen for cooking in, but there was enough bench space to create salads, healthy 'guilt free' snacks and wraps. I created 'super smoothies' and made fresh fruit and vegetable juices, way before the juice bards became a thing in every shopping centre. I tapped into the contacts I'd established over the years who ran vegetarian catering businesses so I could include some of their offerings. One such business, run by a Jitendra Bhatia, was Vegetable Creations. They supplied organic vegan sourdough pies, pastries and burgers, many with an Indian flavour. Jitendra has remained a good friend to this day. We've run cooking classes together and have been involved in other business ventures since then.

Even though I couldn't have an official kitchen, we still had a portable stove with gas cylinder. So, along with having a rice cooker on hand, I had everything I needed to make brown rice and tofu burgers that could be cooked in a wok on the portable stove. These were served with my favourite home-made tahini, miso sauce.

SANDY'S TAHINI MISO SAUCE

Use as spread, as topping for steamed vegetables, noodles, or as dip.

Ingredients:

- 4 tbsp   White miso paste (Shiro)
- 2 tbsp   Tahini
- 2 tbsp   Lemon or lime juice
- 2 tbsp   Mirin (optional)
- ½ cup   Water

Method:

- Mix with whisk in a glass jar and keep with lid on in refrigerator. Keeps for 1 week. Add water for thinner consistency if required.

And can I tell you? These burgers were a hit!

The cafe proved to be very popular with the stars of the tennis world when the Australian Open came around again. All the big names were coming in now, not just to top up on their supplies, but to stop for a coffee or light meal. The tennis players weren't the only highflyers who frequented the store though. When 'Mission Impossible' went into production in Melbourne, some of the cast and crew staying at the nearby Como Hotel also became enthusiastic regulars.

The cooking classes continued as well. Only now, I could bring them into my *own* venue when it suited, a place that I owned.

SANDY'S TOASTED SEED MIX

Makes 2 cups. Keep 1 glass jar.
Best use within one week.

Ingredients:

- 1 cup   Sunflower seeds
- 1 cup   Pumpkin seeds
- 1 tbsp   Tamari

Method:

- Preheat oven to 150°C
- Place seeds onto baking tray and toast in over about 15 minutes
- Switch off oven and remove baking tray with seeds
- Add tamari to seeds and mix through
- Place back into still warm oven for 5 minutes
- Remove to cool
- Place seasoned seeds into a glass jar and cool before closing the lid.

I came up with the idea of doing monthly product information evenings in the store. These allowed me to share knowledge with customers regarding ingredients, how to cook them and their health benefits. Each month between ten and twenty people turned up to learn, eat and mingle. A wholefood community was developing. Although still considered 'alternative' back then, the more time went on, the more mainstream healthy natural foods were becoming.

There was so much happening. I'd never been so happily busy in my life! I had the store, the cafe, the Japanese Cuisine Company, the Vegetarian Cooking School and, to top it off, I was still helping out with some of the marketing for Spiral Foods.

CARROT, BEETROOT ARAME SALAD

Ingredients:
- 1/2 cup arame seaweed
- 1/3 cup beetroot grated
- 1/3 cup carrot grated
- 1 spring onion diced
- 2 red radishes slivered

Ingredients:
- 2 tbsp toasted sesame oil
- 1 tbsp mirin
- 1 tsp tamari
- 1 tbsp brown rice vinegar OR Japanese plum vinegar (Umesu)
- 2cm ginger grated
- 1 clove garlic pressed
- 6 sprigs chopped parsley or coriander leaves & stems
- 1tbsp diced red chilli or dried chili flakes (optional)
- 1/3rd cup toasted pumpkin or sunflower seeds for garnish

Method:
- Soak arame in hot water for 10 minutes until softened. Strain and allow cooling to room temperature
- Grate Beetroot and carrot
- Chop spring onion
- Chop radishes into small slithers
- Combine ingredients into mixing bowl
- Combine dressing ingredients, mix and dress salad

In an effort to keep costs under control, I tended to do a lot of the work associated with the store myself. After all, I had my accountancy experience, so it seemed pointless to spend money on having someone else looking after the books. I was doing a hell of a lot though. In hindsight, considering that I was still finding my way regarding how much my body's immune system could cope with, it would have been sensible to have had more help. I was doing the ordering, marketing, organising and conducting the cooking demonstrations, setting up the product information evenings and doing the bookkeeping. Yes, I did have staff, but they were too inexperienced to do the work I was taking on. To top it off, many of the small local suppliers didn't deliver and I really wanted to sell their produce. So, I was running around and personally picking up much of the stock. The bread came from a bakery, the fruit and vegetables from a market, vegan treats came from another local baker.

I was pushing myself hard... and loving every minute of it.

But it's not until you take on more than any one person can do on their own that you really start to appreciate your limitations. And my compromised immune system tightened those limitations.

By early 1991 it became clear, I was overextending myself. I'd been pushing myself way too hard and was starting to pay the price, both physically *and* mentally. I needed help but didn't really have anyone, other than Mum, to support me. And she did her best. On many occasions she'd help pack nuts and dried fruits for me. Lilli helped out at times too – but it simply wasn't enough.

Why hadn't I realised that I was taking on more than was humanly possible?

What was I thinking?

So what if I was a qualified accountant?

Why was I putting myself in a position where I was trying to do my bookkeeping when I should have been sleeping? Or, was it more that I was sleeping when I should have been doing the bookkeeping?

I took a much-needed holiday, a quick trip to Bali, hoping my staff would take care of things back at the store while I got an essential rest.

TOFU POUCHES (INARI SUSHI)
makes 12 pouches which if sealed well can be kept in refrigerator for 2 days/

Ingredients:
- 1 quantity cooked brown sushi rice (see recipe below)
- 4 Shiitake mushrooms, dried
- ¼ Carrot, julienned
- 2 packets Fried unmarinated bean curd (can be found in frozen section of Japanese supermarkets. Also called abura age)
- ¼ cup Mirin
- ¼ cup Tamari
- 1 cup Dashi stock (use a sachet) or shiitake soaking water stock
- 1 tbsp maple syrup or any liquid sweetener of your choice
- 4 Green string beans
- 3 tbsp Pickled ginger, to taste
- pinch Sea salt
- 1–2 tbsp Toasted sesame seeds

Method:
- Soak shiitake mushrooms for at least 30 minutes in 1½ cups warm water from the kettle or for even better flavour, soak overnight.
- When mushrooms have softened, discard stems then slice mushrooms caps. Strain shiitake soaking water and keep to use as stock.
- Place julienned carrot, sliced shiitake and tofu pouches in a small saucepan with mirin, tamari, dashi stock or shiitake soaking water and sweetener and simmer for approximately 15 minutes. Cool. Drain. Squeeze tofu pouches to remove excess liquid.

> - Thinly slice beans on the diagonal then blanch in salted boiling water for 1 minute. Drai
> - Mix chopped pickled ginger, string beans, shiitake, carrot and sesame seeds into cooked sushi rice and stuff into cooled marinated tofu pouches.

Oh, how wrong I was!

When I returned and went through the stock and the books, I noticed discrepancies. Products were missing with no record of their sale. Not cheap items either, these were products like expensive natural cosmetics. Either my staff were helping themselves to the products, or there was a sudden major issue with shoplifting. Sadly, it gradually became clear that it was a staff member taking advantage of the trust I'd placed in them. The person had to be sacked as a result.

And talking about staff, I *really* needed to employ more. It also became clear that I just didn't have the energy levels for the amount of work I was taking on. But there was a Catch 22. To pay the staff I needed more money. To get more money, I needed more staff... and more customers.

Manna Natural Health Foods was everything I'd dreamed of and everything I believed a good health food store should be. However, my little store was ahead of its time - by Australian standards anyway. As much as I had an enthusiastic regular clientele, and as much as tennis and Hollywood royalty appreciated the quality of what I was providing, it simply wasn't enough to keep the business viable.

I didn't need my accounting background to see how crazy the situation had become and how unsustainable it was. I was burning myself out, physically, emotionally and financially. I was faced with just one real option.

COOKING BROWN RICE FOR SUSHI

Use this for making nori rolls and nori pyramids (Onigiri) too. (See MY WHOLEFOOD COMMUNITY COOKBOOK for recipes)

Ingredients:

- 1 cup Short grain brown rice
- 2 ¼ cups Water
- 2 tsp Tamari or shoyu

Sushi Vinegar Mix:

- 3 tbsp Brown rice vinegar
- 2 tbsp White sugar (we do use sugar for this traditional method) or use your preferred sweetener
- 1 tbsp Sea salt
- 6 cm Kombu (optional if available)

Method:

- Wash rice in cold water, stir and wash away floating husks. Wash several times until the rinsing water is clear, then place rice in a saucepan and add measured water and tamari or shoyu.
- Soak for at least 30 minutes.
- Bring to boil then cover and lower heat to simmer for 30 minutes or until all the water has been absorbed. Don't stir.
- Turn off the heat and leave it to steam with lid on for another 10 minutes.
- Place vinegar, sweetener, sea salt and kombu (if using) in a small saucepan and simmer gently until sugar is dissolved. If using kombu, remove from mixture before using vinegar mixture to make sushi rice.
- Place cooked rice in a hangiri wooden sushi rice bowl, or, if you don't have one, a glass bowl (don't use plastic) and slowly add the vinegar mixture.

- Cool the rice by lightly tossing in the vinegar mix until it reaches room temperature. Don't put the rice in the refrigerator to make it cool faster as that will damage the rice. You can, however, use a fan as you toss.
- Cover with a clean damp cloth until you're ready to use it – use within 2 hours.

It's best not to store cooked sushi rice in the refrigerator as it loses flavour and becomes dry and hard to eat. For proper hygiene and the best-tasting sushi, always make fresh sushi rice and use promptly.

VARIATION: Use a natural ready-made sushi vinegar instead of making your own. I recommend Spiral Foods sushi vinegar.
For a tasty different flavour, you can use Japanese plum vinegar (Ume Su) instead of brown rice vinegar.

With great reluctance, I put the store on the market, hoping someone with greater energy levels than my own would be able to build on what I'd created.

It was one of the hardest decisions I'd ever had to make, but I really had no other choice. I placed a 'for sale' advertisement in the business section of the local newspaper.

I can't begin to tell you how relieved I was when a potential buyer soon showed up.

"I really like what you've done here," he said. "The product range is just amazing, I especially like the focus on organics. They're so hard to find in Melbourne, even in other health food stores. I'm looking to buy it for my daughter to run. She's right into all the natural foods and stuff like that."

"Thank you, and that's really nice that you want to do that for her." It was reassuring to know that someone who wanted to purchase my store appreciated what I believed a health food store should be like.

He put down a deposit and asked if he could spend time with me over the ensuing weeks to get a handle on how to operate the business. It seemed like a sound idea, a way to ensure a smooth handover.

I introduced him to all the regular customers and took him with me on my rounds to pick up the produce. I wanted to ensure that he had a good idea of what to do.

Then, after three weeks, disaster struck.

He pulled out of the sale.

"What happened?" I asked him.

He seemed evasive. "Oh, my daughter doesn't really seem that interested anymore. I'm not going to go ahead with it if her heart's not in it."

Devastated, I called Jim. "Have you got any ideas? I feel like I've tried everything. There must be something I can do."

"I'd love to help you, Sandy, but I'm flat out here. You know what it's like. Hang in there, someone will come along. You just need to keep going until they do."

"Michael's saying I should just close it down and walk away. That I should just cut my losses before it gets any worse."

"Oh, no, no! Whatever happens, don't close it. Hang in there Sandy. You've got this."

Yes, Jim's right, I told myself. *I just need to hang in there.*

There'd been a potential buyer not long after the store had gone on the market. Surely there'd be another waiting in the wings. I just had to be patient.

Each day, I found the energy to get up and put my best smile on to greet the customers. With each day, it became harder. And the stock seemed to be continuing to disappear.

Michael was adamant. He saw it as a problem that was just leaking money everywhere. I tried explaining that all I needed was the extra funds for improvements and some more experienced staff. But it was a simple black-and-white decision in his mind. Every day that the store remained open was another day that money was walking out the door. He'd watched as I'd poured my heart and soul into the business since I'd bought it over three years earlier. The solution was so straightforward in his eyes. "You've done everything you can. It's time to close it up and walk away."

I didn't have the strength to argue anymore. This particular *recipe for living,* while having been full of seemingly the most delicious and wholesome ingredients, simply hadn't turned out as I had hoped it would.

I closed the doors, covered the windows in newspaper, and began the humiliating process of returning all the unsold stock to the suppliers.

CBD Health Cafe

As devastating as it had been to walk away from my store, I was still walking away as someone who had grown from the experience. That's so much easier to see with hindsight. It was a short burst of energy and an amazing flurry of activity – a flame that shone brightly before its fuel ran out.

I was, however, exhausted. And the windows of my showcase – of all I had learned from so many – were covered in newspaper. Every time I drove past it in the following weeks was a terrible reminder of how difficult it had been to make that final decision. Had I hung in there for just one more week, maybe there'd have been another buyer? Or maybe it would have dragged on for months, or even years? I will never know, and it's certainly not healthy to dwell on such thoughts. The decision had been made and it was time to move on, in a forward and positive direction.

It took weeks to get to all the suppliers and return their unsold stock. Every day I swallowed a little bit of pride as I packed up my car and returned the items to where I'd bought them from. When faced with such a difficult task, it's reassuring to find out how understanding most people are. And as hard as that process was, it allowed me to leave Manna Natural Foods behind with my integrity intact.

I spent the following three months processing what I'd been through. During that period of self-reflection well-meaning phone calls and letters flooded in from people who'd come into my life as a result of the shop.

There was much I still had to be grateful for though. Having walked away from the store, I still had the other businesses I'd established beforehand while working with Jim. *The Japanese Cuisine Company* and the *Vegetarian Cooking School* were still viable in their own right.

And there were other opportunities opening up. Opportunities that were emerging as a direct result of what I'd been doing in the previous twelve months.

One of the most important ingredients in *recipes for living* is remaining open to those opportunities and recognising them when they appear. It would have been so easy to slip into months of despair after closing the shop. It was such a gut-wrenchingly difficult thing to do. Instead, I chose to focus on what I'd walked away with. I'd met so many people and made myriad connections in the health and nutrition scene. People you meet end up talking to other people about you and you start to develop a positive reputation.

So perhaps it shouldn't have come as a surprise when, just a few months after closing the shop, I received a phone call.

"Hello, could I speak to Sandra Dubs please?"

"You're speaking to her. How did you get my phone number?"

"It wasn't hard to get your number. It's listed in the Yellow Pages. I was both a customer and supplier at your shop as well."

"Oh, okay."

"Are you familiar with the plans to open a Daimaru Department Store in Melbourne's CBD?

"I've heard about it, yes."

"I'm doing some consulting for them. We want the food available there to include healthy options, as a reflection of our broader philosophy. Ultimately, we'd like it to include a health cafe and juice bar. I immediately thought of you. Are you interested in applying for the position?"

Yes, I certainly was interested and, as it turned out, I was the only applicant.

There were months of preparation involved that had me working there, on site, long before the department store opened its doors to the public.

There was the menu of healthy foods and juices to develop, signage that needed to be designed and the seating layout for thirty that had to be planned. I had a budget for the purchase of kitchen equipment, crockery and utensils. I also had to contract suppliers of organic fruit, vegetables and vegetarian ready-made foods (these were crucial as the cafe lacked a proper kitchen).

'Sengi-kon' or 'service before profit' was the ethic that Daimaru told us they expect all their employees to adopt.

I'd been learning so much about the Japanese approach to diet and nutrition and now I had the opportunity to manage a health food cafe in a Japanese department store... right in the heart of Melbourne... my hometown! What a wonderful way to move forward and build on the experience I'd gained throughout the eighties... and this time I was an employee with a leadership role.

On the first of November, just two days before my thirty-fifth birthday, the uniformed staff were all preparing for the first day of trading when an address came across the in-store speaker system.

The store will open in two minutes. Please stand in your position, ready to greet customers with a friendly smile.

Everyone took their positions and looked towards the entrance.

Please open the doors now.

The doors opened and the first customers flowed in.

Good morning and welcome to Daimaru.

There were smiles all round. The staff all felt they were part of the beginning of something special and unique, a new era in Australian retailing. And for me, it resurrected my self-confidence.

My health food cafe proved to be a hit with the clientèle.

But would it be just as much of a hit with the company's management?

After a few months I discovered that the philosophy of 'service before profits' had caveats. There were monthly budget targets to meet that were based on the previous month's trading and results experienced in cafes, unlike mine, in Daimaru's Japanese stores over many years. The expectation was that each month, the café would increase its turnover. Not by a figure that I worked out, based on what I was experiencing on the ground, but based on figures calculated by an accountant who had more than likely never even visited my cafe. As a qualified accountant myself, with an extensive experience in owning and managing food businesses by this stage, I found it totally bizarre.

But I persevered, and my customers were happy with the food. They kept coming back, and management kept sending me budget targets that simply didn't match reality.

My relationship with management was soon to get its biggest test though.

The brief when I had started the job was to establish and run a health cafe and juice bar. I was preparing seasonal wholefood meals based around macrobiotic principles, using organic products wherever possible.

Then came the bombshell.

"We want to put a Coke fridge in your cafe."

"You what?" I couldn't believe it! Of all the products to sell in a health food-based cafe, they expected me to sell Coca-Cola and other soft drinks from the Coke range.

"It will help you meet your budgets, which you've been consistently failing to do."

"I won't do it. I will not sell Coca-Cola products, and nor do I want their fridge in my cafe."

"You have no choice in the matter. There will be a Coke fridge."

Well, the fact is, I did have a choice. We all have choices when it comes to these things. Sometimes those choices lead to us seeking employment elsewhere.

Needless to say, Daimaru's desire to install a Coke fridge in the cafe I'd set up for them led to the company and myself parting ways. That was one decision I have no regrets about. I'd given all that I could and had created a wonderful café. Probably the saddest part is that its revenue had started to grow by then. But you know what? Integrity is one of the most important ingredients in any *recipe for living* and I had no intention of sacrificing mine.

Interestingly, I found out the day after I handed in my two weeks' notice that Daimaru were retrenching two hundred staff, and I would have been one of them anyway. The retrenched staff received quite a bit of extra pay. As I had just resigned, I missed out. It would have been nice if my manager had let me know before I'd handed in my resignation. It came as no great surprise when Daimaru's Melbourne store closed down completely not long afterwards.

Life in Bali

After the experience and drama of leaving the *CBD Health Café* at Daimaru, a holiday seemed the most appropriate recipe for a bit of a reset.

Bali beckoned.

Being back on that beautiful island, I felt inspired to make a significant change to my lifestyle... one that supported my health and wellbeing even more. The cost of living in Bali was way cheaper than living in Melbourne, in those days. It was a time when the Australian Dollar was seen as a valuable currency in Indonesia. When I spoke with friends and other contacts, I saw that there were people from Australia and other Western countries managing to make a good life for themselves by setting up little businesses that didn't need a huge turnover to earn a decent income, by Balinese standards anyway. There was an abundance of creativity and entrepreneurship going on in Bali. I saw an opportunity to get by making my own creations and choices. No more being an employee, I'd developed the confidence to be my own boss.

It took only a few calculations to work out that if I was to rent out my house in Melbourne, the money left over after paying the council rates and other costs would be enough to get by while I organised a business up there running macrobiotic and vegetarian cooking classes. After all, I had my accounting skills and had established myself somewhat with the cooking classes already.

I returned home, found a tenant for my little cottage in Malvern East, then embarked on an exciting new adventure. A whole new life awaited me on an island paradise, filled with unique and varied experiences while immersed in another culture. Although, I must admit, there was a degree of hesitation due to the challenges my immune system might face, concerns my family didn't hesitate to express. But I'd shown strength handling the myriad challenges I'd dealt with previously.

There was a small expat community living in Bali. Everyone within it sharing a passion for tropical Bali life, a love of the Balinese people and their Balinese-Hinduism and customs. People were making clothes, art, furniture, jewellery and running food businesses. There was yoga, meditation, a thriving music scene and the parties were fabulous! Every afternoon before sunset at the beach in Seminyak, likeminded people met to sit, talk and be together watching the sunsets. This is where I met some cool people who became friends.

In those days we relied on fax machines to maintain contact with friends, family and business associates in our home countries, sending and receiving them from places like *Rudy's* and the *Krakatoa Restaurant*. It was in these venues that all the expats ended up meeting and getting to know each other.

It was always easy to find somewhere to stay. Invariably someone would always be offering a room. I bought a little Vespa and rode into Rudy's or Krakatoa daily to check for messages from home.

My creative juices started flowing. How was I going to make money with my skillset? After I made posters offering cooking classes, the owner of a health food café contacted me and I was soon running classes at his venue.

There was no way to find supplies of the necessary ingredients other than riding around on my Vespa and stopping to ask the locals at various shops for help. There was a Japanese grocery store on the way to Sanur and the local supermarket Alas Arum also had some of the ingredients. It took several weeks of navigating my way around before I finally found everything needed.

Half a dozen or so people came to my classes; while I was packing up at the end of a class one day, an American woman approached me. "This is great!

Can you teach a few Balinese people working for me how to cook? They're great housekeepers, but they've got no idea how to prepare a decent meal."

I looked up and smiled, "Sure, I can do that."

"My name's Ginger by the way." She was clearly fit and healthy with long blonde hair and an infectious smile..

"Hi Ginger, I'm Sandy, Sandy Dubs."

After that first meeting, we soon became friends. And her housekeepers? I soon had them cooking wonderful, plant-based meals. At that time, if you were a Westerner living in Bali, you'd generally have one or more Balinese locals employed to look after your house. The pembantu (Balinese for housekeeper) were paid around thirty Australian dollars a week and saw that as a good living wage. Having a person in the house was actually crucial from a security point of view as well. Most houses had little in the way of windows, and sometimes not much in the way of walls either. It was open-plan living that fully embraced the tropical gardens, making it wise to ensure you always had at least one person there to watch over the place.

Once I'd been living there for a while, I wanted a place for myself – rather than continuing to jump from one expat rental house to another. It wasn't that I was overstaying my welcome with anyone, I just wanted the privacy and independence of having my own space.

One day, while I was sitting at a table drinking coffee at Rudy's, a German woman who'd joined me at the table said, "You can have my place for a few months."

"Oh?"

"You can have it for half the rent that I'm paying. I've got to go back home to Germany for four months. It's on Rum Jungle Road near the beach. Are you interested?"

"Oh yeah! That's sounds great."

"Just one thing though," she said. "You'll need to share the house with my two dogs."

I sat there as this sank in, wondering what that would entail. I probably should share with you that I've never really been into cats or dogs. I'd had a cat when I was young, but discovered I was allergic to them. In Balmain my housemates had a dog who I enjoyed walking at the local park. While doing that I'd even connected with another dog... and his sexy owner, someone who ended up becoming a wonderful lover!

And now, here was this woman offering cheap rent on the condition I babysit her dogs. She set out to put my mind at ease. "It's okay. My boyfriend... he'll come over every day and feed them. You won't need to do anything. They're really well trained, quiet and well behaved."

If the boyfriend was going to come over to feed and walk them each day, I couldn't see why it should be a problem having to share the house with them. It was a two-story, large house with a beautiful garden near the beach. I'd have it to myself for four whole months at half rent. What could go wrong?

As it turned out, quite a lot. The dogs were large. Don't ask me what breed. As I say, I'm not a dog person. There was a lot that I didn't know about dogs before then. Like, did you know that dogs can suffer from separation anxiety if their owners go away? I certainly didn't. And the boyfriend? He didn't end up showing up every day. There were no phones, so I couldn't call him. I ended up having to feed them myself. I took them for walks when I could, but they were strong dogs and pulled me along. It was a huge relief when the boyfriend *did* show up and take them for a walk... probably for the dogs as well.

A couple of weeks after the owner left, the dogs' behaviour changed. Every night, after I'd fed them, they'd start going berserk, demanding more and more attention. It didn't seem to matter how much I tried to placate them; they were hanging out for their owner to come back. Bit by bit, they started to tear into the furniture throughout the house. I ended up resorting to barricading myself in my bedroom. It was awful. I was trapped by the freaking-out dogs! I couldn't relax in the garden and the cushions on the couches were shredded. And the boyfriend? He didn't seem too interested in helping. The money that'd been left for food wasn't enough. So I had to pay for more food as well. For a person who's not into pets, it wasn't the greatest experience.

Despite that, most of my other experiences were positive.

Living there allowed my entrepreneurial spirit to flourish. After a few months, I was talking to one of the friends I made there, Stevo. He was one of many Dutch people in Bali, due to its history as a Dutch colony and he had a business exporting traditional Indonesian furniture and artefacts to Holland. "Check out these cool little bottles I picked up!" he said.

"Oh, they're interesting." I held one up to the light. They were only a few inches long and had little cork stoppers in them. They were made in Java from recycled glass. "I can see real potential in these."

Stevo raised an eyebrow.

I said, "these would make lovely and unique little bottles for massage and essential oils."

Stevo nodded – I could see he found the idea interesting.

"And the tiny glass ones, I could make jewellery with them. All they'd need is little silver caps, made up to hang them on necklaces."

"What about packaging?" asked Stevo.

My mind was racing. "I've seen small boxes... made from bamboo. They'd be perfect." The ideas just flowed. I thought about messages in a bottle... I'd always loved that song by The Police. An idea flashed into my mind. "Little zodiac scrolls! We can create little star sign write ups on little slips of coloured paper, and put them in the bottles with a couple of little flowers." I'd already found a good printer where I'd had my fliers designed and printed for the cooking classes and I could see the possibilities. People I'd met on my travels often spoke about astrology and I'd also become interested. Perhaps my Scorpio creative energy and desires were kicking in?

Although Stevo already had a successful business that included sending the bottles to Holland, he seemed enthusiastic about selling them to me as well for my new business. "You really think people will go for them?" he asked with a smile.

"Oh yeah. I know people in the giftware business, both retail and wholesale. I'll get in touch with them and get this going. I can sell them at the gift fair in Melbourne too." The trade fairs in Sydney and Melbourne were a great way for people to make connections with retailers. Homeware and giftware retailers attend the trade fairs in search of unique items. In those days, everything in Bali was so unique and inexpensive to make. Clothes, giftware, furniture... there were people making good money selling all of it.

Stevo was also selling candle holders made from broken, recycled glass. They were a translucent green. I just loved them and could see a market for them in Australia too. He showed me platters and pots made in Lombok. There was a small pot set on metal with a candle holder under it. It was a great idea for using with aromatherapy oils, as they could be used in the pot – a few drops of oil in warm water with a candle burning underneath. This was around the time the aromatherapy and massage oil craze was just starting. I could see the potential for all of them.

But what was I going to call my new business? I walked along the beach the following afternoon. *Who am I?* I wondered, *what do I aspire to?* I looked out over the ocean, feeling my feet in the sand and conscious of how blessed I was to be part of this world. I was a good networker, at ease meeting new people, and I had plenty of contacts in business. Just before the sun disappeared over the horizon it came to me. The next day I registered the business name *Whole Earth Network* and my Bali import business got off the ground.

It only took a month to get products and packaging sorted, so I could take samples to the trade fair in Melbourne where I shared a stall with a friend. The zodiac bottles were a great success! And the other products? Small retail outlets were happily ordering the recycled glass candle holders and aromatherapy bottles as well.

It was so successful that, after returning to Bali, I joined Stevo on a trip to the bottle makers in Java. It was a gruelling trip for me. My immune system was breaking down due to the energy I was investing in the new business. Stress, heat and the damp of the tropics were also taking a toll. While in the car with Stevo as we travelled from Bali to Java, an infection broke out on my face. It didn't clear at all during the week that we were away. I was dabbing it with diluted tea tree oil and a tonic we found in a local pharmacy called jamu, that contained turmeric. Poor Stevo didn't know what to do. I did my best to smile and underplay the situation. We made it to the Borobudur Temple, the largest Buddhist Temple in the world. It was extraordinary. But did I bother taking photos? Not while my face was in such a state.

We did, however, manage to get my order in for more bottles. Although, seeing the recycled bottle blowing factory left me feeling concerned for the workers' health. Despite my success with the giftware sales, I didn't end up continuing with that aspect of the business. It didn't feel right.

Stevo was also exporting huge food-grade Lombok ceramic plates, sealed ceramic trays and pots. I showed samples to people I knew who ran a large homewares store in Melbourne and were keen to stock a range of the products. I even had an order from a large catering company for the food-grade platters that filled a whole shipping container

I revelled in organising the shipping with my Balinese crew. It wasn't a smooth operation though. Each item had to be well packed, a process that took days before the items could be loaded into the container. But it was still great fun. I was creating something that felt special while working with the kind and wonderful Balinese people.

What a great lifestyle! The cooking classes continued to be popular, and each day included trips to the beach or the gym. It was a lifestyle that just wasn't possible back in Australia. And the adventures! There were plenty of those.

"I've met this guy," Ginger said one day. "He's got a boat that he normally uses to take surfers out to the offshore breaks."

Okay, so that's not such a big deal, I thought to myself at the time.

"Have you heard of Komodo Island? You know, the one where the Komodo Dragons live?"

"I think so. It's volcanic, isn't it?"

Ginger continued as though she hadn't heard me. "I want to get some friends together so we can hire his boat and go there."

"Oh, wow! That's sounds cool." My enthusiasm was as obvious as the huge grin that spread over my face as I asked, "Can I come too?"

There it was again, without hesitation.

Can you blame me though? I mean, hey… we're talking about the one place on Earth where you can go to see *real* dragons in the wild.

I wasn't going to miss that for anything. I'd been sailing and was up for the adventure. I volunteered to organise the food, with everybody chipping in to cover costs. It took a few days to get the menu together and drive around in a rented car to collect the ingredients from my favourite speciality stores.

When we met up at Ginger's a few days later we had a crew of twelve, all ready for the week-long voyage.

We headed off from there to the jetty where Brett, our captain for the voyage, was waiting with a tender. He took us out to where his boat, a sixty-five-foot yacht painted green and bearing the name *Ann Judith II* was waiting for us. Seeing it was normally used for taking surfers to the outer breaks, it'd been decked out in a basic, no-frills manner. I was pleased to discover a couple of Brett's deckhands could cook. They also caught fresh fish that we could cook with a grill on the deck, which was where most of us preferred to sleep. We were a motley crew made up of Australians, Americans, French, Dutch and Indonesians. Oh, and one other important aspect of our preparations… we all took seasickness pills.

We set sail and lazed the days away eating, drinking, smoking joints and playing music. Along the way, we stopped off at a few islands, one with the most incredible soft pink sand from corals. It was wonderful, swimming naked then lying on the beach for hours, visiting villages and taking in nature.

It felt good to be back onboard the yacht after meeting the dragons

We sailed through one night with a dancing trail of phosphorous thrown up by the bow, highlighting the dolphins swimming alongside the boat. Then, at nine-thirty in the morning, we entered a shallow bay on the island of Medang. Some of our contingent chose to go for a scuba dive, others took the tender into shore. Me? I *swam* to shore. That swim was just so refreshing, and the island was home to a beautiful village with houses on stilts laid out in neat rows. The villagers were incredibly friendly, and we enjoyed a delicious lunch before heading back to the boat and pulling up anchor so we could continue on our quest to find the Komodo dragons.

On the third day we woke up to discover our intrepid skipper was weaving a course for our boat through an extensive nest of extinct volcanic islands rising up from the ocean, some draped in rainforest and others protruding from the depths like jagged, rocky teeth. The dark waters were turbulent with raging whirlpools and masses of white foam, created where currents from the myriad outcrops of rocks collided with each other, each struggling to push the other back. It could have been a set for a movie! Brett navigated us safely through and into a bay on Komodo Island. Somehow, we'd made it. Brett dropped the anchor then headed into shore so he could register for a guide at the ranger's station, a small shack on the beach.

"No guides today," the ranger told him.

"What? You've got to be kidding me." Our intrepid skipper was livid. "We've spent three days at sea. I've got twelve paying customers on board."

"I'm sorry that you've travelled so far to get here. There's no guides today."

A great deal of negotiation ensued before Brett returned to the boat and we were able to board the tender and head to the island for our date with destiny. After several days on the high seas and navigating through the treacherous rocky reefs surrounding this small group of islands, we would be setting foot on an island that was home to Komodo dragons! This was definitely *not* a typical tourist destination.

Sailing off to adventure

The Anne Judith II.

We passed the shack, and the ranger joined our fearless troop. "Are there any menstruating women among you?" he asked.

"What business is that of yours?" asked Ginger in response.

"The dragons, they can smell blood. If a woman is menstruating it attracts them. Very dangerous."

"Oh, okay..." I couldn't help but wonder if he was telling the truth or if he was just playing with us.

He held up a stick, the sort you might use to poke a small campfire. "I'll use this to ensure everyone is safe."

Are you kidding? I thought, *you're going to keep us safe with that?*

We headed towards a large cement sculpture of a dragon next to a an equally large 'Komodo Island' sign that seemed like a weathered relic from a theme park ride.

"Oh my god! It's huge!" exclaimed one of the girls from our crew. "I never thought they'd be that big."

The girls all screamed, except for me that is.

The islands along the way were pure magic.

"Um, that's a statue," I said.

"Ohh..."

Not far beyond the sign it appeared that there was yet another cement statue.

As we approached all sorts of comments were spilling out from our group who were starting to feel concerned the trip may end up a bit of an anticlimax.

"Why so many statues?" asked one.

"You'd think they could make them look a little more realistic," complained another as she approached it, bending over slightly to get a better look.

The supposed statue's tongue flicked out.

We all froze before the group let out another collective scream.

Not me though, I simply retreated... slowly and quietly... probably in a bit of shock.

Then we all turned and went running back to the beach.

The ranger must have thought we were hilarious!

We watched from a distance as the first dragon any of us had laid eyes on ambled down to another part of the beach.

Aware now that all dragons that appeared to be statues should be considered as more than likely the real thing, our courageous group set out to explore the island. "Make sure that you stick together," said the ranger as he reassuringly held up his one metre stick.

At this point I probably should mention the nickname that one of our group had given me. Tom, whom I'd originally met through my friend Stevo, was a Scot who lived in Melbourne but had been living in Bali for a few years. He had a wicked sense of humour and liked to dub each of us with a nickname that reflected his observations of our personalities.

"You're Alice," he said to me one day.

"Alice?" Where'd that come from?

"Alice in Wonderland." Seeing my confusion, in his thick Scottish accent he offered an explanation. "You're excited about everything, whether old or new. You don't seem to have any sense of fear or danger. Whatever happens, you always seem to be walking around with wide eyes and a cheesy grin that spreads from ear to ear. If someone was to tell you they were going to Hell for the weekend you'd more than likely grin and ask them, 'Can I come too?' I've never met anyone quite like you. Particularly not here in Bali. Have you ever noticed that all the other expats seem to have something they're running away from? Something in their past they don't want to talk about? Half of them are more than likely fugitives in their own country. But you just walk around the place with a wide-eyed sense of wonder."

Alice in Wonderland, huh? Well, Alice was wondering as she wandered around an island with real dragons inhabiting it. And the island itself was different from what I was used to in Bali. It felt prehistoric, but not like the jungle-covered islands in Indonesia that I'd become so accustomed to. Komodo is the remains of a volcanic mountain, sticking up out of the ocean. There's something inhospitable about the place. Instead of jungle, the island

Our intrepid crew in search of dragons

There be dragons... albeit baby ones.

is covered in sweeping areas of long grass between stands of trees. Grass that's long enough to get lost in. Long enough for someone who's wandering around with wide-eyed wonder to inadvertently turn to the left while everyone else has gone to the right. Long enough for 'Alice' to get lost.

Can I tell you something? It's scary when you realise you're lost, wearing nothing but a sarong and a bikini, and on an island inhabited by deadly dragons. For anyone who doesn't know, the bacteria in a Komodo Dragon's saliva is so toxic that you'll most likely die within forty-eight hours of being bitten. When a dragon bites you, it'll walk away straight afterwards, comfortable in the knowledge that its meal will have died and started to decompose when it returns a few days later to enjoy a feast. And they will very happily choose people as a meal.

I'd been wandering alone for what seemed like hours (in reality it was only fifteen minutes). *Where is everyone?* I thought *I'm not lost, I can't be... surely not.*

"Where are you, Sandy?"

The voices of my companions calling out to me were the only means I had of finding my way back to them. It was a huge relief when I could finally see them again, rather than relying solely on hearing them to get my bearings. As it turned out, I hadn't drifted that far off. It was just so easy to get lost in the long grass. And my colleagues? Well, they could actually see where I was all along. One of them even took a photo of me walking through the long grass, a photo that now hangs on my wall at home. I look at it every day when I wake up, a reminder that even if I *think* I'm lost, I'm not really.

As we made our way back to the beach, we saw plenty more of the real live dragons we'd travelled so far to see, and they were big too. It was as though word had got around that there was a group of hapless Westerners wandering around the island that had the potential to provide the kind of feast they hadn't enjoyed in years. One after another spilled onto the beach as we were hastily boarding the tender, trying as best as we could not to look like we were

Lost? Well, I thought I was at the time.

panicking. Of course, we had nothing to fear. The ranger had a stick that he could use to protect us.

Brett wasted no time pulling in the anchor and getting the motor started once the last of us was on board. I looked back toward the beach at the ranger waving to us, seemingly oblivious to the hoard of dragons surrounding him on the beach now. It was as though they knew instinctively that ranger meat was off limits. Maybe it was their fear of his stick.

Being able to decide from one day to the next to go on these sorts of adventures was a big part of what was so special about Bali.

One of the great things about travelling is experiencing these cultures that are so different from our own. And yet Bali had this expat community that really came together at times. One of the most memorable instances of that phenomena I experienced was when Passover came around. The feast to celebrate the Passover is incredibly important in the Jewish calendar. It doesn't matter whether you're a believer or a total atheist, to anyone brought up in a Jewish family the Passover feast is as integral culturally as Christmas is to people from Christian backgrounds.

As the time of Passover approached while I was living in Bali, it turned out that there were quite a few amongst the expat community who were Jewish. We ended up having one of the most memorable Passover feasts of my life, all of us taken by surprise at just how many of us there were. Around fifty Jewish people were invited to one of the family's homes. Most of us brought a dish, all vegetarian. One attendee even brought a *matza* meal with them from Sydney, contributing special matzah balls for the vegetarian soup. All the symbols of Passover were there. We sat at a long table and read from the Haggadah, the Jewish text that sets out the order of the Passover ceremonial meal. It tells the story from the Book of Exodus about God delivering Israelites from slavery in Egypt with a strong hand and an outstretched arm. It blew my mind. There were Jewish people there from Brazil, Italy, Israel, Australia, America, Holland and France… all knowing the story, the songs and the traditions. It was a huge coming-together and sharing of the traditions. No matter where people were from, the humour and idiosyncrasies were on display. The evening was full of wonderful and vibrant ingredients for some delicious *recipes for living*.

I was lucky enough to have been sponsored by a business associate of one of my Melbourne friends who was living in Bali, which had allowed me to get my business permit. However, Indonesian law still required that I leave the country and return to Australia for a while every four months. For a business like the one I was operating this was actually quite handy. The trips back and forth provided opportunities to attend trade fairs and engage in other marketing ventures in Australia.

It was approaching the time for me to return when my friend Henry, whose sister was involved in the organising committee for the Dalai Lama's 1992 visit to Australia, got in touch with me via fax. His message prompted me to give him a call. "Hi Henry, how are you doing?"

"Sandy! Good to hear from you. Hey, did you know the Dalai Lama's coming to Melbourne? I'm helping the organising committee. I've been told we need to organise preparation of the food for His Holiness. I suggested you... seeing you're a vegetarian cooking specialist and all that. Would you like to cater for him? Will you come back for it? Given his vegan diet, we can't think of anyone who'd be better qualified to do it than you."

What an amazing offer! I may come from a Jewish family, but I'd always found a great deal of appeal in Buddhist teachings and had spent plenty of time at the Tara Institute in Melbourne practising Buddhist meditation. What an extraordinary offer Henry was making.

"Oh, yeah! You can count me in for sure on that one."

The Dalai Lama was going to be staying at what was then the Rockman Regency. It was where all the touring rock stars, and anyone else who was really cool, generally stayed while they were in Melbourne. Much of the committee also had a good relationship with Irving Rockman, the hotel's owner. So it made sense for the Dalai Lama and his entourage to stay there.

Returning to Australia not long after Henry's call, I was both excited and nervous as I got to work preparing menus. Then came a call from another member of the committee. "Hi, Sandy. We've just received word from His Holiness. He said he doesn't want to put anyone to any trouble... that he doesn't really eat that much, so he's happy to just eat whatever the hotel chefs are able to prepare for him."

"But the menu... I was almost done preparing it!"

"I'm so sorry, Sandy. But we'd still love to have you on the committee."

And so it was that, on the day of the Dalai Lama's arrival, Henry and I drove along the Tullamarine Freeway to the airport in Henry's blue Combi-style van as part of the official convoy of vehicles, the rest all being maroon sedans, matching the colour of the Dalai Lama's robes (It also happens to be my favourite colour and is associated with life force and preservation). All the vehicles had the official Dalai Lama flags. We had a good laugh as I hung onto one that was sticking out the window of my side of the van while Henry had stuck one on the driver's side.

Having arrived at the airport we made our way to the special lounge and waited for His Holiness to get off the plane, accompanied by his entourage of monks and assistants. There were warm greetings and much bowing, everyone was beaming with joy. A truly magical moment!

We escorted them to the baggage carousel where Henry collected all their luggage onto trolleys, then we took them out to the van. One monk, who acted as the Dalai Lama's personal assistant, joined us in the van so he could ensure all the luggage was transported securely.

The three of us were sitting abreast in the front seat, the Dalai Lama's assistant nursing a classic old-style briefcase on his lap, as we sped back down the freeway in the middle of the Dalai Lama's motorcade. With His Holiness being such a highly respected dignitary, the roads had been closed off to regular traffic and we had a police escort, one of the most surreal experiences of my life.

While we were still on the freeway, the Dalai Lama's assistant asked me, "Would you like to know what I've got in the briefcase?"

Before I had a chance to answer, he'd opened it, revealing all the passports and official papers for the entire entourage. He opened up the passports and I was speechless. It was the kind of thing that could simply never happen in today's security-conscious world.

As disappointed as I'd been to not cook for the Dalai Lama, I still got to attend all his talks as one of the volunteers, an experience that I felt grateful to be a part of. Particularly given that Buddhist philosophy had come to be such an important ingredient in my *recipes for living*.

With the Dalai Lama's visit over, it was time to get back to my business operation in Bali.

Some aspects of doing business in Bali took a bit of getting used to. I'd had experience in a range of businesses by that stage and had a keen sense of what was relatively predictable and controllable and what wasn't. One of the areas that I'd always considered to be predictable was logistics, getting products or supplies to one place or another. There were set rates that you could work to. Ships coming and going from ports were known well in advance. It was relatively easy, if you wanted to get a certain amount of product to a trade fair in Sydney or Melbourne, you could plan it. You would need to have the product finished and packaged by date A, transported in a container to the dock by date B so it could be loaded onto a ship that was scheduled to set sail on date C so it would arrive in an Australian port in time for the trade fare on date D. A simple formula to work with, but not necessarily in Bali. Australia's always had a reputation for having a generous number of public holidays. But you know what? Bali makes Australia look positively frugal. There are *so* many holidays and festivals in Bali, and public holidays associated with just about all of them. There was one particular trade fair where I'd planned everything thoroughly to get a full container off to Australia on a ship that would get there with perfect timing. The trouble was, on the day the container was supposed to get loaded onto the ship, it was a festival and, you guessed it, a public holiday. I hadn't checked the dates! No containers were going to be shipping that day. I had no choice but to cancel my booking at the trade fair. The container still eventually found its way to Melbourne and, thankfully, I was still able to sell the products though my established network of retailers. It was stressful to say the least and a mistake I was unlikely to make again.

I found myself having to deal with far bigger problems though. Infections occurred more frequently the longer I was there, and lingered. My immune system needed more support than I could muster while busy with the new business. To make it worse, I was burning the candle at both ends with partying, riding around on my Vespa and living an outdoor lifestyle in the tropics. It all took a huge toll on my health.

At one stage, I was so unwell with infections and fever that I decided to take myself to the airport and board a flight to Singapore. I knew the hospitals there would be better than anything Bali had to offer. I stayed in Singapore hospital for two days while I recovered.

It became abundantly clear I couldn't live in Bali. Not in the long term anyway. My immune system was taking too much of a hit.

Middle Park

Having arrived back in Australia, I needed to reestablish an income beyond the homeware and gift import business I still had going. And cooking classes seemed to be the obvious way to go.. My little cottage still had the tenants there who'd moved in when I went to Bali. Through a friend, I found myself a magnificent apartment to rent with an appropriate kitchen in a block of three others, on Beaconsfield Parade, Middle Park, close to Melbourne's CBD. It was also right across the road from the beach. The front room, which was to be my bedroom, featured a fireplace. It was large enough that I had a lounge in there as well. Huge glass windows overlooked amazing views, framing beautiful sunsets every night. To share the rent, I had a lovely young woman (who was into fashion) join me in taking out the lease.

Now in a new home, I needed to have some more money coming in to add to what I was making from my Balinese import business. Particularly given that it would take a while for the classes to get rolling again. One of my friends from the Goa days told me she was making a lot of money. How? Working on a phone sexline! How hard could it be? Surely I could do it just as well as she could, maybe even better. But what would it be like? It's not like you're actually doing anything with them, and I did like sex. Plus, it would be anonymous... no one would need to know I was doing it. Maybe it'd be a bit of fun? There was only one way to find out.

It wasn't long before I received my first call. I tried hard to get into the groove. "What are you wearing?" was invariably the first question.

"I'm just taking off my undies now. Are you playing with yourself?" I'd reply.

It was usually only a minute or two later that they'd declare to you that they'd just cum.

It was an easy way to make a buck, but the hour or so a day that I did it felt weird.

"Why are you doing this?" I found myself asking them after a while. The phone sex ended up morphing into therapy sessions… not something these guys had been expecting when they made their calls. After about a month, and a thousand dollars or so in earnings, I decided my career in the phone sex industry should come to an end.

Around that time I had a chat with Jenny. "Did you hear that Geoffrey and his wife broke up?" she asked.

"Really? That's a shame. How's he coping?"

"He's alright. He just needs to find a place to live," said Jenny. "It's been hard for him. The new business venture is taking up so much of his time that he hasn't really been able to look for somewhere."

"There's an apartment upstairs that's become available." I replied.

"Oh? I'll let him know. I'll be seeing him a little later this afternoon."

Geoffrey found the time in his hectic schedule to check out the apartment and signed the lease shortly after.

"That's great!" I said, filled with obvious enthusiasm. "We're going to be neighbours! When are you going to move in?"

"I'm not sure just yet," he replied. "I've got to furnish the house and have it all set up ready for when I have the kids. I just don't know when I'm going to have the time to get it all organised."

"I'm not too busy right now," I said, "Can I help?"

"Would you?"

"Of course, I'd love too."

"So, if I give you the money, you could set the place up? Furniture, bedding and all the other basic bits and pieces?"

"It'll be fun!" I said with a smile. I had time available during the day so why not? It's actually really enjoyable going out and spending someone else's money to fit out an entire home. And I was looking forward to having Geoffrey as an upstairs neighbour.

You might also be wondering what this business venture was that was keeping Geoffrey so busy. He'd been involved years earlier in a business that was selling essential oils. The only problem was, his business partner in that venture, who was its passionate aromatherapist and creator, didn't have a good head for the accounts side of things. Geoffrey knew he needed to find a better option for how to make some money.

The nature of how the essential oil business had been run meant he was pretty much hand-to-mouth with his household budget. Then Geoffrey's wife came home one day with a brown paper bag of items that she'd travelled to the other side of the city to buy. Ethically sourced natural facial creams and other cosmetics... expensive ones... expensive ones that they really couldn't afford at the time.

That got him thinking. A product that someone is willing to travel across the city for... that they can't really afford. That's got to be something worth looking into. So he researched the market, looking for an option that was ethical in every way.

Eventually his research led him to a company based overseas called AVEDA. It fitted in with everything he was looking for. Integrity, ethical, holistic. Best of all, they didn't have a distributer in Australia. Geoffrey made the bold move of calling the company's founder and owner, Horst Rechelbacher. After an extended phone call, where they hit it off straight away, they entered into follow-up negotiations to discuss details. Geoffrey had secured the rights to sell AVEDA products throughout Australia and New Zealand!

It was an instant success... which explained how he was able to afford the luxury of more or less handing me a blank cheque to fit out his new home.

And what a great time we had in those Beaconsfield Parade apartments!

By a wonderful coincidence, the young, newly-married couple in the third apartment, next door to mine, had mutual friends. The apartments had a huge back yard and pool, so we had some great times together enjoying each other's company.

You already know that I like to party. Well, Geoffrey liked to party too... and his forty-second birthday was fast approaching.

Do you remember *The Hitchhiker's Guide to the Galaxy* and how the meaning of life, the universe and everything is 42? Well, as Geoffrey was turning 42, that became the theme for the party. I looked after the catering, which as well as a feast of vegan options included such delights as vodka jelly shots (using high quality organic agar jelly of course). It was a wild night outdoors: music, dancing, food, drinks and tarot readers. Right down to the naked fire twirler who was dancing beside the pool.

More importantly though, there were some real movers and shakers of the nutrition and wellness scene that I met through Geoffrey living there, like Doctor Marc Cohen, one of Australia's pioneers of integrative and holistic medicine who would end up heading the Australasian Integrated Medicine Association (AIMA). The people whom I had for so long aspired to be among were now coming to where I lived to gather socially.

Our worlds had collided in an awesome way!

Taiwan

Although I'd had to leave Bali for health reasons, I'd decided to keep my business over there in operation. And, as much as there was a good deal I could do remotely from Australia, there was still the need to go up there from time to time. And so it was that I booked a two-month stay there to plan the next round of giftware creation and export.

I'd been there for a couple of weeks when I received a facsimile from Geoffrey.

Hi Sandy,

I'm in Bali, meeting up with Horst in Ubud for an international sales conference. It'd be great if you could join us. I'm sure you and Horst would really enjoy meeting each other.

Regards,

Geoffrey.

Horst Rechelbacher! Would I like to meet him? Of course I would!

Horst was one of the biggest movers and shakers of the wellness movement anywhere around the globe at the time, being the founder and owner of AVEDA, the company Geoffrey had made the arrangements with. His uniquely ethical company had inspired me since I'd first heard about it in the USA. Horst had worked as a hairdresser from the age of fourteen. By seventeen, he was working in an exclusive Rome-based salon and styling hair for the likes of Sophia Loren.

He worked hard, and he played hard.

By the time he was in his late twenties he was pretty much burnt out. So, he booked himself into an Ayurvedic health spa in India. He was so impressed with the difference it made for him that he set out to learn all he could about this five-thousand-year-old Indian approach to health. One of the fundamental principles of it was the importance of using natural materials and essential oils. Coming from an industry that was notorious for its heavy use of chemicals, Horst could see the potential for a business that applied the same principles to consumer health and beauty products in the west.

And so, AVEDA was born, starting first with shampoo products, but then quickly moving into a range of cosmetic products like lipstick, with all components ethically sourced in a sustainable manner.

Horst and Geoffrey had ended up developing a friendship. Then, when the AVEDA conference was taking place at the luxurious Amandari Hotel in Ubud, an hour's drive north of Denpasar, Horst invited Geoffrey to stay there with him and his family for a couple of weeks.

One day, while meditating on top of a mountain, Geoffrey found himself thinking, *Sandy's here and I'm here with Horst. This was meant to be. They're meant to meet each other. They need to meet each other.*

Geoffrey arranged for us to meet for dinner at the Four Seasons Hotel in Ubud, the wellness capital of Bali. And you know what? He was right to introduce us. Two Scorpios who were both passionate about wellness and sustainability. We got on from the start. It shouldn't have come as such a great surprise. After all, both of us had found that good nutrition and using natural products wherever possible made a profound difference to our ongoing personal well-being.

"I'm heading off to Taiwan when I'm done here," Horst told me.

"Oh? What will you be doing there?" I asked.

"It's a bit of a shopping trip really. A lot of our materials are sourced from there. Bristles for brushes, bamboo for handles… those sorts of things. I like to go and ensure that everything is the best quality and as ethically sourced as possible."

"That sounds fantastic." I couldn't help myself. "Can I come too?"

"Sure, I'd love to have you come along."

Can you believe it? I was going to Taiwan with the founder and owner of AVEDA!

I'll tell you now though, it wasn't cheap. I was very lucky in that Horst paid for my meals while I was there. But the airfare and the room? I had to pick up the tab for those myself, and I was glad it was only four or five days for what was a far more expensive room than I was accustomed to.

It was a wonderful experience, and I had the privilege of sitting in on several of Horst's meetings, providing the ideal opportunity to learn from someone truly inspirational.

By the end of the week it was time to head back to Bali and my little business. Having seen what Horst was doing on a global scale made me feel proud of what I had achieved for myself with my little business recycling materials for export from Bali to Australia.

My connection with Geoffrey and meeting Horst also had positive ramifications for my business. The recycled bottles proved to be ideal for aromatherapy oils that were packaged as giftware. And there were ethically-sourced bamboo containers and boxes made from recycled paper and cardboard that I was able to supply.

Horst was perhaps the most successful person I'd met with regard to making a business out of focusing on sustainable and ethically-sourced natural products. He would sell his company to Estee Lauder in 1997 for a reported $300 million in cash. The father of chemical-free cosmetics had made himself a fortune. He lived well and he shared. Sadly, he passed away in 2014.

Meeting and getting to know Horst had been an extraordinary experience. As a result, I left Bali that time feeling more confident than ever that I could achieve anything I wanted if I put my mind to it.

Sedona Vortex

After returning from Bali and Taiwan, I felt inspired to refocus on my culinary education. I decided to reconsider what I was doing in my cooking classes. I loved to share and inspire, which in turn required expanding my own knowledge. And the best options still lay across the Pacific. I booked a ticket and flew to Los Angeles. I then booked a flight to Sacramento in California so I could get to the nearby town of Oroville, home of the Vega Study Centre, where I attended courses run by Herman and Cornelia Aihara. Herman, a Japanese American born in 1920, had written a long list of books about macrobiotics including, *The Hidden Truth of Cancer, Basic Macrobiotics*, and what was a bestseller at the time, *Acid & Alkaline*. Cornelia had success as an author as well with *Natural Healing from Head to Toe* and her cookbook, *The Do of Cooking* (the word 'do' in the book's title is meant to be pronounced like 'dough') which relates to macrobiotic cooking for the seasons, preparing meals based on what food is available fresh, as well as in season at that time of year. This couple were seen as giants in the healthy food and nutrition scene on the West Coast. Having already read a few of their books, they were like rock stars to me.

There were others at the Vega Centre also sharing their knowledge about macrobiotics. David and Cynthia Briscoe were former students of Herman and Cornelia and were now experts in their own right. David's story of how he discovered macrobiotics is an interesting one. In 1972, at the age of twenty-two, he'd been diagnosed with a supposedly incurable emotional/psychological illness that required constant medication to allow him to function. Unwilling to accept the prognosis that he'd have to live this way for the rest of his life, his mother had sought guidance from Herman. Amazingly, after adopting a macrobiotic diet, David was able to discontinue his medication with no ill effects. The impact of this led him to embrace macrobiotics and build a life around helping others achieve benefits through changes in their approach to food and nutrition. In 1983, David was one of the first people to receive accreditation as a trainer from the Kushi Institute, an organisation established by Michio Kushi, who's been acclaimed as the first person to bring the macrobiotic philosophy to the United States. David's book, *A Personal Peace: Macrobiotic Reflections on Mental and Emotional Recovery* was published in 1989 and focuses on using diet to deal with mental health issues. He and his wife Cynthia ran Macrobiotics America, spreading their knowledge for over thirty years through seminars and chef training courses (Aveline and Michio Kushi also started Erewhon, the USA's first natural food store).

My time at the Vega Study Centre had a huge impact. I spent several weeks absorbing information on the many benefits of the macrobiotic philosophy of using food as medicine. This was particularly evident in the many people I met there who were living with cancer. I was in awe learning about how food affects mood and decided to experiment on myself, paying attention to what I was eating and how it made me feel. We learnt about chewing food properly (we were taught to chew our brown rice one hundred times, something I found quite meditative.) and the finer details of how our digestive systems work. I found myself wondering why this hadn't been taught at school. I resolved to share this knowledge when I returned back to work, even writing a paper titled *I Chew Therapy or The Joy of Mastication*.

It was also the first time I was learning detail about how food effects mood. Other topics covered included the warming and cooling effects of foods in the body, eating with the season, tuning in to body signals, addictions and allergies in an imbalanced system, and more. I was introduced to Do-In: Self Shiatsu, and happily spent time discovering the benefits of the infrared sauna, something that – since asking friends to contribute to purchasing one for my home as my fiftieth birthday gift – I've now made a regular part of my life.

Whole days in lectures were followed by cooking classes, delivered by Cornelia Aihara, that put the theory into practice. Cynthia Briscoe shared her wisdom of eating in season and the ancient Oriental medicine called the *Five Element Theory*. She was intuitive and generously shared her spiritual insights.

After completing my training program at Vega I needed to post all my new books, natural food magazines and lecture notes back home as they would have been way too heavy to carry on the plane. My library was expanding – a wonderful resource to draw on in the future.

While I was there, I also felt the urge to travel around. Oroville itself wasn't the most exciting place I'd been to.

I'd heard a great deal over the years about the Sedona Vortex, a sacred spiritual place and energy hot spot, unique to Arizona's Sedona Mountains. I'd met a guy in Bali called Hareesh who lived just near there and had talked at length about the vortex. Ginger had kept in touch with him over the years and passed on his contact details to me (another instance of connections made through travelling, making further travels easier). With Hareesh being happy to hear from me, I hired a car at Phoenix Airport and drove along the highway for two hours until I reached Sedona, also known as *Red Rock Country*.

I was travelling with a Sony Walkman cassette recorder which I made good use of as I drove along the long straight roads and reflected on what I'd learned at the Vega Study Centre, trying to take stock on what I'd learned while it was still fresh in my memory.

When I arrived in Sedona, everyone I met at the first local café I stopped at seemed to be either a healer, artist or spiritual guide. This was a place where I'd be able to open my mind *and* spirit to discover more about myself in many

VEGA MORNING TEA

Courtesy of Herman & Cornelia Aihara who were my teachers at Vega Study Centre in 1997

Yields: 1 serving

This is a great remedy any time of day for nausea, upset stomach, or to balance the effects of too many sweets!

Herman and Cornelia Aihara originally developed this medicinal tea for cancer patients. It is designed to strengthen the stomach and intestines, and to help you create a more alkaline condition in your body.

It is best to drink Morning Tea on an empty stomach in place of breakfast so that the kuzu can pass through your stomach and into your small intestines. By forgoing breakfast (and thus lengthening your fast), you give your digestive system a chance to rest and become stronger. If you are used to eating breakfast, you might want to experiment by substituting Morning tea (with perhaps one or two rice cakes to help satisfy hunger) for breakfast for a week or two.

If you decide you cannot go without a more substantial breakfast, you should drink Morning Tea first, then wait for a little while (minimum 15 minutes, but 30 minutes or up to an hour or two is best) before eating.

Ingredients:

- 1/3 organic umeboshi plum (or 1/8 teaspoon umeboshi paste)
- 1/2 teaspoon organic shoyu or tamari
- 3 - 5 drops fresh organic ginger juice
- 1 teaspoon spring or filtered water
- 1 level teaspoon organic kuzu (ground to a powder)
- 1/2 cup organic kukicha twig tea, brought to a rolling boil

Method:

- Mash umeboshi into a paste using flat side of knife and place in teacup.
- Grate ginger and squeeze 3 - 5 drops of juice into cup.
- Add shoyu, kuzu and water to cup. Mix ingredients together with a chopstick, making sure kuzu is fully dissolved.
- Bring kukicha tea to a rolling boil, remove from flame and quickly pour into cup. The kukicha must be very hot to ensure that the kuzu will cook and thicken. If the tea is hot enough, the mixture will change to a dark colour. If the mixture remains milky, the kuzu has not cooked completely, and you should start from scratch.
- After adding kukicha, allow the mixture to steep for 15 - 30 seconds, then stir with a chopstick. Serve hot.

Variations:
Use less shoyu or tamari for a lighter tea

Notes
All the ingredients of Morning Tea are alkaline forming. In terms of yin and yang, the tea is a good balance of properties.
The umeboshi plums are pickled in sea salt and shiso leaves (beefsteak plant). Umeboshi is a yang alkaline-forming food that aids in digestion, promotes healthy intestinal flora, and has a wide variety of uses in macrobiotic cooking.
Kuzu (or kudzu), a white starch, is a yang alkaline-forming food made from the root of the kuzu plant. As a starch, it thickens liquids, so it is often used in soups, sauces, and desserts.
Kuzu is useful for strengthening the intestines and is a component of many home remedies for diarrhoea.
Shoyu, a yang alkaline-forming food made by fermenting soybeans and wheat with salt, is widely used as a seasoning in macrobiotic cooking. Tamari is a wheat free alternative.
Kukicha twig tea, unlike many teas that are acid forming, is a yin alkaline-forming food made from the leaves and twigs of the Japanese tea plant.
Ginger juice is a yin alkaline-forming food made by grating ginger root and squeezing the juice from the pulp.

deep and profound ways. At one stage I found myself sitting with a guy who did my Tarot reading. I don't actually remember the details, other than that he was passionate and became quite excited about one of the cards. "This is why you are here!" he'd said.

After spending a night at Hareesh's home, that he shared with a few other people, I made my way to one of the seven vortexes he'd recommended. It was the *Airport Mesa Sedona Vortex*, the most accessible of all the vortexes, with a three-sixty-degree view of Sedona's breathtaking scenery. It's referred to as having masculine energy, strengthening the internal spirit so one can take charge of their own life and relax in self-confidence. This was important to me, as fostering strength was an essential component of my travels. Feeling energised, I drove to the next recommended location, parked the car and started walking through *Oak Creek Canyon*, famous for its magnificent swimming holes. Roughly following along the river, I walked and I walked but, with no clearly defined paths, found myself feeling uneasy. *I'm lost!* But then I thought back to the last time I'd felt that way when I was on Komodo Island. *It's okay, I'm near the river. I know I am. I can hear it. And there's people nearby. I can sense it.* Sure enough, it wasn't long before I found myself coming across groups of people gathered on the river. They were filled with joy and laughter and left me feeling confident that if I followed my gut instincts I would find what I was looking for, a place where I could sit in solitude and experience the spiritual power of the vortex created by the massive stands of red rock.

I continued walking upstream, keen to find somewhere that I could experience this awesome space in solitude. I walked further, then followed a little side tributary leading to a small rock pool that felt secluded and private. Wanting to experience the vortex in as profound a way as I could, I undressed and slipped naked into the refreshing waters of the rock pool. The water covered me up to just above my waist while I was seated. I fell into a deep meditation.

The vortexes of Sedona are thought to be swirling vortexes of energy that assist with healing and self-exploration; both of these were high on my agenda. As I sat in the pool I felt enveloped in love, an almost overwhelming abundance of love from those close to me in my life. And with that, I felt a deep sense of gratitude. I can't really tell you how long I sat there in that pool before finishing my meditation and I don't recall being conscious of what I was doing as I dressed afterward. All I remember is that I started walking. And once again, I was unsure of where I was going. It wasn't the path I'd used on the way up.

I wandered along, feeling lost once again, but strangely unconcerned. Then I went around a bend and came across a man dressed in nothing more than a pair of shorts. He had long hair, a flowing beard and a biblical style of walking stick. The guy looked at me and said, "Follow the path of least resistance." I intuitively understood and continued walking, following his advice as I went. Where the path split into multiple directions, I chose the one that looked the easiest. I developed a mantra as I walked that day, thinking over how I was lost but not lost: *Take the path of least resistance, take one step at a time and go with the flow.* This mantra has helped me many times since during life's challenges and the forks in the road that so often present.

Before long, I was in the car park. The path of least resistance had worked! But I took his words to mean more than that. Throughout my travels, the idea of following the path of least resistance had always been a key ingredient in my *recipe for living* on the road. I'd never had a clear terminology to articulate it though… until he gave it to me as I descended from the vortex. Or was it that he read it from me and simply spoke back to me what he could see – that I already knew? That was just one of many questions I would ponder as I got back to my rented car and hit record on my cassette recorder. I wanted to ensure I got my thoughts down on tape while they were still fresh in my memory. And I'm glad I did, as I've drawn on those tapes now to be able to talk about this incredible experience.

A unique experience

I spent five magical days in Sedona, hiking a couple more of the vortexes, enjoying my own company and meditating. I also enjoyed hanging out with Hareesh, his friends and all the other people I met in the cafes.

I was ready for my next adventure, driving back to Phoenix to catch a flight to Alburquerque New Mexico – to hire another car for the one-and-a-half-hour scenic drive to Sante Fe. This was along the historic Turquoise Trail. I didn't have contacts in Sante Fe, so spent a little time using maps and brochures to investigate what to do there before heading off in the left-hand drive vehicle. I love to drive and enjoyed the amazing vistas as I drove through old mining towns, the *Sandia Mountains* and the *Garden of the Gods*, a park with breathtaking rock formations.

I kept driving toward Santa Fe, New Mexico, looking forward to immersing myself in the blended cultures of the indigenous, Spanish and American influences. I'd heard about Georgia O'Keeffe, a significant twentieth century American Modernist painter. She was inspired by the stark New Mexico landscape, along with the Native American and Hispanic cultures of the region. On my must-do list was paying a visit to her property, Ghost Ranch, and the museum of her work in Santa Fe.

I found the wonderful historical La Posada de Santa Fe Hotel, an intimate village of Adobe cottages in lush, landscaped gardens. This was the place for me! Having checked in, I went on a search and found a large, impressive organic natural food store nearby.

What more could I ask for?

That question was answered when I had the pleasure of meeting Garry, a health and fitness professional, while shopping at the organic store. We embarked on an affair to remember over the following days, an instant connection. I haven't seen him since, but we still often write long, heart-opening emails to each other.

While in Sante Fe, I also found a Japanese Health Spa called *Ten Thousand Waves*, where I luxuriated while immersed in the waters of an outdoor hot tub and relaxing in the steam room. Best of all was the opportunity to enjoy my first experience of Watsu-hydrotherapy massage. It was the beginning of my long-time love affair with health spas.

The whole experience was such an incredible contrast to the time spent at the Vega Study Centre – one I could never forget.

Passion

The Gawler Foundation was established in 1983 and based in Melbourne. Its mission was to provide innovative, integrated support to those impacted by cancer or other diseases. They were focused on helping people find balance through an integrated approach to health and wellbeing.

On the weekend of March 26-28 in 1999 they held a conference in Lorne: the *Mind, Immunity and Health Conference*. In the months leading up to the festival I was contacted by Brigitte, the festival organiser and was invited to be a speaker talking about *Wholefoods for Wellbeing*. I'd been suggested to her as a potential speaker by Doctor Marc Cohen, who I'd met a few years earlier through Geoffrey.

It was another incredible opportunity to meet some of the biggest movers and shakers of the global health and wellbeing scene.

The main keynote speaker was Doctor Emmett Miller, who'd flown over from the USA to take part and talk on *Deep Healing*. He was considered to be the first to introduce the idea of cassette tapes for guided meditation. Having just come back from my trip to the States where I'd used a cassette to record my thoughts, this resonated with me.

There was also Doctor Ian Brighthope, who spoke about Nutritional Stress Management. Ian was one of the first practitioners of nutritional medicine in Australia, having established the Nutrition Care Company in 1978; it produces a range of products promoting good gut health and other premium grade nutritional supplements. He was also the first integrative medical doctor

I went to see back in the 1980's, and we've both been on the speaker program of several conferences since then. I consider him to be both a mentor and a friend. In recent years he's also become one of the leading advocates for medicinal cannabis.

Doctor Marc Cohen spoke about the Art and Science of Joy. In addition to his medical degree, Marc has PhDs in both traditional Chinese medicine and computer systems engineering. He's published over a hundred peer-reviewed scientific papers, and even a range of children's picture books. He's also a great fire twirler at parties!

In addition, I met Ian Gawler, founder of the institute holding the conference. All of these men were hugely influential in the health and wellness movement. It was such a tremendous honour to be speaking at the same conference as they were. There was a mutual respect and understanding that we all had for one another. It made me appreciate more than ever how important the work I'd been doing – teaching about the philosophy of macrobiotics using foods as medicines and plant-based cooking – really was. And how it was truly at the cutting-edge of developing an understanding of the importance of nutrition in Western society.

Then Marc got in touch with me a short time after the conference.

"I've been asked by Monash University to put together a course on holistic medicine," he said.

"Wow, that's fantastic!" I replied. And it was. The medical schools had always frowned on ideas like holistic medicine before then.

"It'll be an elective for the first and third-year med students. It'll have a strong component based on nutrition."

"That's so good to hear." My understanding was that nutrition was only ever given lip service by medical courses at the time.

"I was hoping you might be interested in delivering some cooking classes and demonstrations as part of it?"

"Of course, I'd love to."

This was like a dream come true, and such an incredible endorsement of my wholefood philosophy, one that I could never have imagined even a few years earlier.

My apartment in Middle Park had led to mixing in social circles that introduced me to plenty of people I hadn't met before. One of the more memorable ones was Yvonne Rowe.

As we got to know each other, we realised that we had much in common regarding our attitudes toward health and nutrition.

"I want to set up a health food shop," she told me one day.

Rather than buy an existing business and adapting it, like I had done, Yvonne, working with her son Ned, wanted to set hers up from scratch.

They found a warehouse space near South Melbourne Market. It was and still is a perfect location for an eco-living, organic health food store. The two went all out, installing a proper kitchen, extensive shelving, fridges, counters for the best quality products and produce along with everything else required to make a successful health food store.

When it opened, the new *Passionfoods* also became another venue where I could run a few cooking classes. I'll be forever grateful for the experience of Yvonne and the support she gave me.

The store still stands in the same spot today, albeit with a new owner. It's a testament to the great job Yvonne did in establishing it. An inspiring woman… meeting her was a wonderful ingredient in *my recipes for living*.

Finding a Voice

For years I'd been reading Annemarie Colbin books, ever since my macrobiotic mentor, Michio Kushi, had first told me about her. I'd enjoyed the single day courses I'd done at her Natural Gourmet Institute on my previous trip to New York, and was keen to do the full courses she had available.

Financially, it simply wasn't viable. What I could afford though was five weeks over there, enough time to do some of the individual courses. I had decided to sell my little cottage to fund my new business, *Ozfoodtrainer*, and travel adventure. I wanted to go and grow. I'd revelled in the sense of fulfillment I'd achieved running the cooking classes – and I knew that, if I was to continue doing them, I needed to expand my own knowledge so I could take them to the next level.

I called the *Natural Gourmet Institute* and they sent their brochures. Within a week I was planning which classes to attend and asking my New York City friends if they could ask around for a place for me to stay.

While not all the food within the courses was vegetarian, the vast bulk of it was. The individual courses included everything from knife skills to Chinese medicine, and food writing.

There was something else I really wanted to do before going over to the States. Inspired by Annemarie's *The Basics of Healthy Cooking* video, I developed the idea of producing something similar in Australia using ingredients available here, *Sandra's Whole Cuisine*, something of substance

With Annemarie Colbin in New York

that I could take with me to the States. In addition to having a cooking video of my own to sell through my website, could there be a better way to let people in the USA know what I had to offer? Ideally, I was hoping to actually have it running on my website. But this was back in 1999, when most people were still relying on dial-up connections. With ADSL2 not even available in Australia until sometime in the year 2000, it would be a few more years before streaming videos online would be a viable option.

I knew who would be the best person to approach about shooting the video. Way back when I'd visited Israel in 1978, when I'd gone there from Goa, I'd met a talented couple, Suzette and Shulka. A photographer, Suzette was originally from Melbourne. Shulka was from Israel and had been involved in film and television production. I'd caught up with them in New York in 1985 when they were living there, but they'd since moved to Melbourne.

When I contacted Shulka, I asked what it might cost. His response?

"I think this is a great idea. I just want to see it done. I'll do it for the love of what you're trying to do. It's important." I hoped there'd be enough sales to cover expenses... and a share for them too.

I gathered the plant-based recipes from my cooking class recipe file, making sure to include as much nutritional information as possible and a glossary of ingredients. There were easy-to-follow instructions for beginners as well as experienced cooks.

We set up and prepared to shoot at Shulka and Suzette's house, with Shulka directing and Suzette looking after the camera and lighting.

"Okay Sandy, we're rolling... and one, two, three..."

"Hi, I'm Sandy..."

I got a few sentences in when all of a sudden Shulka calls out, "Cut!"

I stopped mid-sentence and looked to him for the reason.

"You said 'um'. You really need to try and watch that."

We rolled again. I got a little bit further this time before I heard him again. "Cut!"

"What was it this time? Did I do it again?"

"Yeah, you've got to be really conscious of it."

I wanted to be relaxed and roll through the whole thing like I would in one of my classes, but I ended up so self-conscious about the dreaded 'um' word that I started to become robotic with my delivery. So, it was like, "Hi... I'm... San... dy... Dubs..."

Regardless of how nervous I was, we got through it – and when I look back on it today, I feel immense pride in how far ahead of its time the video was with the recipes I chose to include. They were all plant-based, vegan and even gluten-free. Recipes like cooking with quinoa, Miso Soup and Vegetarian Brown Rice Nori Rolls – the sort of recipes you see everywhere nowadays. But back then they weren't well known.

"Have you given much thought to the cover design yet?" Suzette asked me between takes.

"Not really. I need to work out the branding for it too."

"I know a designer who's really good – Irene. She's health conscious too, so I'm sure she'll be in tune with what you're doing. I'll send you her details if you like."

Irene and I hit it off straight away. We ended up deciding to brand it as being from *Whole Earth Cooking*, a variation on the business name I'd developed for the business I'd been running in Bali. She was so interested in what I was doing that she started attending the classes herself.

I got in touch with Yvonne from Passionfoods Health Food Store and asked if I could do the video launch in her shop.

"I'd love to have it launch at Passionfoods," she replied.

After almost a year creating the ninety-minute video with twenty-seven tried and tasted recipes, on July 28th 1999 my cooking video, *Sandra's Whole Cuisine*, was launched.

Thanks to Irene, the cover and booklet insert looks fabulous. I ran off VHS copies and took them to some of the local health food stores, but most importantly organised NTSC copies to take with me to the States. This was crucial, as Australia used a different video standard at the time.

I'd also realised by then that the internet was set to be fundamental to the success of almost any business in the future. Having just been a speaker at the *Mind, Immunity and Health Conference*, I was aware that my profile within the Health and Wellbeing community was building, making it critical to establish an online identity in what was essentially a global movement. Fortunately, Ginger had set up a business in San Francisco that focused on the new digital technologies and had all the skills necessary to build a website for my *Ozfoodtrainer* business.

I emailed her the design work Irene had done, along with the text files to be included and the website came together! It put me way ahead of so many others in the health and wellbeing space. As I mentioned, the internet was still based around dial-up, and speeds in Australia were still very slow. But ADSL had just started to roll out in the USA, making concepts like video streaming feasible. Even though it would be another six years before YouTube would stream its first videos, I could see that was where it was all heading, and I wanted to ensure I was ready to be one of the early adopters from a business point of view.

While the website was a huge step forward, I wanted more: I wanted to get to get back to the States. But first I needed a buyer for my house to make my plans affordable.

At the same time, I was running my classes at the Centre of Adult Education (another opportunity to promote my newly completed cooking video). One of the attendees, Jody, came up to me at the end of one the classes. "Have you ever thought of doing a television program?" she asked.

"What, like a cooking show?"

"It could be more than that. It could be a show that looks at all aspects of a healthy lifestyle, with you and your cooking as a central theme. I've got a friend who works at Channel 31. I think it could be a real goer."

Having always enjoyed watching Sex and the City I suggested, "We could call it *Health and the City*."

The idea had a lot of appeal to me. Channel 31, which still operates today, is a community-based television station in Melbourne. Some major small-screen personalities have got their big break from working there, and I could certainly see the potential.

I envisaged a program with half hour episodes that would include interviews with some of the big names in the health and wellbeing community I'd come to know over the years, as well as the obligatory cooking session in each episode.

Jody's friend was keen as well. So, we set out to pull together a pilot.

Sadly, it didn't quite work out the way I'd hoped. Jody had taken on the role of producer and had a different vision on the direction the show should take. The first hint of this came when she said, "I'm organising uniforms for us, so everyone on air has a standard look." She was also looking to make it a much broader-based lifestyle program than what I'd had in mind.

We produced a pilot that involved Jody interviewing me outside a café, along with a few cooking demonstrations, but the momentum was falling away as we continued to struggle with agreement on some of the fundamentals. While the pilot did go to air, the show didn't move forward.

In the meantime, a buyer had come forward for my house, making my plans to study at the New York Natural Gourmet Institute viable.

Finally I was able to book flights for my 2000 trip overseas. The Y2K bug had proved to be a non-event. So, despite *Health and the City* having been a non-starter, things were looking positive.

Once in the States, I headed up to San Francisco and called a friend I'd met at a conference the year before and asked, "Hey, I'm in town for the next few days. Would you like to go to dinner?"

"I'd love to, is there anywhere in particular you'd like?"

"Yes. Have you heard of Chez Panisse?"

Chez Panisse was founded by Alice Waters in the early-seventies. Having been in operation for over fifty years, it originated as a place where people could meet to sit around the table and eat great food while discussing politics, art and culture. In those early days, there was a set menu which changed daily, depending on the available produce. Alice and her chefs were totally focused on the 'farm to table' concept. They had their own market garden, but also travelled around the local farms seeking out organically grown produce that was appropriate for the season. Over the years the range of suppliers expanded, all of them offering only the most ethical of produce.

Chez Panisse now features both a cafe and a fine dining restaurant with expansive menus. It's famous not just for its early adoption of farm-to-table dining, but also for its relaxed atmosphere where no one feels pressured to finish their meal and leave. I'd wanted to eat there since first hearing about it a few years earlier, and now I had my chance.

I also stayed with Ginger for a few days while I was in San Francisco. It was a great opportunity to visit her office where my website had been put together. It was also a good reminder that when you take big chances in life, like I had done with my time living and working in Bali, you meet other people who also take chances that put them at the cutting edge.

But my main purpose had always been to head to New York and train at the Natural Gourmet Institute. I enrolled in several courses and they didn't disappoint.

I was able to sublet a small apartment from a theatrical couple who'd gone away on tour, making my stay more affordable than if I'd had to book into a hotel room.

Having been in New York before, I was well aware of just how much it had to offer culturally. Aside from being spoilt for choice with plant-based cafes and restaurants, I spent plenty of time in art galleries including MOMA and the Guggenheim. And the music! There was always so much choice. One particular highlight was a night when WBLS Radio were putting on a special night at the Exit nightclub.

I rocked up on my own and joined the long queue, not thinking much of it. I heard a voice behind me saying, "Are you alright there, honey?"

I turned around and saw a concerned look on the face of a very tall, bejewelled black woman standing behind me in the queue.

"You do realise that you're the only white girl waiting in this queue?"

It hadn't even occurred to me until then that I was in the queue for a black nightclub. "I hadn't noticed until now to be honest."

"I've got to hand it to you, you've got some balls. Stick with me, honey, and I'll make sure no one gives you a hard time."

As it turned out, I felt perfectly safe once inside. The music was fantastic: Mary J Blige and Sisqo, both of them riding a wave of success at the time.

I was sitting at the bar when this handsome black guy came up next to me. "What's that you're drinking?"

"Nothing alcoholic, it's cranberry juice."

"No way!" he held up his glass. "That's what I'm drinking too."

I responded with a big smile.

"I hope you don't mind me saying this, but we don't get a lot of white girls in here usually."

"I can't see why not, the music's great."

He gave a little laugh. "I like your style. What's your name?"

"Sandy."

"Well, it's nice to meet you, Sandy. My name's Tony."

We talked and we danced, and then Tony asked if he could drive me home. I felt safe in his presence and so my instincts said yes. He ended up coming back to where I was staying, leading to what was one of the most wonderful casual affairs I've ever enjoyed, one that I would revisit each time I returned to New York in the years ahead. It still gives me shivers and puts a smile on my face whenever I think about him. I made a wonderful friend for life.

When I returned from the USA this time, I had another problem to face. Relations between my landlord and myself had soured. So much, that I ended up suing her for $5,000 at the Victorian Civil and Administrative Tribunal, for lack of providing services as laid out in the lease and for disruption to our lives on weekends – and other harassments. This money came in handy, as by this stage, Geoffrey had already moved out, and with relations deteriorating so badly with the building's owner, I decided it was time to move on. I needed funds to cover the cost of moving. It also provided enough for another trip to Bali.

As it happened, an investment property that my parents owned in Caulfield North was available. I decided it might be a good option in the short term while I looked for somewhere else (little did I know at the time that I would spend almost twenty years living there).

During this time I turned my skills in another direction, another means of getting my message of nutrition to the community. I wanted to share my knowledge with others via publications. The problem though was: where should I begin this new adventure?

Vegan Voice was a magazine produced out of Nimbin from 2000 onwards. While reading the magazine, I felt like it might be a good fit for my message, so I submitted an article titled *Use Your Noodle*. It spoke of how, after a busy day working as a food consultant at Prahran Health Food Store, I loved nothing more than relaxing with my own form of meditation... cooking! The story was followed up with three recipes. It seemed like a novel way of presenting them and it boosted my confidence.

There was a growing number of publications coming out that focused on wellbeing and nutrition. I could see this becoming another part of my ongoing effort to help people find a healthier version of themselves.

In 2002, I had the great opportunity to study with medical practitioners and natural therapists in Swinburne University's *Graduate Diploma to Applied*

Science and Nutrition and Environmental Medicine. Professor Avni Sali AM created the course to educate practitioners in evidence-based complementary and alternative medicines and to emphasise the principles and practical application of nutritional and environmental medicine to common clinical problems.

Having moved into a whole new level of my involvement in the world of healthy nutrition and cooking, I was keen to build on my educational qualifications. It can also make a significant difference to both your confidence and the optics when you're booked as a speaker at international conferences and writing articles for publications that have a wide circulation.

As I continued the course, one of the subjects happened to relate to dealing with menopause, a golden opportunity to do some quality research. Why? Well, I was going through the early stages of menopause myself. I could be my own test subject looking into the impact of nutrition and traditional herbal therapies on hormonal changes during menopause. I'd also had a lot of women by that stage asking me for advice on how to deal with this important life change. It was important to me that I pass on to them the best possible information. Going through the experience myself would give me greater confidence in understanding their needs.

I started by getting a bioidentical hormone test carried out taking the results to an integrated medical general practitioner. The doctor was able to then prescribe a range of creams that would help with the hot flushes. Then I pored through notes I'd accumulated over many years of studying macrobiotics and nutrition, searching for the best options that would help to keep my body in balance.

I experimented with different foods, taking note of their impact, spoke to natural therapists on the topic and attended multiple women's health seminars collecting whatever evidence I could find. Much of it was anecdotal.

One of the resources I drew on during this time was a book called *Hormone Heresy*, written by an American friend living in Australia, Doctor Sherrill

Sellman ND. Her book was considered to be very radical, but it has opened many people's eyes, to think and say, "Hold on, there's more to this than periods coming to an end and feeling terrible." It's actually a period of your life where you can shed a good deal of emotional baggage and embrace the beginning of a whole new phase.

The course continued through until 2004, when I graduated with a *Diploma of Applied Sciences for Nutritional and Environmental Medicine*. Subject titles included:

- Safe Application and Toxicity of Nutritional Therapies
- Biology of Nutrients
- Environmental Medicine
- The Importance of Nutrition and Behavioural Medicine
- Nutrient Therapy in Toxicology and Skin Problems
- Nutritional Approaches to Men's Health and Endocrine Problems
- Nutritional Approaches to Women's Health and Paediatric Problems
- Nutritional Approaches to Cardiovascular and Respiratory Problems
- Nutritional Approaches to Musculoskeletal Problems and Sports Nutrition
- Nutritional Approaches to Gastrointestinal Problems and Behavioural Problems
- Nutritional Approaches to Neurological and Degenerative Disorders and Aging Problems

Bangalore

Before I'd moved out of Middle Park, Marc had come over to visit Geoffrey in the apartment upstairs and I was invited, as I so often was, to come up and join them.

"I'm going to speak at a conference in Bangalore in January," said Marc. "It's called the *Global Holistic Health Summit*. Horst will be speaking there as well. It's a special event that's attracting all the premier people in holistic health. Deepak Chopra is going to be one of the keynote speakers, and the Dalai Lama is going to be addressing the conference on the first day."

This was a big deal. The author of over ninety books, Deepak Chopra, a physician by education, is a popular proponent of a holistic approach to wellbeing, incorporating yoga, meditation, and nutrition, along with other new-age therapies. Another speaker was Gurudev Sri Sri Ravi Shankar, a humanitarian, spiritual leader and ambassador of peace and human values. He'd previously worked as an apprentice under Maharishi Mahesh Yogi, founder of Transcendental Meditation. His conference speech would be about the art of living.

It didn't take long before I ended up asking Marc the obvious question, "Can I come too?"

As it turned out, with a bit of help from Geoffrey and Professor Ian Brighthope, Marc was able to make it work. He already had his wife and children accompanying him, along with his mother. I became another part of his entourage. It was indicative of how highly respected Marc was that he was able to extend an invitation to the conference for me, along with accommodation, although I did have to pay my own airfare.

A good friend of mine, Nina, was helping me prepare for a cooking class a few days later. A naturopath and practitioner of using foods as medicines, her response was very much like mine when I told her about it. "Can I come too?"

To Nina's great joy, she managed to make it work and was able to join us.

The conference ran from the 12th - 17th of January, 2003. But I decided to stay on for a couple of weeks extra, returning in early February.

This was a conference filled with movers and shakers of the global health and wellness scene. Everyone I spoke to there had an inspiring story to share. There was a couple I gravitated to who shared their dream with me. As I got into a discussion with the husband one day, he talked lovingly about his partner and about his dream of setting up a holistic and spiritual retreat in the south part of Koh Samui, Thailand. They had the land and the vision and I was certainly impressed with their passion. However, I wondered if this could be real. I'd met so many people by then who dreamed of running a health resort (including myself), but when I visited Koh Samui later in 2005, I actually went there and saw it under construction. Plus, I had a guided tour of the place. They'd done it! Now, Kamalaya is a multi-award-winning wellness sanctuary and holistic spa, using ancient Eastern health traditions with Western medical research in a stunning environment.

On the final night there was a big dinner for the keynote speakers, and the organisers went to great lengths to ensure the speakers felt appreciated, putting the dinner on in an accredited seven-star hotel. And, being part of Marc's entourage, I was invited to attend. How cool is that?

As Nina and I walked in we looked around and marvelled at how there seemed to be gold everywhere, gold and pink pillars, gold frames on every panel. Even the ceilings were adorned with imagery of Shiva and other Hindu gods. I wondered if perhaps we were in a building that had been a palace in the days before it became a hotel. In every corner of every corridor an Indian

Arriving at the conference

stood dressed as though they were the Maharaja, waiting for their services to be needed. From the doorman to the waiters, the staff were dressed immaculately. There were half a dozen long tables laid out in a big undercover outdoor setting for the dinner. Everyone from my group ended up scattered among the different tables. It was luxury like I'd never experienced before or since.

Many owners and the staff of high-end spa resorts in Asia were there, as well as government dignitaries and all the conference speakers. Several people at my table talked about one resort in particular, a more traditional Ayurvedic low-key favourite. Somatheeram in Kerala. It seemed almost everyone on my table had either been there or was planning to go there. As I had a few weeks to go in India after the conference, I thought, *hmmm... can I go too?*

The conversation was flowing at all the tables when suddenly a hush swept through the room; everyone turned to watch as the keynote speakers made their entrance together, with Deepak Chopra in the lead. Each of these people on their own had the sort of charisma that turns heads as they entered a room, but combined it was compelling. Their very presence demanded attention.

It was amazing in so many ways, some of these speakers had the sort of following that rock stars have in the west. Particularly Gurudev Sri Sri Ravi Shankar, who had a sea of what to western sensibilities might appear to be groupies, who followed him everywhere he went.

After the summit, Marc told me that he and others were invited to go to Sri Sri Ravi Shankar's Bangalore Ashram and that I was welcome to join them. It was an opportunity to gain a better understanding of why he attracted so much attention. There was also a major celebration taking place there at the time, with around ten thousand people attending. It was worth going there even if just to experience the festival. But you know what? After a couple of days, I realised that following gurus just isn't for me. I hung around for the spectacle of the celebration then moved on, spending a few days at a nearby small Ayurvedic health retreat in Bangalore that was recommended by friends

Outside Sri Sri Ravi Shankar's Bangalore Ashram

in Melbourne, before catching a flight to my next adventure in Cochin, home of a small Indian Jewish community. I was fortunate to find a homestay there and had a great time wandering the streets and checking out all the vegan cafes. At one of these I met a couple of backpackers who explained to me how to find my way to 'Jewtown Street' as they called it. Even though there were only eight Jews left in the town, they still had a synagogue. When I arrived, the synagogue's caretaker was happy to let me in and have a look around.

I caught a train from there to Kerala in South West India, where I'd booked into the Somatheeram Ayurvedic health resort I'd heard so much about on the coast of the Arabian Sea. Ayurveda is a medical philosophy that has its origins in India. The translation from Sanskrit is words to the effect o 'knowledge of life'.

When I alighted from the train after a four-hour journey, I was assaulted by the noise, the mixture of pungent odours and the general bustle that you'll find in most Indian cities. There was a shuttle waiting at the station which took me to the resort – where the contrast couldn't have been greater. This time as I left the shuttle, I felt like I was being caressed by the sea breeze with its salty aromas. There was an abundance of coconut palm trees everywhere I looked, and the distant sound of the waves rolling in created a gentle soundtrack for the moment.

I stayed there for a week and found it lived up to every expectation. Each person's diet and treatment while they stay is customised to match an analysis of their body type. I had a long and private consultation with the Ayurvedic doctor, sharing my health challenges and lifestyle choices. Then I indulged in all the therapies, yoga, the steam room, and the specialised massages.

My room was a self-contained cottage with a thatch roof and a hammock that was almost right on the beach. I spent most of my time just in a sarong or a light cotton dressing gown as I relaxed between treatments. I mixed with some of the other guests, joining a table for dinner or the like. But for the most part I enjoyed my own company as I luxuriated in the treatments on offer.

A lot of my time was spent on the beach, either walking along and watching people fishing from the shore, or sitting in a private area that included service from the resort. Elephants – animals that are much-loved and revered in India, roamed through the grounds, some adorned with bejewelled headdresses and other ornamentation.

There were some treatments that stood out. The sweatbox... oh, how I enjoyed that. So much so that I took multiple photos of it in the hope I could work out how to build one for myself on my return to Australia. Another favourite was a treatment called Shirodhara, part of the Panchakarma cleansing treatment (Panchakarma being a five-stage cleansing process that is a cornerstone of Ayurvedic practice). In Shirodhara, a treatment said to help the nervous system, herbal oils are poured on the forehead.

Then there's the massage. There's a big difference between regular massage and an Ayurvedic massage. It involves use of special oils and is focused on the skin and circulation system as much as it is on the muscles, helping with lymphatic drainage as well as muscle tension.

My four weeks in India was inspiring. It grounded me in what I would continue to do and added a great deal to my knowledge base. I was confident I could share what I'd learned with those who came to my classes and had an interest in learning more about self-care and wellbeing. It was especially essential to my own health, as I gained a deeper understanding and awareness of what works for me.

On arriving back in Australia, I returned to running my classes at the Centre for Adult Education. This had become my core business, and primary source of income. So, it was quite welcome when I was approached by Shaun Fincham, asking if I could run courses in nutrition and cooking at the Box Hill Institute of TAFE. My reputation was building, and my work diary was filling.

2003 was also a year where I enjoyed several casual affairs. One with a member of one of Australia's most prominent bands from the sixties and seventies. Another with a young guy from down the road who used to stop by and help me with my computer from time to time. None of them were ever going to lead to anything bigger, but they were a lot of fun. These were all great times that I had with nice people, but there was never that depth of emotional connection with them like I'd felt with the likes of Ian, Peter, or Jim.

I find it interesting that for some people, it seems so important to them to be in a relationship. But me? I'm actually quite comfortable with my own company. It's not that I don't want relationships. Each of the big relationships I've had in my life has been very special and important to me. And each of them has ended with a lifelong friendship resulting from the time spent together.

There are a great many experiences in my life that may never have happened had I been linked inexorably to a significant other half. Plus, I've been able to enjoy a great many casual relationships throughout the years that introduced me to a broad range of interesting personalities.

It would probably be fair to say that, for me, the emotional freedom I've gained from travelling solo through my life, has been a fundamental ingredient in my personal *recipe for living*. For others, the love they share with a partner may be one of their crucial ingredients.

The vital ingredient has been to develop the relationship with myself – for me, committed relationships have proved again and again that they aren't the be-all and end-all.

Aloha Hawaii

When 2004 came around, I was excited by the idea of another trip to the States to attend more courses at the Natural Gourmet Institute... and to experience more of the adventures and good times that accompany travelling.

Ginger had moved to Hawaii with her husband, Hank and my sister-in-law had a cousin in Honolulu on the island of Oahu. So, a stopover while crossing the Pacific was a must!

I stayed a few days with Lilli's hospitable cousin, having a lovely time eating, drinking and sightseeing in Honolulu. Then I boarded a plane for the short flight to The Big Island, also known as the Island of Hawaii or Hawaii Island.

I embraced Ginger in a warm hug when she greeted me at the airport before leading me to her car, exchanging all the pleasantries on the way that go with seeing a friend for the first time in years. "We'll have to stop by Costco and pick up some groceries," she said as we left the carpark.

This was long before Costco had set up any outlets in Australia, so I had no idea what to expect. As we walked in it was a revelation. The place was enormous: want a small punnet of blueberries? Well, sorry... you'll have to buy the supersize one kilogram pack. Need a couple of toilet rolls? You'll have to get a pack of fifty. We arrived at the fresh seafood section, and it seemed like Costco must have explained the "bulk" concept to all the sea creatures of the oceans as well... the frozen wild Alaskan salmon were gigantic!

And they weren't the only super-sized observation I made. I'd never seen so much obesity on display as the customers browsed the aisles.

Having picked up on my surprise, Ginger said, "The only place I can get something healthy to eat around here is Subway." My heart sank at the thought.

"Are there any good restaurants?" I asked.

"The Four Seasons has a good menu; we'll go there if you like."

It was a wonderful escape from this unfamiliar confrontation with the unhealthier side of American culture I was experiencing.

But that confrontation was set to continue.

Ginger was into canoe racing and was competing the next day. Naturally, I chose to go along and watch. There was this guy standing next to me with a bag of 'Dunkin' Donuts' that he was happily consuming while watching the super-fit paddlers racing each other.

He looked across at me and asked, "Do you know any of the racers?'

I pointed toward Ginger as she worked her way through the field and said, "Yes, my friend over there in third place."

He nodded then asked, "Hey, do you want a donut?"

I shook my head as I replied, "No, thank you. I'm not into eating donuts"

He gave me a weird look then shrugged his shoulders as he turned back to watch the race. It was the last I'd hear from him.

When Ginger and I caught up after she'd finished her race, I recounted the story to her.

"You did what?" she asked, her tone suggested I'd somehow done something wrong.

"I politely declined his offer of a donut."

"How could you be so rude?"

"But I don't eat them. Why would I want to accept his offer when I don't eat donuts?"

"Sandy, he was being kind and you rejected his offer." Seeing the look of confusion on my face she continued. "Look, if someone offers you something, the polite thing to do is accept it gratefully. It doesn't matter whether or not you'd normally eat donuts. It's just plain rude to reject someone's generosity."

I was lost for words. I didn't mean to be rude. lesson learned.

"Hey, do you want join us going scuba diving tomorrow?" asked Ginger in an effort to change the topic and the mood a short time later.

"Okay…" I replied tentatively. In 1996, I'd managed to get my scuba PADI diving license in Bali. I'd done the course as a fortieth birthday present for myself. I hadn't done any diving since then though, so I was a bit cautious.

"There's a fantastic reef just off point that we go to. You'll love it."

I nodded as I took a deep breath, trying to ensure my apprehension wasn't apparent.

The next day, we were scrambling across rocks, carrying our scuba gear. I watched as the first diver in our little party jumped off the rocks and into the choppy seas. I turned to Hank and said, "I might need a hand getting in… it's just so choppy."

Hank gave me a reassuring smile as he held firmly onto my hand while I eased myself into the water.

Scuba diving is an amazing experience. It's almost as though you're cruising over the surface of some alien world. But right from the outset, I wasn't feeling comfortable. This was so different to the scuba diving I'd done in Bali, where the waters were calmer. *Steady breaths*, I thought to myself, conscious of the importance of maintaining a steady flow to my breathing. *Steady breath in, steady breath out.* It was no good.

Two hundred metres out from our starting point, the panic set in. I couldn't do it. When we returned to the point I watched in awe as the others pulled themselves from the water onto the rocks with the grace and confidence of a sea lion. And me? I had to be hauled out. It was embarrassing and painful. All I could think of afterwards was how I'd clearly overestimated my abilities, but at least I'd tried.

Back in the safety of dry land at Ginger's home, I went for a dive of a different kind, deep into the internet dating app, jDate... a dating app designed specifically for the Jewish community. In a few days I was going to be in LA, and thought that it would be good to meet up with someone while I was there.

My cousin, Oren, picked me up from the airport and gave me a lift to my usual accommodation when in the City of Angels, the Venice Suites in Venice Beach. They were directly across from the beach made famous by the muscle men, who like to work out there and the arty market stalls along the boardwalk.

I loved hanging out with Oren. He knew all the groovy night spots and his handsome features made him look like he could have easily been cast as James Bond. His brother, Nir, who happened to be visiting from Israel, joined us, another great-looking guy who had the appearance and air of a sports star. They both love surfing and, even though they live so far apart, they're very close. I can tell you, when I was out with these two stunning, tall men (both younger than me) heads would turn as we entered the room (and perhaps someone noticed me as well).

During the days I'd check out Venice Beach and Santa Monica, revelling in the choices of healthy cafes with vegan options. And the wholefood supermarket? That was my Nirvana. There must have been at least ten checkout lanes, and always packed. I spent a whole seven hours there one day, just immersed in the cornucopia of what was on offer... and so many tasty vegan foods to eat while there.

I'd also decided to book into the Beverly Hills Hilton for a four-night special offer I'd seen online. It's right by Rodeo Drive with all the high-end stores and stylish people, including the chance to spot well-known Hollywood stars. It provided some great opportunities, like hanging out at the hotel bar where, being an 'Aussie', I was a bit of a novelty, a unique attribute that led to some riveting conversations with the other guests.

It was also an opportunity to meet up with a few of the guys I'd been chatting to on jDate.

Online dating was new to me, so I approached it with an open mind. It was, after all, a good way to have company while eating in some cool LA restaurants.

I met the first guy at a Japanese Restaurant on Abbott Kinney Boulevard. Dinner was delicious and the banter was fine. You know how it goes when indulging in small talk with a stranger. It's easy to find things to talk about. Then, when he took me back to the hotel, he said, "Can I walk you to your room?"

"It's okay, I can find my way," I replied. "It was a lovely dinner, thank you."

"No, really… I insist…"

It felt awkward, but, rather than have a scene in the hotel lobby, I relented and let him accompany me to my room. Then, as I unlocked the door, he slipped inside. Before I had time to react, he'd pushed me on to the bed. No pretence of tenderness, just a push.

"NO!" I said as forcefully as I could. He got a shock from the firmness of my response and scurried out the door. Wow! It was good that my instinctive reaction was so strong… and that he was actually quite a wimp.

There was one guy, though, Jeff, who was a charming man with impeccable manners. We enjoyed a lovely dinner, one that felt comfortable and easy. We ended up having a memorable although brief few days together during my stay at the Hilton, and he remains a friend, someone I only have fond memories of.

Thailand

In 2005 I had the honour of being invited by Doctor Marc Cohen and Ingo Schweder (the group director at the Mandarin Oriental Health Group) to be a speaker at the Mandarin Oriental Hotels Spa Conference, to be held that year in Thailand. The conference was focused on training the hotel group's staff from around the world, to ensure the high standards of spa and wellness treatments and services in all their hotels would be of a consistent standard. All the staff were well-trained professionals in their particular fields.

My airfares, accommodation and expenses were all paid for during the conference. This was a big deal for me... the hotel was the Mandarin Oriental in Bangkok! I arrived a few days early so I could settle in and attend some of the hotel's special cooking classes being held across the river, taking advantage of the opportunity to further enhance my own skills while I was there.

All the participants radiated good health as they arrived. I did find myself feeling a little overwhelmed by the hotel culture, but was happy to be there and meet new people. The conference was held over the course of two weeks and spread across three locations. I was scheduled to speak during the third leg of the conference and was able to enjoy the luxury that accompanied the first two stages as well.

After stage one at the Mandarin Oriental was concluded, we travelled by organised cars to the historic Railway Hotel at Hua Hin for a few days. At the time it was known as the Hotel Sofitel Grand 'Railway' Hotel Hua Hin, a magnificent hotel with over a century of history, charm and elegance. I loved experiencing the style of this resort and the beauty of its grounds on the west coast of the Gulf of Thailand. I especially enjoyed a few fun evenings at the local market tasting new delights with Marc and his family.

From Hua Hin we flew to Chiang Mai in Northern Thailand, and the venue I was scheduled to speak at. Managed by the Mandarin Oriental Group, the Dhara Dhevi was based on the design of an ancient Mandalay Palace with stunning teakwood architecture. Its seven-tiered roof was designed to represent the seven steps to Nirvana and the attainment of spiritual and physical perfection. How poignant for me that this was to be the venue for my presentation. By this stage I'd developed a better friendship with Ingo, who was coordinating the group's spas. We had similar world views, which helped give me confidence as I stood in front of a room of fifty people delivering my PowerPoint presentation… no cooking demonstration accompanying it like I was so used to.

It felt so strange without my kitchen bench and the associated props that my demonstration style relied on so much. Despite knowing that I had the well-studied knowledge and experience to share as I had done so often back in Melbourne, I felt quite nervous about how I would come across compared to Marc and Ingo who were such charismatic and professional speakers.

And yet, here I was. I'd achieved this next level, presenting a training session for professional staff at an international luxury hotel chain's conference. It was the fulfillment of another dream! Some of the participants even came forward later to let me know my session had inspired them to choose better quality ingredients when cooking for themselves into the future. I worried, though, that my presentation might have come across as stilted; I kept dwelling on a particular moment when I'd become sidetracked by a question and Marc took over, something that left me feeling less than totally satisfied.

But my biggest concern was my fear that I might not be able to sustain working at this international level, where there is such enormous pressure to be at the absolute top of your game. That meant constantly having to be up to date on everything happening within the health and nutrition scene. I could see that the travelling, the hotels rooms, and constant networking (while maintaining my own health with rest and self-care) simply wasn't sustainable with my compromised immune system.

I'd made it to this level, an extraordinary achievement that went beyond what I'd ever imagined for myself.

But staying at this level? That would be another thing altogether.

It had been a massive learning curve. And I felt completely run down after the intensity of the conference. So, once it was over, I decided to treat myself to some extra time in Thailand. Koh Samui, Thailand's second largest island, home to some of the world's best health and wellness resorts, was my destination of choice.

I spent five restorative days at the tranquil village retreat of the Spa Resort Village, a detox and wellness retreat. It offered peaceful isolation in what felt like my own private mountain retreat. Yoga, a vegetarian restaurant, massage, a steam room within a cave, magnificent walking tracks and lush gardens, along with a pool and fresh air.

It's a popular destination for people wanting to detox, a program that involved things like coffee enemas and fasting. But that wasn't for me. I leaned into the nourishment and nurturing of modalities and all that the facilities on hand had to offer. No need to detox... more a need to build up the strength of my mind and body while enjoying the location. I have to say though, the main incentive for me to stay there was the food that I'd heard so much about from others at the conference.

On my final night there I sank into the comfort of the private herbal steam bath and thought about all that had happened since I was first invited to speak at the conference – and its toll on me, physically and emotionally. The time I spent on Koh Samui really brought home to me the need to focus more on self-care. I'd been pushing myself beyond what's reasonable for someone with a compromised immune system and my history of cancer. I'm forever grateful to have been invited to share my knowledge. Staying at these top-end hotels was a treat and something that I will never forget. Spending time with Marc and his family and other new friends was an honour and so much fun. As a lone traveller it is an essential ingredient for me to spend time with like-minded people.

There was now a very real need to be careful about how I approached my work when I returned home. I needed to make it as stress-free as possible. Continuing the cooking classes was a way to continue sharing the knowledge without putting myself under too much pressure. When I returned home, I'd have a new opportunity waiting for me with a new course I'd be delivering at the Box Hill Institute of TAFE.

A Helping Hand

There are some people you meet in life who are destined to have a profound impact. Sometimes these might be movers and shakers, people who facilitate a change in thinking or the way we approach different aspects of our lives. Other times they are just people whose down to earth honesty and inherent goodness inspire you and make you feel more whole when you're with them.

The latter was to be the case when I needed an assistant for the cooking classes I was about to run out of Box Hill Institute of TAFE where there was a well-established chef culinary school.

I'd previously received the call from Shaun at Box Hill Institute asking if I'd be interested in setting up short courses in plant based/vegan and traditional Japanese Cooking at the their TAFE facilities. This was an opportunity to teach in an environment designed for the purpose: a commercial cooking venue.

The venue featured a cooking demonstration lecture room with overhead mirrors on the kitchen bench and seating in front with an easy view to the preparations on the bench. There was even a small preparation room on the side.

In the past, I'd employed my own assistants and sometimes was lucky enough to have volunteers wanting to assist me so they could learn more about the ingredients, cooking techniques and nutritional information.

At Box Hill though, I was fortunate in that they were going to provide an assistant, someone who would prepare the ingredients for each part of the class.

These needed to be freshly prepared for the demonstration (experience had taught me that, rather than spend class time chopping, it was more efficient and entertaining for my guests to have an assistant prepare the ingredients prior to their use in the demonstration, ensuring the demonstration aspects of the classes flowed smoothly).

Arrangements had been made for the assistant assigned by Box Hill Institute to meet me in the carpark with a trolley to help me get everything from my car to the allocated room.

No sooner had I got out of the car than I heard a voice, "Hi, are you Sandra?"

I turned around and was greeted by a radiant smile framed by long wavy locks that draped well past her shoulders. "Yes, that's me." I replied.

She extended her hand and said, "I'm Gabrielle. Would you like a hand getting your things out?"

"Nice to meet you Gabrielle. Is it okay if I call you Gab? You're welcome to just call me Sandy." Right from that first greeting, everything with Gab just seemed so easy, which added to my excitement about teaching in this new venue. "Do you do much cooking?" I asked.

"Yes, I actually work here through the day as a campus cook," replied Gab. "I've recently finished my cert four in cooking as well."

"That's great!"

When we arrived at the room where I'd be running the class, I showed Gab the recipes that were going to be prepared that night and she got straight into the preparations, cutting up ingredients and placing them in bowls so they'd be ready as I needed them. Meticulously cut onions, carrots, sweet potatoes, fennel, well-washed greens, soaked sea vegetables, shiitake mushrooms and more were set up on my cooking bench in a timely manner.

"These are different," she said while soaking the sea vegetables. "I've never cooked anything with seaweed in it before."

"It's pretty common in traditional Japanese and macrobiotic style dishes," I replied.

Running a class with Gab's Assistance

Although Gab's experience was mostly with French cuisine from her certificate four course, she embraced the opportunity to learn about a different style of cooking.

By the end of that first cooking session together, I felt elated in the knowledge that I had found not only an assistant that I knew I could trust to understand my meticulous instructions, but also that there was an easy vibe between us. I could tell straight away that this wonderful human would become a reliable and dear friend, which she has been ever since that first night.

"Would you be interested in assisting me when I run classes from other locations as well?" I asked.

"Yeah, I would. I really enjoyed tonight's class. I got a lot from it. And I *really* appreciated how well you'd planned everything out. It made my job easy."

That was 2005, and Gab has been there with me ever since. Whenever I ran private and corporate cooking classes, demonstrations at food expos and health food shows and catering for functions, she has been by my side. She has also stood by me through personal tragedies like the loss of my beloved mother and through my own health challenges, always willing and able to cater to my health supportive nutritional needs in the best way possible... with love and care.

The classes at Box Hill continued from that first night in 2005 until 2013. They included courses in vegetarian cooking with a wok, traditional Japanese cooking, and individual courses for vegetarian cooking for spring, summer, autumn and winter.

It doesn't matter how many masters of health and food preparation you meet. Those things don't really add up to much without having people like Gab in your life.

I hadn't been back from Thailand for long when I received another important call from Marc. "Hey Sandy, remember last year's AIMA Conference?" He was referring to the *Australasian Integrative Medicine Association*.

"I sure do. It was great. Are you doing it again this year?"

"Absolutely, the theme is going to be the Art and Science of Holistic Health."

"I really like that." I replied. "It's recognition that good health isn't just about science, it's about spiritual and cultural wellbeing too." Marc is a living testament to this. An absolute dynamo, he's always worked hard at the cutting edge of bringing nutrition and general wellbeing to the populace.

The next thing Marc brought up took me by surprise. "Would you be interested in being a speaker?" What a relief! After my stilted presentation in Thailand he still had confidence in me and what I had to offer.

"Of course!"

But there was more. "We also need someone to help Anna, the conference organiser. It's become too much for one person, and I can't think of anyone who'd be better than you to give her a hand."

What an incredible honour!

AIMA's conference was Australia's most important annual gathering of international movers and shakers from the holistic health community.

Anna had all the skills necessary to organise a conference, and I was enthusiastic to assist in any way I could: like taking on the role of liaising with the hotel chefs about what foods to provide; leaning into wholefoods with a big emphasis on plant-based ingredients; brown rice rather than white rice; more legumes and greens; adding sea vegetables and fermented foods, and offering dairy-free alternatives along with gluten-free foods. With our like-minded approach, Anna and I worked comfortably with each other as we pulled the conference together. She had the perfect temperament for dealing with the details of planning a conference, and I learned a great deal from following her lead.

I delivered a presentation about Maintaining a balanced life: *Health Supportive Wholefoods for Wellbeing,* and found myself feeling far more comfortable than I'd been when presenting in Thailand.

Despite my concerns over whether I could maintain this level of activity with a compromised immune system, I was thriving in the moment. And my reputation was growing.

To top it off, on October 27th, I was invited to speak at a corporate seminar for Shell at their Australian headquarters in Hawthorn. The staff member who'd booked me had said, "If we can get our staff to eat properly, their productivity will improve, and we'll have fewer sick days." It was basic and pragmatic business sense on one level, but also a recognition that people were generally keen to learn more about the benefits of good nutrition.

I made super shakes for them that day, a simple demonstration of how easy it can be to improve your wellbeing with quality ingredients and very little preparation.

Shell was not the only organisation I made presentations to. The courses I was delivering at the Centre for Adult Education and the Box Hill Institute had led to my reputation spreading more broadly at a time when there was a growing interest in corporate wellness programs and staff training for workplace improvements.

These presentations took me into yet another completely different sphere, one I hadn't presented in before, and it boosted my reputation for sharing the information I was so passionate and knowledgeable about.

Kramer

I was flipping through the local newspaper while enjoying lunch at the Albert Park Deli with my friend, Shraga, one day.

"Do you watch Seinfeld?" he asked.

"I love it!" I said with a big smile, "always have." Then the most amazing coincidence happened. I turned the page and saw a promotion: *Win a date with Kenny Kramer!* Yes, that's the *real* Kenny Kramer, the one that Kramer in Seinfeld was based on. The real Kenny Kramer lived across the hallway from Larry David, co-creator of Seinfeld. And Kenny Kramer was coming to Australia in early 2006 to do a series of shows with a group of other American comedians. As a Valentine's Day promotion, Melbourne's Herald Sun was running a competition where you could win a Valentine's date with him. I found myself thinking, why not have a go?

I can't remember the exact words, but it was something along the lines of: *super excited because I love Seinfeld... I'm Jewish... I owned a health food shop.* I also popped a photograph in with the entry and sent it off.

Needless to say, I won!

So, February 14th comes around, I meet him at the designated location. He brings a rose, doing all the right things. His comedian buddies who'd come over from the States with him were all sitting at another table nearby, which you'd expect. I mean, he didn't know anything about me. So it becomes a bit of a safety backup plan. But he told me later that he'd ended up quite relieved when I rocked in. I suppose that shouldn't be surprising given that I was an attractive, well travelled chick who'd done cool stuff like living in Bali. He called his buddies over and we all ended up having a great night together.

As it turns out, they were all here for a few days and we continued hanging out together. I became friends with Ron Maranian (who seemed to take a shine to me). So, being a good ambassador, I got them some pot and you know, all those things you do when you feel comfortable with people.

So Kenny said, "Sandy, when you next come to New York, I run these *Kramer Reality Tours,* taking people on a bus through New York and showing them all the significant locations from the show, like the Soup Nazi's kitchen. You should come along. I'll make sure you have a good time." He went on to explain how he hadn't made anything out of Seinfeld, but Larry David and Jerry Seinfeld had let him use the naming rights to run his bus tours, which had in themselves proved to be quite successful.

And it just so happened that I was planning a trip to the States in June. I now had more people I could connect with when I got there!

Back to the States

Another great opportunity that had come from the Box Hill Institute was when they asked me to develop a certificate four course for them in Wholefood Cookery. This made it feel more important than ever to make another trip to the States to hone my skills and learn more from my mentors there. Especially Annemarie Colbin at The Natural Gourmet Institute in New York City. Of all the professional training cooking courses, these were my main inspiration for developing something similar for the Box Hill Institute.

I was making connections in preparation for the trip and was still regularly in touch with Peter, a good twenty-five years after we'd first got together. We had by then both become comfortable with the realisation that we cared deeply about each other, but just didn't seem to be able to make the relationship thing work between us.

"I'm off to the States in June," I told him one day.

"Oh? I'll be there around then too. Where are you going to be staying?"

"I'll be arriving in LA on the 14th. I've booked a room at the Venice Suites."

"Oh, cool. I'll be in Vegas. I should be able to get up there for a couple of days if you want to catch up."

My flight landed at 11am LA time. Oren was there to pick me up at the airport and drive me to Venice Beach so I could check in and get some rest. We arrived and I checked in, only to discover that my room, being on the ground floor, had bars over all the windows. It didn't matter that I was tired, I wasn't going to be able to relax in that environment. Somehow I found enough energy reserves to negotiate an upgrade with management so that I was on a higher floor looking over the Venice Beach boardwalk and all the action happening on the beach. It may have cost another twenty US dollars per day, but one of the things I've learnt during my travels is that the quality of your accommodation becomes an ever more important ingredient in good *recipes for living*.

With the upgrade sorted, I went for a walk to find somewhere for lunch. I may have been jet-lagged, but I was hungry too. As I walked along the boardwalk, memories of being there in 2000 came flooding back, and I found myself at the iconic *The Rose Cafe*, where I ended up getting lunch... and then to *Wholefoods Market* for supplies (my room had a small kitchen); it all felt wonderfully familiar. I went back to my apartment and drifted off into a deep sleep for a few hours before heading out for a meal with Oren at a nearby Japanese restaurant. I can't begin to tell you how good it feels to arrive in another country and have a welcoming person there to help you settle in and feel at home.

The next day, a nice young guy, (a few years my junior) I'd been talking to on Jdate picked me up at noon and drove me around LA doing the full tourist guide thing for me... City Hall and the like. We hung out at his apartment for a while then headed off to *Real Food Daily*, a vegan restaurant on Santa Monica Boulevard. I really enjoyed the meal and hanging out with him, so it was an easy affair. Why not? A single woman having fun. He came back to the suites with me and the next morning I lay in bed after he'd got up and gone to work. I was listening to the sound of the waves rolling in on Venice Beach when the phone rang. I picked it up as I looked out onto the palm trees and rich blue sky. The sound of seagulls completed the perfect picture.

"Hello, Sandy?"

"Peter?"

"Are you settled in, okay?"

I couldn't help but smile as I lay there gazing out at the picture-postcard setting. "Yes, thank you. I got in a couple of days ago."

"How are you placed if I come over on Saturday?"

"That'd be great. You're welcome to stay here if you like. That is, if you're happy to sleep on the couch."

"Works for me," he replied.

When I hung up the phone, I found myself feeling a special kind of contentment. It felt wonderful to know that, despite some of the difficulties Peter and I had had in the past, we were able to look forward to spending time together as friends while travelling.

When Peter arrived, we drove around LA with Oren discussing the buildings his architectural firm had designed. Peter got right into it and the two of them had a great rapport.

We had a lot of fun, particularly the day when we came across the Hustler store on Sunset Boulevard. You know Hustler magazine? Well, this was a store with a wide shopfront and big window displays proudly showing off their sex toys and other paraphernalia. We may not have been in an intimate relationship at the time, but we certainly knew each other's tastes. We had a ball going through and making suggestions to each other. We were like kids in a type of Disneyland of sex, and both walked away with a little bag of goodies. It's a reminder I guess of one of the most important ingredients I've come across in *recipes for living...* the importance of maintaining the friendship part of a relationship, wherever possible, when the romance has gone. I feel glad that the bigger relationships I've enjoyed throughout my life have invariably ended in this way, leaving me with a group of very special friends who have been such an important part of my life and whom I still stay in touch with to this day. A few days later I was on a plane headed for the East Coast.

In New York, through a friend's recommendation and a fortunate piece of timing, a couple of people who ran a theatre group were going away, so I was able to sublet their apartment.

It was near the centre of the city, just off from the corner of Madison Avenue and 30th. An old building with real character, exemplified by the cage-style elevator. I pulled the door shut and pressed the button to take me up to the third floor, hoping it wasn't going to jam up between floors. If elevators have personalities, I'd have to say that this one was cranky.

I got out of the lift, walked down the corridor, then opened the door onto a small, quirky apartment. The kitchen was tiny with a small fridge and two-burner cooktop, and the apartment was filled with what New Yorkers refer to as *tchotchke*, a term borrowed from Yiddish that's used to describe bric-a-brac. It was everywhere in this small apartment.

As I looked around, I thought, *oh, what have I done?* As I continued my investigation, I came across what you could be excused for thinking was a closet. Needless to say, it was in fact the bedroom, a bedroom where the bed literally took up the whole room. So, I sort of had to crawl over the bed to get in and out the bedroom door. And the shower? That was really small as well. But, hey, I was in New York, and this was how these people lived, along with so many others in that magnificent city.

Even though I'd never met them, they left me a welcoming letter:

Wiring is not up to code specifications. While air con is going, please don't use hair dryer or the microwave oven. I'll be coming up to New York once a week to get the mail and water the plants. I'll sleep on the living room floor and try not to be in the way.

Air con? Yes, that would help deal with the stuffiness in the place. Once I'd switched that on, I was so tired that I just crawled into bed and fell asleep.

Coincidently, Benny was going to be in New York at the same time. He booked into the hotel across the road from the apartment I was renting. We'd meet up for breakfast and went out at night sometimes, to catch some of what New York is so good for: the music, food, hanging out at Washington Square and just walking... and walking. When I'd been in New York in 2000, Benny and I had gone to see the Jackie Mason show, *Much Ado About Everything*. We'd smoked a joint before the show and didn't stop laughing the whole time. It was brilliant! On this trip we went to see a fantastic exhibition at MOMA together, *Dada Lives*, before having a bite to eat at the NBC Rockefeller Centre.

Afterwards, I'd arranged to meet another guy I'd met on jDate, Aly. It was all kind of funny when we first met up. You see, he's a chiropractor, so of course, I'm like, "Oh, great. Can you give me a quick fix up for my back?" So, on our first date, he's taking me to his office, laying me on a table and adjusting my body. I guess that's a good way to get to know someone. It certainly seemed like a good way to start at the time.

We went out for sushi at a local restaurant and hung out a bit. He was a part-time musician and I went to hear him play at an open mic. Then he says to me, "Hey, I've got tickets to Bruce Springsteen... at Madison Square Garden."

My response came out like a reflex: "I don't like Bruce Springsteen." I was so blunt that he had every reason to be offended. It's a bit embarrassing when I look back on it now, and in hindsight I kind of regret having knocked back his offer. As much as I'm not a fan of Springsteen's music, the concert would have still been an incredible experience.

Irrespective of my rudeness regarding the tickets, Aly and I went on another date, dinner at a well-known vegan restaurant, the *Zen Palate*, on the corner of 9th Avenue and West 47th Street. Part of a chain of three restaurants, it had developed a huge reputation (sadly, in the ensuing decade it apparently went downhill, even being closed by the health department at one stage in 2013 and then closing altogether in 2014). We initially got a table upstairs, but I wasn't comfortable with the vibe. So, we tried downstairs and had to wait for a table; by the time we finally got settled there, I was starting to lose my appetite.

"Not enjoying your meal?" he asked.

"Oh, the food's fine. I'm just not all that hungry now."

"Well, don't worry too much about that," he said, brimming with confidence. "I've got a special treat in mind for when we leave here."

"Oh?" I smiled at the thought that he was keen to impress. "What might that be?"

"It's a surprise." A huge grin spread across his face. "You'll love it. It's really quite famous."

So, we left the restaurant and started heading south down 9th Avenue.

Now, I probably should mention that, not being fully accustomed to the idea of walking everywhere in New York, I wasn't aware that New York women generally wear comfortable shoes, shoes that are good for walking. Because that's how people generally get around in New York, they walk. So, here I was, dressed up in high heels, being taken for this walk by my date.

We crossed West 45th, then 44, 43... the numbers kept ticking down. I was really starting to regret wearing high heels by the time the countdown reached West 21st Street, and it kept going, my feet in more pain with each street we crossed. Once we'd crossed West 15th, we veered left onto Hudson Street. I could tell from Aly's excitement that we were getting close. "You're going to love this place," he said. "It was made famous by *Sex and the City*." I sort of grinned in response and kept on walking, trying to make sure my expression looked like a smile rather than a grimace of extreme pain. Every step of the forty-five-minute walk was agony by the time we'd veered left again onto Bleecker Street and walked the final few blocks, when he announced, "Here we are!"

Magnolia Bakery... specialising in... cupcakes!

Nothing gluten-free.

Nothing dairy-free and nothing sugar-free.

What there was a lot of was colourful icing, hundreds and thousands (or sprinkles as they're referred to outside Australia), and all other manner of sugary toppings. I couldn't fake it. I couldn't pretend to be thrilled, and my feet were in agony. Clearly feeling a bit deflated by my obvious lack of enthusiasm Aly asked, "Can I buy you a coffee?"

I got a cab home feeling disappointed and that, despite Aly's best intentions, there'd been such a definite lack of connection. I was tired and uncomfortable and, after having arrived in New York City just a few days earlier, it was a lot to take in. I needed rest.

My feet had blisters all over them for days afterwards. Despite all that though, Aly and I did keep in touch. One day we met up with my friend Jackie, whom I'd met when she was living in Melbourne. Being a foodie herself, she knew what I love. "Would you like to visit Chelsea Market?" she asked.

"Oh yeah!" Did I really need to say it though? My smile had already answered for me. If you weren't aware, Chelsea Market is a huge food hall and marketplace located right in the heart of New York City. It's become internationally famous for both the fresh produce and the culinary options. You can buy the best ingredients to help with your home-cooked meals and also have something to eat while you're there. The three of us spent the day going from store to store – and I found so many fresh, healthy and tasty options and everything else that was on offer. It also gave Aly an opportunity to discover the sort of foods and experiences I enjoyed.

The next day, I met up with Annemarie Colbin for lunch, one of the main reasons I'd wanted to go to New York on this trip. I'd had the occasional brief chat with her when I'd done some of her courses on previous trips. Now, she was interested in coming to Australia. So I suggested we discuss it over lunch.

Teaching courses in another country involves a few hurdles, and Australia is no exception. Working Visas are needed and it's a great help if someone sponsors you for that visa. "I can help you," I told her. "My friend, Jim from Spiral Foods sponsored Michio Kushi when he came out to Australia. I'll speak with him and see if he'd be happy to do the same for you."

"It sounds promising."

The idea of having such a leading figure in the natural foods and holistic health field coming to Australia was compelling. Sadly, it turned out to be more difficult to arrange than I'd imagined. I talked to her about the cooking courses I'd been running and how wonderful it would be to establish a branch of her cooking school in Australia. We met several times to discuss the possibilities, and we both tried to make it work. But, in the end, the logistics just became too difficult.

However, the seeds had been sown and I continued to ruminate about what a wholefood cooking course at Box Hill Institute could be. I had done so many courses at the Gourmet Institute and had discussions with chefs about the courses they had done. I made notes about a potential course outline for future reference.

On the social side of things, I still needed to catch up with Kenny Kramer, to go for coffee and book in for his Kramer Tour. When I gave him a buzz though, he seemed a bit nervous, "I've got a girlfriend. I think it's really important you know that."

"That's great," I replied.

Some guys find it difficult navigating friendships with women. And I guess people who have a bit of fame may frequently have to manage expectations from would-be female friends.

In the end we did meet up for coffee and I arranged two tickets for his tour. The other being for Benny.

Kramer's Reality Tour For Seinfeld Fans was a quirky, fun trip. Kenny "The Real" Kramer, took us on a theatrical multi-media stage, bus and video tour of New York City, visiting the sites made famous by the world's most popular sitcom. Of course, there was a stop for soup at that famous soup stand. Kenny Kramer answered questions, shared backstage information and revealed how many story lines and characters' names came right from real life.

Natural Therapies Expo

After I came back from the States I was writing more articles for publications such as *FACE* Magazine and *Pointers*. My profile had certainly been building.

While overseas, I'd arranged with *Wellbeing* Magazine in Australia to write an article about healthy eating in New York City. They'd liked the idea and said that if it was good enough, they'd publish it. This was a project that gave me a sense of purpose while checking out the multitude of delicious and well-known vegetarian and macrobiotic health food cafes and restaurants. I had a list of recommendations along with my own research, and working through them all was a most pleasurable mission. I met the passionate, professional chefs running them and pored over the menus, trying myriad dishes that I later had the great joy to write about. As a result, my own repertoire of possible recipes was expanding and I looked forward to trying some new ideas out in my classes.

Two articles I'm particularly proud of from the time were for Australia's *WellBeing* Magazine. One was titled *Wholefood Wisdom*. It focused on how to choose the right combination of wholefoods for an ideal acid/alkaline balance in the body and included some of the ways that goal can be achieved.

The other article was one that's especially close to my heart, *A Healthy Bite Out of the Big Apple: From Ayurvedic Menus to Vegan Meals, New York's Endless Eating Options are all Good.* Having just returned again from the States, it was an opportunity to share information on my favourite restaurants and cafes from a city that I'd fallen in love with.

After my experience in Thailand and then as assistant organiser at the AIMA conference, I'd gained extra knowledge and confidence. So when the opportunity was presented to be one of the organisers of the Natural Health and Therapies Expos in Melbourne and Sydney, I grabbed hold of it with both hands.

I was asked to put the seminar program together, as well as helping with the general duties of running the expo, a two-day weekend festival featuring naturopaths, health food companies and other allied health professionals, with a big launch on the Friday evening. Co-ordinating the seminar program was a terrific opportunity to call on my network of health care professionals to present a seminar. I processed the other applicants as well and created a program covering a broad range of health-supportive subjects. I should also mention that these presenters weren't paid, but were no less enthusiastic to participate and share their knowledge.

Once the Melbourne Expo was over, the organisers flew me up to Sydney to do the same for their Expo there.

All this was followed up by the opportunity to speak at the Gawler Foundation's 2006 conference. It was only a year since I'd delivered my presentation in Thailand where I'd felt so unsure afterwards whether I had it in me to regularly do the international conferences – but in Australia I felt like I was riding a wave of opportunity that had opened up as a result of what had culminated in that Asian presentation. I'd become someone conference organisers could turn to with the confidence and trust that I would help deliver a stellar program!

Red String

Without inner peace, how can we make real peace? - Dalai Lama

His Holiness, the fourteenth Dalai Lama had announced he was coming to Australia for his first visit in over ten years. Once again, I was able to put my hand up as a volunteer.

The status of the Dalai Lama had grown dramatically since his 1992 visit. He'd spoken at indoor venues back then. This time, for his 2007 tour, the crowd was going to be much larger. So, the Carlton Football grounds had been booked to support the larger numbers.

Security on the day was going to be looked after by the volunteers.

The volunteer coordinator started to address the group. "We need someone for security on the VIP section."

I immediately put my hand up. I knew quite a few of the people who had paid to be VIP guests, so I figured it wouldn't be too onerous. Everyone else was delegated their roles, our hi-vis vests with "Dalai Lama Tour Crew" printed on the back were handed out, and we went on our way, confident that we all knew our roles.

It wasn't until the day came and I was standing at the narrow entrance to the VIP section that the reality of my situation dawned on me. I was the only one who had been assigned to being security for the VIP section. And there were a lot of attendees who seemed keen to occupy one of the two thousand or so chairs that had been positioned front and centre for the Dalai Lama's talk.

The criteria seemed simple enough. Those with orange wristbands had paid the required price to be in the VIP section – but the crowd entering the grounds didn't seem to care about queuing up in an orderly fashion to show those bands.

I frantically waved my arms around, trying to be in several places at once, while doing my best to control this enthusiastic but pushy crowd. In their efforts to get the best spot to hear the Dalai Lama speak about loving kindness and peace, they were disregarding polite behaviour! I tried to get the attention of other volunteers to let the volunteer coordinator know that I couldn't handle the agitated hoard of peace-lovers on my own. I was sure that I was just moments away from being trampled when the reinforcement arrived. She was a quiet girl, a bit shorter than me and with a slighter frame.

"Hi Sandy, they said you need some help?"

That was it... between the two of us, we had to hold back the crowd and ensure only those with the correct wristbands got through. The attendees tried everything.

"But you don't understand... my friends are already in there. I have to join them."

"I'm meeting my companion at our seats... he has both our wristbands."

And of course, there were those who even tried to ignore you and just barge through.

Somehow, perhaps with the aid of the universe chipping in to lend us a hand, we managed to hold them back and let the genuine VIPs filter through and take their places.

The Dalai Lama gave a memorable presentation, and all the impolite jostling for position seemed to be in the distant past... for the attendees who'd done the jostling at any rate. I looked around the VIP sections to see huge smiles on everyone's face, the anxious scramble to get seats now forgotten. I too smiled in relief.

At the end of a long day when the crowds had departed, the Dalai Lama called together the volunteers for a special audience where he expressed his gratitude. His Holiness did this not just with words, but by gifting us all red strings (which he blessed and handed out to each of us. This simple red string has become perhaps my most treasured possession. I have worn it on my left wrist every moment of every day since then and it has remained intact. I did think I'd lost it a couple of times but fortunately found it both times, once in my car and the other time on my bedroom floor. I do have a spare just in case, as His Holiness had blessed three strings for me. I gave one to a friend and kept two. In all my travels, I have connected with my red string to remind me of my blessings. It's stayed on my wrist through all my medical treatments and surgeries too. It holds much meaning for me, of strength and protection – a constant reminder, in the humblest of objects, of the Dalai Lama's speaking of how loving kindness and peace are the pathways to happiness.

It was without doubt the main highlight of 2007, but there were other highlights that year as well. Like what my nephew Marlon's friend, Daniel, who'd always been proactive on issues regarding the environment, had done. In High Street Prahran, there was a petrol station that was about to close. Seeing this as an opportunity to do something positive for the environment, Daniel took out a twelve-month lease on the station. His dream was to establish a petrol station that specialised in making biofuel options available, something that was well ahead of its time for Melbourne, Australia.

You may be wondering what this has to do with my story? Well, petrol stations have shops, and Daniel was keen to ensure that what was stocked in the shop was as ethical as possible. Even back then, there were actually quite a few healthier options available that could be sold as snacks in that sort of situation, and so I was more than ready to do what I could to help people make better food and nutrition choices. Also, the shop stocked magazines on health and wellbeing and information on water filters, eco-friendly household products as well as healthy drinks and snacks. Stocking these items was right up my alley and I felt proud to be part of this forward-thinking project.

The station was called Conservo. In addition to selling E10 fuel – regular unleaded petrol with 10% ethanol – the station sold a bio-fuel that was suitable for use in standard diesel engines that was made from 100% bio-fuel.

The business got plenty of good promotion, particularly when a significant captain of business was photographed filling up his Bentley there.

The fuels produced fewer toxic emissions and were soon adopted by other companies that operated chains of petrol stations. But none of these other outlets picked up on the other side of the business... a convenience store that focused on nutrition and wellbeing. It was a concept way ahead of its time.

Daniel operated the business for three years with support from the biofuel supplier while they were building their market share. He then sold the Conservo concept to another company to develop further so he could focus on becoming a barrister specialising in environmental law.

Part III
Staying Alive

"Your spirit is a part of you that is drawn to and feels like hope"
—Carolyn Myss

Mammogram

I'd recently reconnected with a friend I'd made in Sydney after she'd returned to Melbourne.

She'd just received the results from her mammogram after discovering a small lump in her breast. She was devastated. "It's cancerous." This was late 2012, and we were hanging out a lot together. We'd become even closer as friends than when we'd known each other in Sydney. When she got the results of her mammogram, it was a potent reminder that perhaps I should get one myself, particularly considering that I'd noticed I was getting fatigued more easily than usual.

Two weeks later, I'd made my appointment and my ever-supportive mother was there by my side as I sat waiting. But what about my friend? She was going in for surgery to remove the lump, the doctors being confident that they'd got to it early enough and that there'd be no need for chemo or radiation therapy.

A couple of weeks later, I went to see my doctor to get my own results.

"There's a small lump in your breast."

Those words reverberated.

It took me back to how, when the second lump in my neck area had been found years earlier, the first thought that came into my head was that it must have been related to the mantle radiation from my original treatment. Opinions from medical professionals were varied regarding the cause – but the connection seemed hard to ignore.

I sought multiple opinions from a range of doctors, both Western and complementary. I spoke at length with them all as I went through all kinds of tests and scans.

"Breathe deep," I was told as I was mechanically drawn into the MRI machine.

There was nothing else to do while I lay inside the machine.

I breathed in.

I breathed out.

In...

Out...

I found myself in a deep meditative state by the time they slid me back out of the machine.

"Sandra?" In what I knew must have been a dream, a handsome face floated over me, beckoning me to join him. "Sandra?" His voice was more insistent, his face drawing closer. Then reality invaded my dream and I realised the handsome features hovering over me belonged to one of my doctors—that I was in a hospital rather than some exotic holiday resort.

All the medical professionals, from all backgrounds, had the same opinion. While they weren't happy to commit either way regarding the source of the cancer, my history suggested that the safest course of action would be a double mastectomy, to remove the problem before the cancer had a chance to metastasize.

"I'll need reconstructive surgery."

"Of course," came the response from one doctor after another.

"I really don't want anyone to know." I'd managed to keep my previous encounters with the big 'C' confidential, with just a few trusted friends privy to what was going on. This time it would potentially be a lot trickier. How effective would the reconstructive surgery be? Would people be asking if I'd had a boob job? These were things that were beyond my control. I had no choice but to see how it played out. I needed to stay strong and maintain my privacy. There was no need to have random people knowing my business, or to be faced with the inevitable question of, 'How are you?' I certainly didn't want to be known in public as *Sandy with cancer*.

Mum and I went to my pre-surgery appointment, holding hands and saying nothing. I was being strong for her, and she was being strong for me. No histrionics, no overt anxiety. We met the experienced nurse Kathy who Mum took an immediate liking to. She would be the main one looking after me through the two-week recovery process.

I was booked into Cabrini Private Hospital from January 2013. They told me I'd more than likely be in there for eight to ten days. It really helped that I had a family member, Ted's daughter, Michelle, a doctor on the staff there at the time. She helped reassure my mother and I with good recommendations.

It's only when the wheels start rolling on these sorts of procedures that you realise how many people become involved in the medical team specific to your case.

My surgeon would be Doctor Jenny Senior, a breast surgeon specialising in oncology surgery with expertise in all areas of breast cancer treatment. Once my breasts had been removed, they'd be reconstructed by Doctor Nicholas Houseman, a talented plastic surgeon who also had a lovely bedside manner.

And very important to me was the understanding and support that I received from two integrative medical practitioners, Doctor Christopher Bagot and Professor Avni Sali. They guided me through how I could best support myself in using complementary medicines and natural methods as I went through the procedure and the recovery.

I thought long and hard about how to handle who should and shouldn't know what was happening this time around. When I was twenty, I had the cover story of a car accident, which I was still using to explain away the massive scar from my splenectomy. Then I used a scarf to hide the scars from the thyroidectomy. This time, my boobs were going to be completely reconstructed.

And what about support? The first time around I was lucky enough to have Ian by my side, even lying with me in my hospital bed. I would need to keep Gab in the loop. There was no way I could hide what was happening from her. I knew I could count on her to make sure I had food and especially miso soups while in hospital and when I came home.

There were a select few I'd told about my previous cancers in the years since. I chose carefully who among those that I trusted, and who else I should let in on my very private journey. I loved my friends, and I wanted to have a bit of emotional support while remaining discreet.

Technology had come a long way by then and provided far more options than it had in the past. I could write a blog, one that was only visible to the select few whose emails were added.

On December 28th, I wrote the first instalment of *'Salubrious Dubstars - Circle of Trust'*. I took a deep breath before hitting the send button, in the hope that it would lead to support—a circle of friends that I could connect with online both during my hospital stay and the recovery. I figured that it could be a very special *recipe for living* with this latest chapter in my ongoing cancer story.

In that first post I shared the broader background of my medical history, without going into detail. I talked of my path to gaining and then sharing my knowledge and passion about nutrition. I explained the pathway to recovery my medical team were planning. I let them know what was happening and the plans I had in place to deal with it.

New Year's Eve came around and my Salubrious Dubstars ensured that my last opportunity to have dinner with friends before my stay at Cabrini would not pass by. Shraga, Ruth, Fay, Henry and Stacy all ensured that I got to share the enjoyment of indulging in some of my favourite foods... cooked by someone other than myself. We went to a great restaurant and enjoyed a truly memorable meal... and a couple of cocktails. It was the celebration of a new year, with a focus on celebrating life in general. The dessert was fresh apple sorbet and to wash it all down, we had wine and my favourite Campari soda with a twist of orange.

The New Year's feast behind me, I checked into 'Hotel C' on the 2nd of January. It seemed so appropriate to refer to it as that. 'C' related to both the hospital's name and, of course, cancer. And hotel? Well, I intended to do everything within my power to ensure as comfortable a stay as possible.

Mum accompanied me to the check in. Then I had the luxury of being taken in a wheelchair to the nuclear medicine unit. Fortunately, it was the off season. So, we didn't need to navigate through too many crowds in the corridors.

Once settled into my room, the nursing staff ensured I was comfortable. I had brought my pillow, my special wool travel shawl, iPhone loaded with music, iPad, blender for making smoothies, and my supplements in powder form… Vital Greens and vitamin C being essential. I wanted to create a warm atmosphere in my private room as I was about to embark on days and days of living on the bed.

I was fortunate that Mum was by my side when the admitting physician, who I'd never met before, chose to demonstrate his severe lack of bedside sensitivity as he insisted, without warmth, on me running through my full medical history for him—one he had ready access to if he bothered to look. Does that sound like an imposition? Perhaps, but it actually helped me appreciate, while rattling off the litany of challenges I'd conquered, just how much I had managed to turn my situation around, developing an understanding of health and nutrition that had allowed me to live a far more adventurous life than I'd dared to dream of when I was younger. Not only that, but I was also teaching others how to tread the same path. At the end of the day, his blunt communication skills probably did me a great favour.

My admission interview was followed up by my introduction to the latest fashion accessories sweeping through the Hotel C… pressure socks, the sexiest of accessories to enhance one's appearance when being wheeled through the hotel corridors.

No sooner had I tried them on than the hotel cuisine was brought right to my room. Such extraordinary service. Boiled asparagus, cauliflower and something that they insisted was in fact fish. How could I complain though? In less than twenty-four hours I was going to be in the intensive care unit. And when I came out a couple days later, life would once again be different to how it had been before.

I was wondering, as they wheeled me in, if there was a party in the operating room. They were laughing and chatting. It seemed like there were far too many people in there for it to be just my own little operation. There must have been around ten of them, all standing at their stations surveying readings on an array of high-tech machines. I couldn't help myself, "There's a party in here!" The reply was delivered via a prick in my arm. No one asked me to count backwards. There was no mask, just that little pin prick.

The next thing I knew I was in ICU. The party was over, and I'd clearly slept right through it.

The Hotel Cabrini

I woke up after the eight-hour operation in a haze, unsure of where I was. The last thing I remembered was lying back under the bright lights of the operating theatre with tubes going into my arm as the anaesthetic was administered.

Lying on the hospital bed, I noticed there were now four new tubes draining fluids from various locations on my body. There was also an intermittent pneumatic compression device wrapped around my legs, helping prevent harmful after-surgery blood clots, and a mask over my face to deliver oxygen into my lungs.

Something that helped in dealing with the post-op reality was the ever-attentive nurses supplying a steady flow of pain relievers that kept the pain at bay. I developed a connection with these specialist breast cancer nurses, particularly Kathy. I was also pleased that they were eager to learn what I could share about dealing with food intolerance and other diet-related issues. All of them had stories of a loved one experiencing some sort of problem that they hoped could be improved through good nutritional advice. Meanwhile, they helped me in whatever way they could to maintain my planned regime of probiotics and other supplements I'd brought with me to the *Hotel C*.

And Mum? Well, she spent hours every day with me, knitting in a chair by my bedside and smiling while we did our best to chat despite my persistent discomfort. Between her and Gab, I had a pair of guardian angels who'd been briefed meticulously on how to support my dietary needs during the post-op recovery. Having already ensured I had an alkalizing water jug by my bed, they also brought supplies of green soup with miso, coconut water, yoghurt, organic figs, dates along with organic carrot and beetroot juice.

The room was a massive contrast to the couple of days in intensive care immediately after the operation. Lights on all the time, privacy coming only when a curtain was around the bed – and constant, sometimes disturbing noises coming from the other patients and staff. It all made it feel uncomfortable and stressful while trying to get sleep and rest.

Thankfully, my stepsister Michele had a friend who was an ICU nurse and did what she could to help make it more bearable.

It was a relief when I was able to be moved to a private room on the second floor.

So, there I was, with all manner of tubes hanging out of me; but despite it all, I was managing quite well. I dove into an update on my Salubrious Dubstars Blog, updating friends about progress, posting photos and creating a record of my time there, which in turn has enabled me to share it with you now. It was therapeutic and I believe it aided me in my recovery.

There was one unexpected post-surgery side effect in particular that was difficult to deal with: my body's reaction to the multitude of bandages. No one had warned me about the potential for this. After the double mastectomy and reconstruction, my entire chest was wrapped in bandages, and my skin reacted to them badly. The itch was driving me insane. But the nurses... how wonderful are they? Nurse Kathy had a tried and tested solution that her years of experience had bestowed upon her. Mylanta! Yes, you read it right. Mylanta actually relieved the itchiness from the bandages... and a couple of injections of Phenergan antihistamine definitely helped as well.

Due to my wishes to keep my hospital stay private, Mum and Gab were the only outside visitors who came during my two week stay at the hospital. Meanwhile, the visits from Doctor Jenny were always enjoyable (the impressive and kind surgeon who removed my breasts), along with the visits from the

Kale Miso Soup

Serves 4-6 big bowls
Keeps refrigerated for up to 3 days. Good to keep some in the freezer for the times when you don't feel like cooking.

Ingredients:

- 1 medium Onion, medium diced (during chemo I recommend using fennel instead if there is an onion sensitivity)
- 5 Shiitake mushrooms, dried
- 5 cups Water
- 1 cup Sweet potato, medium diced
- 2 cups Kale, chopped
- 8 cm Wakame, dried
- 1 tbsp toasted Sesame Oil
- 3 tbsp Miso paste (I use Spiral Food Organic Genmai)
- To taste   Ginger juice (grate ginger then squeeze to release juice)
- 1 Spring onion, chopped for garnish (optional as during chemo, taste buds can be sensitive to onions)

Method:

- Soak dried shiitake mushrooms for at least 30 minutes in 5 cups warm water from the kettle or for even better flavour, the longer the better even overnight.
- When mushrooms have softened, discard stems then slice mushrooms caps. Strain shiitake soaking water and keep as soup stock.
- Soak wakame in enough water to cover until soft (approx. 10 minutes), remove stem and chop. Retain soaking water to add to soup. (I toss the stems onto my vegie garden as fertiliser.)
- In a soup pot, sauté diced onion or fennel in oil until transparent.

- Mix in sliced shiitake.
- Add the 5 cups of strained shiitake soaking water, bring to boil, then reduce heat to simmer for 5 minutes. You can add any strained wakame soaking water at this point too.
- Add sweet potato and kale to soup then simmer for about 10 minutes more (until veggies are cooked).
- Add chopped wakame and simmer 2 minutes.
- Remove soup from heat.
- Add miso before eating. Remove 1 cup hot soup, pour into a jug and add miso paste.
- Once the miso has dissolved, return liquid to pot and wait for a couple of minutes before serving. (Best not to boil miso so add it to hot soup last)
- Add ginger juice to your taste.
- Garnish with chopped spring onions – optional

equally impressive and kind Surgeon, Doctor Nick (who'd rebuilt them so beautifully).

It would have been four or five days after the operation when Doctor Jenny seemed to bounce into the room. "Hi Sandy, I've got some good news for you. Your tests are back, and it would seem that you are now cancer free."

"Really? Wow, that's amazing news." And it really was amazing news. While feeling relief, I'd developed an ability to detach myself from having anxiety, due to my previous experiences. I'd also had a strong gut feeling that my body was now free of the cancer. So, as welcome as this news was, it came as no surprise.

Doctor Jenny was buoyant as she continued, "I have to say, your physical and mental strength are incredible. I'm really impressed." And *I* have to say, her words were comforting and most welcome.

Doctor Nick was also impressed with my recovery. So impressed in fact that he suggested I might want to write up a new suggestion/protocol for pre-op preparations geared toward people in similar situations to my own. I hesitated to take him up on it though, as I was focused on my own recovery at the time.

My plant-based diet excluded triggering mucus-forming foods like processed foods, dairy, wheat products and sugars, which helped in my recovery as it meant less likelihood of stressing the lungs with coughing, while also dealing with a bandaged, surgically-affected chest area.

As positive a picture as the doctors were painting at the time though, a lengthy recovery still lay ahead. It wasn't long after the cheerful surgeons had bounded around my 'hotel room' that the physio rocked up. He seemed intent on walking me up and down the room and imposing a regime of other exercises that my body tried desperately to tell me I wasn't quite ready for. Having said that, my reluctant body performed admirably, getting a big tick from the physio for its efforts.

The Oxycodone that I'd been given to keep the pain at bay was also causing some incredibly vivid dreams. I woke up after one feeling quite disoriented. I'd been at an international airport preparing to catch a flight, but realised that I'd left my luggage behind at a five-star international hotel, one that I hadn't been to in real life. While racing around in the dream searching for my bags, I kept running into people I knew who seemed unconcerned about my plight and wanted to talk to me.

"Sandy," said one of them from behind me.

I turned to see who it was, but they were gone.

"Sandy," called another. I turned only to see they were gone too, leaving me feeling totally disorientated.

"Sandy," I opened my eyes to see a nurse gently trying to wake me as she prepared to take my blood pressure... not exactly the usual way to greet the day.

Mum had already been for her morning visit, dropping off my hair-straightening irons for my first hair wash post-surgery. It was perfect timing, as it gave the nurses an opportunity to fuss over me. They administered the full pampering, allowing me to sink into the luxurious pleasure of a full hair wash and styling. Such a relief after so many days of being unable to tend to it. You can't appreciate it until you're in a situation, such as recovering from major surgery, just what a profound difference something like that can make to how you feel.

The next day rolled around, sunshine streaming in through the window at just the right angle to sit in the chair next to the bed and soak up the warmth. I couldn't help but have a little laugh when I looked down at how sexy my legs looked in the long white pressure socks I'd worn since being admitted.

I'd had a brief glimpse at how my body was looking when the bandages were changed. I'd been wrapped in copious amounts of cotton (seeing my skin seemed to reject contact with any of the other bandages). When the cotton had come off, it was not a pretty sight. But I guess that's only to be expected so soon after such a major operation. It made me grateful for the painkillers… and my resilience.

When recovering in hospital you need to keep your mind active. Having my laptop loaded with videos, the Salubrious Dubstars blog to keep up to date and books that had real meaning to me were all crucially important, helping to keep me focused on creative pursuits.

The secret to success in this regard was explained succinctly in one of my favourite books on Buddhist thought, *Freedom Through Understanding*. The title in itself largely sums it up. And, while on the topic of freedom, my recovery was going so well that the hospital staff had begun discussing the possibility of sending me home a few days earlier than originally planned. I wasn't keen on the idea, as I worried it might put an unreasonable burden on Mum to look after me while I still required a good deal of assistance.

"You've got a strong will," said Doctor Jenny.

BROCCOLI AVOCADO SOUP

Serves 2 or 3
Keep refrigerated. Best used within 3 days.
Can be frozen too.
This is a big favourite!
It's super tasty and quick to make in blender. Only need to steam broccoli. Good as a sauce on cooked rice, steamed veggies, pasta and noodles.

Ingredients:
- 8 Florets broccoli
- 3 Cups water
- ½ Avocado
- ½ Fennel, roughly chopped (or use red onion if tolerated)
- 1 Stalk celery, roughly chopped
- Handful spinach leaves (or kale)
- 3 Cm wakame sea vegetable, dried
- 1 Tsp ginger, grated
- 1 Large garlic clove, minced
- 1 Tsp cumin, ground
- 2 Tbsp miso paste (any type is ok)
- ½ Tsp black pepper, ground
- Garnish roasted almond pieces
- Optional lemon juice or plum vinegar (I use spiral foods plum vinegar – ume su)

Method:
- Wash broccoli, celery and spinach leaves very well.
- Soak wakame in enough water to cover until soft (approx.10 minutes), remove stem and chop. Add strained soaking water to blender.

- Lightly steam broccoli (in a bamboo steamer is best) over a pot filled with 3 cups water for 5 to 6 minutes, until softened. Keep steaming water.
- Place steamed broccoli in blender with the rest of ingredients (except garnish and optional ingredients).
- Add steaming water as required. For a thicker, sauce-like consistency, use less water
- Serve with roasted almond pieces and, if desired, a few extra pieces of avocado and lemon juice.

"I've got a carefully laid out nutrition plan that I prepared to help me recover quickly," I replied.

"It's just incredible!" exclaimed Doctor Nick, "you've really demonstrated how having a positive attitude contributes to recovery."

"Having a really good diet and understanding the right supplements to use has prepared my body to get through this." ...but I might as well have saved my breath. For all the platitudes I'd heard from him before about how I should perhaps prepare nutrition plans for others, I wondered if he'd fully appreciated just how big an impact it was having on my own body's ability to recover.

And the talk of an early departure seemed all the more surreal since it was happening while there were still various surgical tubes draining stuff out of me. But then the first tube's removal was just one day away. What a huge relief!

I woke up on day eight to sunshine streaming into the room highlighting the magnificent view of the mountains. Looking for company, I turned on the television and discovered that I agreed with a good deal of what Judge Judy had to say. And the nurses, oh how wonderful they were, particularly when they removed two more of the draining tubes from my body. That left just one to go.

Time passed. I watched videos, typed up a post on the Salubrious Dubstars blog, slept, read my health and spiritual books, watched more videos, slept some more. Before I knew it, the sun had risen on day nine. It was a beautiful sunrise, one that I was grateful for being awake to witness. Gab and I exchanged text messages, and arranged for her to stock up my fridge at home on the following Tuesday when it was 'fresh day' at the Prahran Market.

The bandages finally came off, revealing my new body. Thanks to the swelling there were lumps and bumps in all sorts of places you wouldn't expect. And my old bras? Well, the size twelves and fourteens didn't have a hope of fitting, I was now a size twenty! - but this swelling was expected to subside over the coming days and weeks.

Doctor Nick made it clear that I'd need to continue seeing him over the course of the following six months so he could ensure his sculpting of the new breasts was brought to completion without complications.

I received a text message from Melma, who'd been a favourite customer from the Manna health food store days.

> *Hi Sandy,*
> *Hope you're recovering from the scar tissue surgery.*
> *I was wondering if you could advise me on the best blender for nut milks, smoothies etc?*

It was a reminder of how few people I'd shared the full story of my situation with. Melma was a real sweetie, one of my favourite friendships with a customer that had developed from my time at Manna. She'd been following a healthy lifestyle for many years before I had the health food store. She was fifteen years my senior and I admired her positive vibe and good nature, her large family life, business sense and interest in all things health and wellbeing. Despite this, I couldn't bring myself to tell her the full story. She was one of the few outside of my Salubrious Dubstars who was aware I was even in hospital. Did I disclose the full reasons? No, I told Melma I was having surgery to deal with scar tissue. It seems a bit ironic, given that the mastectomy and breast reconstruction were leaving me with a whole new collection of massive scars. I gave Melma the best advice I could regarding the blender, and she ended up buying one for me as well. How generous is that? I still use it, a regular reminder of the special relationship we shared, right up to last year when she sadly passed away.

Day ten of my stay at Hotel C came around and I was looking forward to checking out. For all their efforts to wrap me in cotton and protect me from my allergic reactions, the bandages still itched. And my gigantic bra? That was even worse. But it wasn't all just happening around my chest. I had a stylish elastic bandage around my lower abdomen, the result of Doctor Nick taking some fat from where I had some to spare to sculpt my new breasts. Actually, it was probably more like a girdle… a really tight one at that. The nurses had put great effort into smearing my body with enough Mylanta to relieve the itching, wrapping more copious amounts of cotton around it as well. I can't imagine how bad it would've been had the nurses not gone to such lengths. To be totally honest, the post-op recovery was far easier to deal with than the problem of my skin choosing to reject those bandages

Unable to tolerate the girdle-like bandage anymore, I managed to get approval from the nursing staff to remove it, providing at least some relief. But the discomfort in general was still unbearable.

The next fashion item to go was the white pressure socks. As I stripped away the Hotel C fashion accessories, I was starting to feel more like something resembling a human again.

Feeling desperate for connection with the world outside I tried calling Mum. I'd tried the night before, but the line had been busy. Guess what? It was busy again. I tried later. Still busy. This required some lateral thinking. My stepfather Ted was into technology, way ahead of most people in his age group. Usually when he was at his desk, Skype would be open so he could make or receive video calls. Perhaps I could call Ted on Skype and ultimately reach Mum that way? The plan worked. Not only did I get to speak to both Ted and Mum, but I got to see them as well.

"I tried calling you, Mum."

"Really?"

"Yes, last night and again today. The line was busy."

Ted turned to Mum. "Maybe the phone was off the hook. I'll go and check."

Sure enough, that was the problem. Thank goodness technology now allowed for other ways to reach people.

That Skype session had left me with a warm feeling. I'd just spoken to family and felt more comfortable with the reduction in my enforced body wraps. Then, Nurse Kathy entered. "Hi, I'm really sorry, but I've spoken to the doctors…"

"The bandages?"

"I'm so sorry," replied Kathy. I could see in her eyes that she felt terrible about having to be the bearer of unwelcome news. The sense of new-found freedom was stripped away, but there was also a degree of resignation. It wasn't her doing and she was doing her best the soften the blow.

"The good news is we've managed to work out a compromise. It's just the waistband, and it only needs to be the one layer. You won't need the pressure stockings."

Closing my eyes, I nodded in approval. "Thank you, I really appreciate your help." Acceptance… I'd be going home soon, hopefully the next day. I could deal with the discomfort, and the single layer felt a lot more comfortable than the previous girdle with its cotton padding.

I woke up the next morning filled with excitement. Time to check out of Hotel C and head home. I put on my Lululemons and marvelled at how well they concealed the wobbly evidence of surgery. Knowing my cover wasn't likely to be blown, I made my way downstairs to meet Mum. "I'm really hungry," I said once we were on our way. "Can we stop by Malvern Central? I'm craving some vegetarian brown rice sushi."

What a wonderful relief to walk through my front door, to unpack and fall into the comfort of my own bed then drift off into a peaceful slumber. A couple of hours later I was up again and enjoying some takeaways from the Global Vegetarian that a friend had kindly dropped in. I logged into the Salubrious Dubstars blog and typed a simple message in the heading for the day's blogpost. "I'm Home!!!!"

I settled in to watch Lleyton Hewitt battle against Janko Tipsarević in the first round of the Australian Open. Poor Lleyton went down in straight sets. It was still a good game though – so often the scoreboard doesn't tell the true story of the game. I may not have been able to watch it live at the stadium like I normally would have, but at least I could watch it live on television in my own home.

Despite having stayed up watching the tennis until 11pm, the next day I woke at 5.30am, beating the sunrise by half an hour. The really good news though was that I was able to cook my own breakfast, even after successfully showering myself. Despite the fact that I couldn't raise my arms yet, I was able to look after myself within my home environment! Gab came over after she'd picked up my goodies at the Prahran Market and stayed for a few hours preparing some super-alkalizing green soup, cutting up some summer fruits and tending to some of my house plants that had copped a bit of a scorching while I'd been in hospital. Meanwhile, I pottered around and spent a good deal of time demonstrating how well I could stretch out on the couch and relax.

My nephew, Marlon, and his wife, Jacqui, stopped by later in the day after he'd finished work.

"Is there anything you need?" he asked.

"Actually, there's a few bits and pieces I need from the health food shop up in Carlisle Street." I grabbed my bag so I could give them some money.

"No, don't worry. We'll pay," insisted Jacqui.

"Are you sure?"

"Yes, it's no trouble at all."

It was an unexpected act of kindness that warmed my heart. Those gestures make such a huge difference and are always deeply appreciated, whether they come from family, friends… or even strangers. After they returned, my pantry was stocked with everything I could need to get through my convalescence.

Late in the day a text came through from one of my nurses, thanking me for a gift basket I'd sent them, and commenting on how amazed all the medical staff were at the pace of my recovery. Despite the sensitivity to the bandages, the pace of my recovery had taken the surgeons by surprise.

One week later and the reality of my recovery well and truly presented itself. It was wonderful to be home and good to be back in my own bed, but my nightclothes were very different to what I was accustomed to. Wearing a bra and big undies with a pressure band at the top to sleep in was not in any way comfortable. I still had to accept being wrapped up like that for a couple of weeks, but at least I was home and cancer free. And the swelling that had enveloped most of my body had started to recede. But most of all, it was a relief not to be consumed by the previous itchiness. Looking in the mirror made me laugh out loud; even though it hurt like hell, I simply couldn't help it. You've heard about various 'lifts'? Facelifts, breast etc. Well, no one had told me that I was getting a 'private parts lift'. You see, the surgeon had used belly fat to reconstruct my breasts, and had to create a new belly button in the process. The result being that it lifted the whole area below my new belly button. An unexpected but quite interesting little discovery.

Slipping into an early morning routine was pure joy. Making a morning anti-inflammatory kudzu drink, showering, dressing, preparing supplements and super smoothies in the new blender. Then soaking nuts (almonds are my favourite) to make some nut milk and soaking brown rice for a few hours to prepare it for cooking – something that could go with whatever I might have been intending to prepare later in the day. After that I could settle into checking emails and enjoying a slice of gluten-free toast, spread with a little umeboshi paste and avocado.

What better health spa could a girl hope for? My mind drifted, taking me on imaginary retreats to some of the great health and wellness retreats I'd discovered over the preceding years. I dreamed of Somatheeram Ayurvedic Retreat in Kerala, India and Five Senses in Thailand.

It would've been easy to get lost in those daydreams, but reality beckoned. It was time to try and reactivate my creative instincts and start preparing for my 2013 cooking class program. I was past the uncertainty I'd felt in the earlier stages of my recovery and was feeling motivated. Both the Centre for Adult Education and the Box Hill Institute had confirmed dates for my next round of classes, and I needed to prepare. I came up with a few catchy ideas for new classes like, 'Alkalize for life' and 'Wholefoods for Good Moods' and 'Cancer-fighting Vegetarian'. I made a note to include adding the use of my new blender in my new classes and demos.

I felt like I'd turned a corner that week; I was sleeping better, and felt confident going out in public again, especially after Mum took me to the hairdresser for a wash and style. I treasured the quality time that Mum and I were able to spend together during that recovery. Our true colours were shining through for each other, with no dramatising the situation. We handled it all in our stride with good humour, even though deep down it was very challenging. We didn't need to speak about all the details and spent a lot of time just smiling at each other.

Focusing on enjoyable experiences and events was a powerful aid to recovery. I settled down to watch Andy Murray and Roger Federer fight it out to see who made it to the final of the Australian Open. Earlier in the day Australia had made it into the mixed doubles final but had been knocked out of the women's doubles; one of the players in that match being a young player by the name of Ash Barty. Another Australian youngster, Nick Kyrgios, had won the boy's semi-final played that day.

As I watched the game that night, I reflected on how successful my idea for the Salubrious Dubstar blog had been. I'd put a good deal of faith in my 'circle of trust', believing those closest to me would take an interest in following my journey and slipping in words of support along the way.

It can be dangerous to build up your hopes with these things sometimes.

Yes, there were a couple of responses on my blog, however, comments became sparse as my stay rolled on.

Had people read my posts but lacked the time to respond?

Did they feel there was even a need to?

Were they not able to be creative in cheering me up?

These are questions I'll never know the answers to. Maybe the idea would be more understood now than it was then. Today, it would be so much easier, using social media and setting up a private group. Perhaps the blog was ahead of its time then? Don't get me wrong, I loved writing it and have it as a record to be able to reflect on and share now and I really appreciated every comment I received. But at the same time, it was a bit of a reality check regarding thoughtful input in support of a close friend who is going through a major medical procedure.

For the Love of Music

Every year, Adelaide hosts a four-day festival during March called the WOMADelaide Festival of Music, Arts and Dance. And, being a lover of multiple music genres, I'd been attending every year since 2000 and continued to do so until 2019.

Throughout my life, music has always been one of the most important ingredients in *my recipes for living*. And live music is something else. It fills your being and enriches the soul.

My first big concert was the Rolling Stones at the Kooyong Tennis Centre in 1973, which I attended with Michael and Lilli. It was outdoors, and from the very first note I was enthralled. The sight of Mick Jagger sliding across the stage during *Gimme Shelter* will forever remain crystal clear in my memory, along with my favourite song of the night, *You Can't Always Get What You Want*. I've since been to see the Stones on three more occasions when they've toured Australia (1995, 2006 and 2014). They still know how to hold an audience.

Another truly memorable concert from my youth was Bob Marley and the Wailers, at the Melbourne Festival Hall in 1979. The stage was still shrouded in darkness when Bob started to sing the first notes of *Positive Vibration*. Then the lights came on and the entire crowd, myself included, stood up on our seats, the distinctive aromas of marijuana filling the air as a multitude of joints were passed around. It was an electric moment. I looked around and saw that everyone was singing along. By the time he finished with *Exodus*, the entire hall was buzzing on his message of love.

Arriving at WOMADelaide

These experiences have been powerful, and since then, I've made sure to enjoy live music whenever I could. Some of the other standout live concerts I've had the good fortune to attend were, Prince (1992 & 2006), Lady Gaga (2008), Leonard Cohen (2010 & 2013), Beyonce (2013), Coldplay (2016) and Paul McCartney (2017 and 2023). All of them so different to each other, and yet each has been equally enriching.

But festivals like WOMAD? They're special. I'd heard so much about it ever since it started back in 1992. Listening to Melbourne's Progressive Broadcasting Service community radio (PBS) for years had already exposed me to the kind of musical diversity featured at the festival.

But this iconic open air festival in the heart of Adelaide's stunning Botanic Park was something else. A magnificent celebration of world music and cultural diversity.

The most special aspect of WOMAD was the opportunity to discover new music that I'd not been previously exposed to. The list of favourites that I saw there is extensive and includes the likes of Salif Keita, Sean Kuti, Ziggy Marley, Cheik Lo, Christine and the Queens, Sinkane, Ozomatli, Richie Haven (the guy who sang the first song at the original Woodstock), Sinead O'Conner, Toumani Diabate, Youssou N'Dour, Hugh Masekela, Jimmy Cliff, Mariza, Miriam Makeba and so many more. No doubt among those names there are those whom you've heard of, and those you haven't. I get to relive the joy of those festivals regularly when I listen to the festival CDs (now through a streaming service) that were released each year.

It's a festival that means so much to me that I even attended the year of my double mastectomy, just six weeks after the operation.

There was another festival though that was further afield, one that I'd always wanted to attend: the Montreux Jazz Festival in Switzerland. Founded in 1967, it now attracts a quarter of a million people every year and has become renowned for legendary performances from some of the music industry's biggest icons.

Brigette, who'd run the Gawler conference, had become a good friend but had moved back to her homeland of Switzerland and was living there with her partner, Peter. *This is my chance*, I thought, *I can visit Brigitte and take the opportunity to attend Montreux*. I was also wanting to visit Israel again to see family and worked out with a travel agent that I could easily do both. The only problem was, when I looked at the Montreux Festival website, the tickets were expensive, beyond what I had expected. So, I developed a plan that would hopefully help me be at the festival.

At the time, my friend Henry had spent several of the previous years producing a show called *The Shtick* on Melbourne's community television station, Channel 31.

"I want to be able to say I work for you... at the station," I told him one day.

"Really? Why?" He could tell I was up to something.

"I want to go to Montreux, but the tickets are just so expensive."

"Go on," he said.

"When I was looking at the website I noticed the press option. Members of the press can apply for a free pass."

The silence on the other end of the line told me he was waiting for the details.

"I could do a story about the food options at the festival, like the story I did on the food options in New York."

"So, you want to be able to say you work for me so you can get a press pass?"

"All I'd need is a business card and a brief letter saying that I'm a producer and you're commissioning me to do the story. I'll organize the card if you can just provide me with a graphic of the logo."

There was a brief pause before he replied, "Yeah, sure... why not."

Getting his agreement was no guarantee that my plan would work... I still had to wait and see if the festival organisers would accept my credentials and issue me with a press pass.

After an anxious wait, the email came confirming my credentials… giving me a free pass to the 2014 Montreux Jazz Festival!

I contacted Brigette to let her know and started booking flights and arranging my accommodation in Israel for the weeks I'd be staying there prior to going to Switzerland. For the first two weeks' stay I'd found an apartment online in Tel Aviv that looked good. It was called the *Rainbow Apartment* and promoted the fact that it had a fully appointed kitchen, something that really mattered to me if I was going to be staying there for two weeks. But there were two utensils that I wanted to ensure were included in what they had, a wok and a blender. No, was their reply. But, to my great surprise, they went out and bought both items to ensure I'd be happy to proceed with the booking. They explained that it was a new apartment they'd just set up and they wanted to be sure that all the likely needs of those who booked with them were fulfilled. Both these items are essential ingredients to help me keep up my healthy nutritional requirements.

The apartment was beautifully appointed and, with its name being the *Rainbow Apartment,* I couldn't help but wonder if perhaps the owners were a gay couple, which may have been apt given that, during the fortnight of my stay, Tel Aviv was holding its internationally famous Pride Festival, part of the international observance of Gay Pride Month. *The Pride Parade,* that takes place on the Friday, attracts over 250,000 attendees.

One of the things that has always struck me about Israel when I've stayed there, is its general inclusiveness and tolerance of groups that are so marginalised in some other parts of the world.

Coming back from Switzerland to Israel, I'd booked an apartment for a week in Jerusalem, where an old school friend, Zel, who'd moved there, showed me a good time and gave me a fantastic tour of the hidden places in Old Jerusalem.

But this story is about my time in Switzerland and the Montreux Jazz Festival.

Brigette lived in Sigriswil, a Swiss Municipality in the administrative district of Thun, not far from Bern. I arrived via train from Geneva and as we headed to Brigette and Peter's home, I could see people in what looked like a festival atmosphere. What was happening in Sigriswil while I was there? A wrestling festival! Not like the Wide World of Wrestling on television back in the 70s and 80s. No, this was an old tradition with men wrestling each other in a round sandpit with a twelve-metre diameter.

Known as Schwingen, this Swiss wrestling and Alpine festival has its roots in the old farming culture. One of the sport's more unique attributes is the shorts, or schwingenhosen, a specialised piece of apparel that must be gripped at all times as the opponents attempt to lift each other from the ground, the loser being the one who ends up with their face pushed into the ground.

Many of the men attending proudly wore Lederhosen shorts. And the food? What can I say? As much as I embraced watching this very physical and amusing scene (to me anyway), the food options basically consisted of bratwurst, sauerkraut and chips... all washed down by gigantic steins of beer. Nothing there I could write about as healthy food options at festivals. I decided that satisfying my appetite would have to wait. It was certainly a different world to anything I'd experienced, but the festival itself was still interesting and a lot of fun. And the countryside around Sigriswil? It was incredibly beautiful. I even connected with a cute lederhosen-wearing guy who was in the competition for wearing traditional outfits while doing their traditional knee-slapping dance.

Brigette and Peter also took me into Bern, where highlights were the Einstein Museum and the famous Bear Pit.

What? You haven't heard of the Bear Pit?

Well, let me tell you a bit about it.

It all started in 1513, when the Bernese soldiers returned from their victorious battle at Novara carrying a live bear as part of their war booty. Initially kept in the moat surrounding the city's main fortification, it was moved two years later to a pit in the town square, the Bärenplatz. Over the years, as the city expanded

Arriving at Montreux

and one bear multiplied to become many, the Bear Pit was relocated several times. In 1857, it was moved to the site of Bear Park, where it remains today, albeit expanded into a 6000 square metre enclosure that was completed in 2006 (although the 19th century pit still remains as well).

As interesting as the history of the Bern bears may have been, I hadn't travelled across the world to see them. I was there for the Montreux Jazz Festival. Founded in 1967, the festival has been held every year since on the shores of Lake Geneva. In 1976, a new venue was built as a home for the growing festival with two large auditoriums (one named after the legendary blues great, Miles Davis, and the other after Stravinsky).

I found a home to rent for two weeks online that was just up the road, and eight hundred steps, from the venue. It was perfect! I stood on the balcony and marvelled at the views over Montreux village, the lake and the festival venue just below me. Those steps were great for walking down past all the traditional Swiss homes. And there were water fountains on the way, with alkalising water on tap. Going uphill sometimes though, especially later in the evening, proved to be a slow process and an arduous journey. Indeed, sometimes I took a taxi

In the press area at Montreux

instead. I can assure you that when I left Montreux, I was a little bit fitter than I when I arrived.

And the festival! What a wonderful feeling it was, walking in there brandishing my press pass, my free ticket to so many of the festival's events. Over the two weeks of the festival I saw dozens of performances, far too many to list here.

There were definitely highlights though. It was the first time I'd heard Ed Sheeran. He walked out onto the stage on his own with just his guitar and a few foot pedals to control his backing sounds. But what a show he put on!

The blues great, Buddy Guy, was such a seasoned performer. Not just working the crowd but entering it and playing to members of the audience as he strolled through the rows of seats, playing and singing as he went. I had the joy, and a photo to prove it, of having him come right up to me as he played.

Among the other highlights were Outkast, Massive Attack, Van Morrison, Pharrell Williams, Morcheeba, Wayne Shorter, Herbie Hancock, Lee Ritenour & Dave Grusin; though the most memorable for me was Stevie Wonder. An incredibly talented, dynamic musician with an incredible back catalogue of great hits – and we all found ourselves dancing and singing along.

There were even some Australians who were performing there, like Flume, Chet Faker, and Julia and Angus Stone.

All up, throughout the whole festival, there were a hundred and sixteen gigs across five venues. It was massive. A wonderful opportunity to see some of the musicians whose work I knew and loved, but also to experience musicians I'd never heard of before.

But wasn't I there to write about the food? Isn't that why I secured my press pass?

Well, you'll be pleased to know that I did indeed write a comprehensive story about the food options, and something I thoroughly enjoyed conducting the first hand research for. There were many plant-based options I was pleased to see and try. Each food outlet was so well presented, and hygiene standards were impeccable. I met some wonderful health foodies. Sadly though, none of the media organizations I sent my article to decided to run with it. Nevertheless, it was an adventure and experience that I will never forget.

If you're looking for ingredients in a *recipe for living* that fills you with inspiration and opens you up to wonderful cultures, a variety of traditions and genres and being amongst happy, music-loving people, I can highly recommend both WOMAD and the Montreux Jazz Festival... or any live music of your choice.

Music continued to play an increasingly important role in my life when Deborah Conway teamed up with Willy Zygier to bring the *Shir Madness* Jewish music festival to Melbourne. The festival had been founded by Gary Holzman in Sydney as a grassroots celebration of Jewish music and performance in 2010. Originally a biannual festival, Deborah and Willy had performed in it previously and could see the potential for rotating it between the two cities.

They asked if I'd be interested in taking on the volunteer role of catering co-ordinator, taking on the task of ensuring there were plenty of healthy, kosher options available for the festival attendees.

Six months of intensive planning followed. Through those meetings I made new and important connections. Like Sharon, the volunteer co-ordinator, who had extensive professional experience organising major events like the *Falls Music and Arts Festival*. The 2015 Melbourne festival was a huge success. This led to Deborah being appointed general manager of the Sydney festival in 2016. Again, she asked if I'd be interested, this time assisting with the marketing.

In 2017 it returned to Melbourne, with Sharon as general manager. This third festival saw me presented with the responsibility of Community Liaison. I made another connection that year as well, Ruth, who had years of experience behind her in entertainment and who is a good friend. It was also the year that Irene became involved. Due to her experience making documentaries, she co-ordinated the film presentation and video aspects of the festival.

Time to do a Cookbook

By this time, I'd already had a multitude of articles and recipes published in a range of publications in both Australia and the United States. I'd produced a cooking video (that was distributed on VHS and DVD) and had dozens of YouTube cooking videos as well. What was missing was a cookbook, something that would package together all the best of what I'd learned over the decades and take that knowledge to a wider audience.

As I looked at the various options it seemed the most obvious pathway would be through self-publishing. I called Irene, who was working for a Melbourne based design company at the time called *The Hive Design*. "I want to do a cookbook."

"Oh, that's a big job."

"Can you help me?"

"Yes, I should be able to… but I think the person you really need to talk to is my boss, Russel. He's got more experience than I have in doing books."

I got in touch with Russel and asked him about what was involved and what costs I was looking at. "Oh, I'd say you're looking at spending at least twenty thousand."

Twenty Thousand dollars?

He explained all that was involved. "You need to understand that it involves photography, design and layout, and then there's the printing. It all adds up quickly."

What he was saying made sense. But where was I going to get that sort of money from?

Fortunately, the exciting new worlds opening in the digital economy presented the answer.

Crowdfunding!

I did my research into the various crowdfunding options, attending seminars and watching online videos while collating the recipes I intended to feature in the book. Eventually, I found the one that seemed the most appropriate, Pozible, which is coincidentally based in Melbourne.

My friend, Brin (who is also my IT specialist), started taking photos of some of the recipes I was cooking. I showed the results to Irene. "What do you think?" I asked.

"These photos give me a good idea of what you can do. I know a specialist food photographer," she said. "I'll get you her details."

I got in touch with the photographer and locked in a date to start shooting. "Do you want to come and help?" I asked Gab.

"Oh yeah… I wouldn't miss it," she replied.

It was a long and very slow day. A very frustrating day. She was spending an inordinate amount of time placing lights precisely. After an entire day we had the photos for just two meals. They were lovely photos, but they felt staged. I wanted a more natural approach… one where I cooked the food and the photographer took photos using the available light so they looked the way the people could expect to see them when cooking the recipes for themselves. I realised that I wanted an easier and quicker process where I could make more meals in a session, like in my cooking classes.

Then I talked to a friend, Emmanuel, who was a professional photographer and lived close by. "I'd be happy to do it," he said.

"I really wasn't happy with the approach the other photographer was taking," I told him. "It felt so staged and artificial."

He nodded and said, "Don't worry. We'll do it all with natural light. It'll look as authentic as it can possibly be."

"That's sounds perfect. When can you start?"

"How about Wednesday?"

And so it was that each ensuing Wednesday Gab, Emmanuel and I would work our way through eight to ten meals... preparing and photographing them.

Meanwhile, Irene shot video footage for the Pozible campaign and helped me put it together. For those of you who have never done a crowdfunding campaign, I can tell you, it's not an easy process. You have to put the effort in to sell your concept to potential investors, making them feel they're getting something worthwhile in return for investing in your proposal. The whole process took months. The campaign was online for six weeks and achieved its target, thanks to the support of friends, family, past students and the general public.

And you're probably also wondering how I went about selecting the recipes to include. There were so many to choose from... when I checked on my computer there were well over a thousand! Some seemed obvious, but for others I consulted some of my students, asking about what their favourite recipes were and what they'd like to see included.

Irene worked on designing the layout, working with Russel to progressively pull the book together. I had faith that she understood what I wanted. She has the Midas touch when it comes to design. Every detail mattered to her. We spoke extensively about details such as what kind of binding the book should have. We eventually settled on it being ringbound to make it as practical as possible in the kitchen setting.

And it wasn't just recipes. I included sections in the front of the book about my philosophy and explaining some of the basics about food groups. I included photos that are important to me from throughout my time learning and putting my knowledge and understanding into practice. And, for the first time, at the back of the book I went public about my lifetime of living with cancer and its consequences.

Eventually, the book was fully cooked, derived from a recipe that involved ingredients coming from a whole team of contributors. It took around a year from conception to receiving the first printed proof.

The excitement of seeing my cookbook on display in a local bookshop

I booked a local gallery space in St Kilda East and, on the 28th of November, 2017, the *My Wholefood Community Plant Based Cook Book* was presented to the world. Mum was beaming with pride and joy. My family, close friends and supporters were all there and Irene gave a heartfelt speech. It was without doubt one of the highlights of my life.

Most copies of that initial print run have now sold, and the book is also available now for print on demand sales online.

The way I see it, every recipe in the book can be considered a worthwhile contribution to a *recipe for living*.

...and Time to Re-energise

I wasn't the only one in my family who had been through dealing with cancer. During the 90's, Mum was diagnosed with breast cancer and ultimately had a mastectomy to remove a tumour. She was all clear for years, but then, around March 2019, she was diagnosed with lung cancer.

Being in her nineties, she decided she'd prefer not to get treatment.

When I stopped by to visit her one day she said, "Take money from my account… today. Book yourself into that health retreat you were talking about." Even as she was near her death, my mother continued to look out for me and my health needs.

I left her room, ready to head home, then looked back at her, lying on her bed. As I continued down the corridor to her front door she smiled at me. I called her when I got home. "Hi Mum, what are you doing right now?"

"I'm preparing Ted's dinner." Perhaps she was still lying on her bed, but more than likely she'd got up to prepare a meal for Ted. She took such good care of him, and feeding him was a sign of her love. "Don't come tomorrow," she said. "The weather's going to be nice. You should go for a walk in the Botanical Gardens." She knew me well and how much that I loved that.

"Okay," I replied. "But I'll come over in the evening." The way that she was always thinking of my happiness made me smile.

I went to sleep early and was woken by the phone ringing. It was 1.30 am on 26 June 2019. It was Michael, sounding distressed. My mother had just passed away. Ted had called his daughter, Michelle. Then she called Michael and Lilli. "What should I do?" I asked, "should I come over?"

Straight forward as ever, Michael replied, "Stay home." He was right, there was nothing to be gained by me heading over to Mum's house when he was already on his way. Instead, I wandered outside and looked up at the to see Mum's face reflected in the night sky's shifting clouds.

Mum knew that her passing was going to be a big blow to me and that I'd need something positive to help with the grieving process and to accept it… to, as she used to say, "get on with it." Even now, so many years after her passing, I feel that she is still looking after me, with a warm hand and a warm heart.

Four weeks after Mum passed, I was floundering, totally wracked by grief and struggling to achieve anything. But I had managed one thing – I'd taken her advice on board and booked myself into the Gwinganna Lifestyle Retreat in Southern Queensland.

The Queensland heat left me feeling breathless as I left the airport terminal, a sensation I was familiar with after so much travelling through South East Asia. I was soon sitting in the back of the Gwinganna minibus with the other strangers on board, all looking to immerse themselves in self-care and rejuvenation.

I felt confident the food was going to be exactly how I like it, and that in itself was important for nourishing myself, as it had been hard to get into cooking for myself after mum passed.

Set on five hundred acres in the upper reaches of the Tallebudgera Valley, Gwinganna is a majestic slice of paradise that overlooks the Gold Coast.

Every aspect of the retreat is designed to leave you feeling at peace with nature and yourself, from the infinity pool overlooking the valley to the timber and glass buildings. It seemed the perfect place to settle in for five days of time spent with myself and nobody else. I was particularly pleased that they offered the option for guests to place a sign in front of themselves while dining to let other guests know they were eating mindfully and didn't wish to indulge in conversation. I had learned from Herman Aihara and Michio Kushi years before of the importance of carefully chewing one's food and being mindful of how one ate, a philosophy very much at odds with the western tradition of discussing the day's events over dinner. And I didn't want to talk to anyone. My mother, the love of my life, was gone. I was there to grieve and replenish myself as I set out to come to terms with my loss.

As much as I wanted to be on my own though, you can't easily avoid contact with other people at these retreats. And so it was that I found myself having to answer a question from one of the other guests. "Hi, my name's David. What brings you here?"

I didn't feel ready to answer questions from people, no matter how innocent they may be. But I also had no desire to be rude. I'd known this question would come at some stage. And, hey, this was a health retreat. Did I really want people to know that I ran vegan, plant-based and macrobiotic cooking and nutrition courses? I dreaded the thought of having people pump me for nutritional information while I needed healing myself. But I had a plan that I'd worked out beforehand. I felt like I was good at creating cover stories. It was a skill that I'd deftly employed since having my spleen removed. I decided to invent a fictitious career for myself, based on one of my other loves. I looked at David and said, "I'm Sandra, Sandra Dubs, but everyone calls me Sandy." I put on my biggest smile as I blurted out, "I'm a comedian."

David jolted back a little like he was surprised. He looked me up and down and then burst out laughing. "A comedian, huh?"

"Yes." I wanted to come up with a quick joke to demonstrate my prowess in my adopted trade, but hadn't quite got that far when I'd formulated my devious deception.

"You really think I'm going to believe that?" His giant grin was infectious.

"Is it that obvious?" His laughter told me the answer. "Okay, I'm a nutritionist. I run cooking classes. But I really don't want anyone to know.

I'm here for private reasons... my mother passed a few weeks ago. I don't want to have to deal with people asking me questions on what they should do. Normally I wouldn't mind, but not now. Not while I'm grieving.

"I get it." And the expression on his face told me that he did indeed understand. "Your secret's safe with me."

"What about you?"

"I'm a business manager. I work for a guy in Melbourne who owns a lot of properties and small businesses."

"Oh, I'm from Melbourne too."

"Small world, huh?"

"What's brings you to Gwinganna?"

"Boss's orders. He suggested I was getting too stressed and that I needed a week up here to get my head together." We chatted a little more then he asked, "Do you want to sit together at dinner?"

"Yes, that'd be nice."

I went back to my room and had a rest until dinner time came around. When I got to the dining room, I'd all but forgotten our agreement. I saw the little sign there in front of me at the table that I could put up to inform others that I was eating mindfully and took advantage of the safe haven it offered.

I took a mouthful of my dinner and started to chew, counting as I went. I wanted to shut out the conversations from the other tables, but somehow the words still penetrated my determination to build a wall through mindful eating.

"Well, I'm just so stressed out, what with work and the kids..."

"I knew that if I come here, I'll be able to lose some weight. I just can't do it at home..."

"I just needed a break, a really good break..."

All the reasons people had for coming to Gwinganna. And they were all perfectly valid good reasons. But I had my own reason.

Then David strode into the room, smiling as broadly as ever. He did a cartoon style take when he noticed my little sign, then proceeded to go into the most bizarre charades routine I've ever witnessed, his actions more apelike than human. I couldn't help it. The silence was broken as I burst out laughing. Who was I to claim the honour of being a comedian when in the company of this man who was so capable of extracting laughs from me while I was trying my best to be so serious and mindful? Ultimately, he did respect my desire to eat in silence, but it was nice to have him sitting there filling the space with friendly warmth. Then, with the meal over, it was nice to chat.

"Did you see that there's a walk up the mountain tomorrow?"

"No, I haven't really looked at all the activities yet."

"Should be a bit of fun. It's an early morning start though. It means getting up before sunrise. Want to come?"

My age-old response of *can I come too?* wasn't going to happen this time. I shook my head. "Sorry, I really don't feel like I've got the energy. I might be good for a walk later in the week, but right now I think I just need to rest."

"Fair enough."

We chatted some more and somewhere along the line the question came out, "So, are you Jewish?" I can't even remember which one of us asked the question, but there it was. Of all the people I could have connected with at the retreat, the one I end up talking to just happens to be Jewish as well. It was another instance of what I'd encountered so often throughout my life, where it's almost like Jews have an inner radar to help them find each other; whether they be religious or secular, it always seems to happen.

There were sixty-five people staying at the retreat. It turned out that three of them were people I already knew, all Jewish and from Melbourne. There was a good friend that I didn't know was coming along, a guy I went to school with and his wife. Small world. We all ended up hanging out together. Then, as the days rolled by, it turned out there were connections between them and others, also Jewish, staying at the retreat. By the end of the week our very funny and earnest crew had grown to around twenty people. Throughout it all though, I continued to eat in silence, helped by the fact that David talked enough for both of us.

The following night, as we chatted after dinner, I asked David what the mountain was like. "Fantastic," he said. "It was quite a vigorous walk, but I loved every minute of it. And the view from the top was spectacular."

"I'm glad." There were different grades of difficulty people could choose, and David was quite proud to say that he'd taken the most difficult grade.

"There's a Tai Chi class tomorrow at sunrise," he said.

"Oh, that sounds nice."

"Want to join in?"

"I would actually. That'd be really good."

But when the sun rose, my head didn't move from the pillow. I was tired. What I needed most was rest. I felt that I already knew David well enough to trust that he'd understand. And what a great place it was to rest. My room had a view out onto an open paddock with wallabies hopping about contentedly. And the bathtub! That was something special, outside on the room's private balcony. There's something that feels liberating about sitting in a bathtub in the open air, just like I'd experienced many years earlier in the hills outside Mullumbimby, but in a more luxurious setting.

It ended up being such a fun week, with one of the highlights being when David decided to join a tribal dance workshop one night. I don't think I've ever seen anyone squat so low while dancing. It was almost painful to watch, but I was impressed by his strength, agility and stamina.

It's not like there was any hint of romance. It was more that we had an instant connection as friends. During our conversations, we were constantly challenging each other. David came from a life that had been very structured and organised. He was a dedicated father of three teens and, though I didn't want to pry into his private life, I gathered that he was about to separate from his wife. So, the more carefree lifestyle I'd lived was something he hadn't really been exposed to before. A fun little coincidence was that it turned out that David's mother had been my teacher in fourth grade. I guess it's perhaps less surprising when you consider that we both grew up in Melbourne's Jewish community, but it still seems pretty amazing.

Meeting David was a gift from my mother. A truly serendipitous occurrence. His friendship continues to be one of my most important. He's a real mensch, a Yiddish word that describes a person of integrity and honour. Plus, he's very funny.

Matters of the Heart

My stay at Gwinganna had been wonderful in ways I couldn't have imagined when I'd made the booking. My five-day stay came to an end, but rather than head straight back to Melbourne, I decided to visit my friend, Fay, from my days in Sydney. She'd been living in Mullumbimby for quite a while by then, and it was fairly close to Gwinganna. So I rented a car from Gold Coast airport and drove to Mullum.

The Byron Writers Festival happened to be on at the time as well. Having already started contemplating the idea of writing a memoir, I hoped I might be able to get some inspiration. With Byron being a short drive from Mullum, Fay had been attending the festival for years and, in her own way, encouraged me to go too.

"A memoir?" asked Fay. "Why would you want to do that?"

"It's important to me. After what I've been through in my life, creating a lifestyle and career to match. And there's also all that I've learned about how to survive cancer treatment with a compromised immune system. I think I've got a story to tell. A story that needs to be told."

"Well, if you really want to do this, you need to go Byron for the festival. We'll go together."

The Byron Writers' Festival is one of Australia's biggest, with over 12,000 people attending the three-day event annually. "You're really short of breath," commented Fay as we walked around the festival. I didn't really think too much about it, being more concerned with wanting to enjoy the festival.

After a couple of weeks I returned to Melbourne and had largely put writing my memoir on the back-burner. I had a feeling that one day it would be the right time to write it, but that time hadn't yet arrived.

It wasn't long after returning that I found myself feeling more tired than I normally would. My mother had been going to a well-respected cardiologist, Professor Dion Stub. So, I made an appointment with my GP to get a referral.

The prognosis came as a shock. "We need to replace the heart-valve."

"Do you think it might be connected with the Mantle radiation I had in the eighties?" I asked. I got met with the same sort of scepticism as when I had my thyroid operation. There's actually quite a few studies that have linked radiation therapy to cardiac issues later in life like Radiation-Induced Aortic Stenosis. And it was then clear that I needed an operation, a transcatheter aortic valve implantation, or TAVI. I remember the actual procedure taking place as it was done under a local anaesthetic. I watched the screen above the operating table throughout the minimally invasive procedure that would help repair the damaged aortic valve. It was fascinating.

The TAVI operation took place just ten days after my sixty-third birthday and just a few months after Mum had passed away. I kept remembering her telling me, "This too shall pass," and, "Be strong and of good courage." (which was my old school motto). *Yes Mum,* I kept thinking as her words ran through my head over and over, *I am.*

It had all seemed to happen in a blur, but I was soon recovering and coming to accept this new implant that I needed to keep my heart pumping properly.

But there are complications that can come from the TAVI operation, as I would soon discover. My life was about to be confronted by new health challenges.

In the meantime, there were other matters to deal with.

Living with Grief

By 2019 I found myself reflecting on all that had transpired since I'd first embarked on pursuing a healthier approach to nutrition and life in general.

Who am I? How did I get here? These were reasonable questions for someone who'd started out on a path toward a life in accountancy, but then deviated into a whole new world. I'd travelled this new world to seek out guidance in how best to follow the principles of zen macrobiotics and wholefood-based nutrition.

From humble beginnings selling sandwiches made in my home kitchen, my career in nutrition had evolved as I'd managed and owned a health food store, a couple of cafes, established a cooking school, spoken at international seminars, produced both a cooking video and cookbook, written articles for a multitude of publications – and so much more.

Having decided years earlier that constantly travelling the world and presenting at seminars was beyond someone whose immune system was so compromised, I viewed the media as a solution… a way of reaching a far wider audience without impacting on my own wellbeing. Despite my immune system, I could still be a mover and shaker and write my articles for the various health and wellbeing magazines, integrative medical journals and the Age newspaper's 'Epicure' section.

I was excited when the opportunity arose to be a guest on ABC Radio Melbourne. Libby Gore (better known to many as Elle McFeast from her television days) was hosting a weekend morning radio show, and was keen to have someone talk about health and nutrition. And it turned out that someone was me.

The first segment lasted almost twenty-five minutes – talking about the whole concept of how healthy nutrition is best achieved through a wholefood plant-based approach. The program got great feedback, so Libby asked if I'd be interested in coming back to do more segments with her. I enjoyed her energy and abilities so much that it was a no-brainer. In the ensuing months I went on her show and spoke about the benefits of tofu and how to prepare it, cooking sea vegetables, Umeboshi plums, how saffron can lift your mood and how ginger is good for migraines; how to use nutrition to fight colds and flu, and the best food to help deal with arthritis.

It was enjoyable talking with Libby and it felt like these segments were destined to be an ongoing, regular gig. I had visions of ultimately becoming a presenter in my own right. After all, radio was such a great way to reach people that were otherwise difficult to spread my message to and I felt confident speaking on air. It allowed me to share the knowledge I'd accumulated over forty years of learning about nutrition and wellbeing without the physical effort of setting up cooking demonstrations and classes as I'd done so often in the previous decades.

But then the tragedy of Mum's passing had struck.

To say that losing Mum hit me hard would be an understatement. Her love and support had been such an important part of my life, a foundation for my own personal *recipe for living*. Her memory is a blessing.

I was consumed with grief and just couldn't bring myself to continue with the radio interviews while still coming to terms with the fact that the most inspirational person in my life was gone.

And there were other challenges that arose with Mum's passing as well.

At ninety-six, Ted was still energetic and essentially in good health, but had already displayed symptoms of the early stages of dementia.

Mum's passing triggered a flare-up in his ability to cope. Basic life skills, like cooking his own meals, were now beyond him. His daughter Michelle and I had little choice but to organise his meals for him. I'd take him pre-prepared chicken soups and other meals that were easy to store in the fridge and reheat as required.

In conversation with Mum two weeks before her passing

But even with the combined efforts from his daughter and myself, he was continuing to struggle. Michelle was spending as much time with him as she could, but it wasn't enough. After a couple of months, we both realised there was little we could do other than start planning his transition into aged care.

The extent of his developing dementia had been less obvious when Mum was around. She'd looked after so many of the everyday matters around the house, so the household had appeared to be functioning quite normally. They'd both continued to do things together like visiting the local grocer. But now, with Mum gone, such things were beyond him.

Then I got a call from Michelle one day. "Ted can't find the switch for the alarm," she said. "He's convinced the light-switch is for the alarm. I pointed out to him where the alarm is but he can't remember the code. He's completely forgotten how it works."

Fortunately, I had the code stored in my phone and forwarded it on to Michelle. The need to get him into aged care had suddenly become far more urgent.

In September, just three months after Mum had passed, Michelle found a space for Ted that was close to where we lived. "It'll just be for a week or two," she'd told him. Needless to say, he would stay there till he passed. I went to visit him once or twice a week.

Mum with my step father, Ted, in 1984

"Ah, Bright Eyes!" he'd say during all my visits to sit with him. "I'm in the waiting room." He still had a cheeky sense of humour and, despite his dementia, was obviously well aware of his situation. I could see that it was a lot better for him there than when he was struggling at home. And, you know what? As he was such a good looking, charming man, all the women staying at the home loved him.

He'd been there for three years when his dementia became noticeably worse. "Someone's stolen my walking stick," he said one day when I went to visit him. A thorough search of his room revealed that it was under his mattress.

"What was it doing there?" I asked him.

"I had to hide it... had to make sure no one steals it." He'd forgotten he was the one who put the stick there. But he had other issues as well.

A few weeks later Michael and I went to visit him. Michael wasn't comfortable at that stage on going to see him on his own. "I don't know what to say," he'd tell me. He felt more comfortable if we went together so I could do the talking for both of us.

When we arrived the receptionist said, "You've timed it well. He just arrived back in the ambulance a short while ago."

"Ambulance?" I asked. "What happened?"

"You didn't know? He fell out of bed and hurt his hip a few days ago. He had to have surgery." No one told us. I was devastated to know that he was lying in a hospital and that I didn't go to see him.

I went back again the next day and saw him as a small, frail man. The man who was by my mother's side for over 40 years, the man who never said a negative word to me and always supported the fact that my mother and I regularly spoke once (or sometimes twice) a day. I sat with him for a while, then Michelle and her daughter came in. Ted was struggling. Michelle, being a physician, was gentle with him and knew what help she could give. I was grateful that she was doing all she could.

The next day, on October 17th, 2022, just two months shy of his hundredth birthday, Ted slipped away.

I miss him.

What about the Lungs?

A few weeks after the operation for the TAVI, I visited my GP for a scheduled check up.

"There's something doesn't feel right" I said to him.

"Oh?"

"It's just... I'm not feeling like I think I should be. I've just had this valve replacement, I'm supposed to be feeling more energetic and better because the blood flow is supposed to be better, but I'm just not feeling it."

The doctor nodded to show he was listening.

"Do you think it may be worth doing a scan on my lungs?"

"Why do you think we should do that?" he replied.

"Well, with all these things that I've had. It always seems to be around the chest... ever since I had the mantle radiation way back when I was twenty. And in all that time, I can't remember anyone doing a scan of my chest."

"Yes, but is there a specific reason?"

"Well, we've done so many tests, and I've had breast cancer, I've had heart issues, I've had thyroid issues. We've done blood tests so we know what my liver's doing, how my kidneys are functioning. But I can't remember there ever being a lung scan. And I'm feeling tired and run down. I'd just like to know."

"Okay," he said. "If you really want a scan, let's just do it."

And you wouldn't believe it, I got the scan and when it came back he said, "Oh, that's a small tumour showing up just there."

Great, I thought, *here we go again!*

My instincts had served me well.

He recommended a lung specialist whom I saw as soon as I could get an appointment.

He had a look at the scan and said, "Yes, there's definitely a tumour there. We'll need to operate." The operation was what's known as a *thoracotomy* where the surgeon creates an incision between two ribs to reach a specific area. In my case, this was so they could access my lungs and remove the right middle lobe. When I came to after surgery the doctor told me, "We're lucky that we got it early. We've removed the margins and we're confident that we got to it before it had a chance to spread. However, you *will* need chemotherapy."

"When will that start?" I asked.

"You'll need to talk to an oncologist."

That's the thing when you get on this roller coaster ride. It picks you up and you just don't know what to expect next.

This is probably an apt time to mention that choosing your oncologist is such an important decision that it really needs to be done with careful consideration. Having been recommended two highly regarded oncologists. I'd gone to see them with my brother who helped me decide who'd would be the better fit for me. We ended up agreeing the best choice would be Professor Gary Richardson OAM, a true leader in his field. And today I'm still absolutely confident he was, and still is, the right choice.

"You've got non-squamous non-small cell lung cancer," he told me.

"Is it serious?"

"It's stage 4A."

That told me that, yes, it was very serious.

"We have some new treatments now that have improved the prognosis." It was hard to focus on his words as *stage 4A* reverberated through my head. "We now use immunotherapy in conjunction with chemotherapy, which has led to significant increases in the chance of remission. But first, we'll need to remove part of the lung where the main tumour is located."

"The mantle radiation that I had when I was twenty... do you think it might have anything to do with it?"

"There's a high probability, yes." After all these years, finally there was a medical professional willing to acknowledge the possible connection between the mantle radiation I'd received when I was so young and the health problems surfacing later in life. This is a consensus that has been confirmed in numerous peer reviewed studies in recent years.

Do I have regrets about the mantle radiation? No, not at all. At the time, it was the cutting-edge treatment. Without receiving it I likely mightn't have survived to do all the things I'd so passionately enjoyed throughout my life. Interestingly, if I were to receive that same diagnosis today, the treatment would be far less invasive with no need to remove the spleen. But there I was, faced with another cutting-edge advance in treatment, another chance at extending my life that wouldn't have been available in the years prior. To put this into perspective, Professor Richardson recently explained to me that when he started in medical school, around forty percent of cancer patients were ultimately cured (cured being a five year period of being cancer-free). Today that figure is around seventy percent. You can't help but wonder what the figure might be in another thirty or forty years.

On top of dealing with my latest diagnosis, it was time to pack up Mum and Ted's possessions and sell their house. It's hard to face such issues while you're still dealing with grief, but it's a reality that only gets more difficult the longer it's put off. Fortunately, I had people who were willing to stand beside me and help out. Gab and Nina were both there to help and, even though I'd only known him for a short time, David also stepped up to the mark, helping with the practical aspects of preparing the house for going on the market. It was something he did with ease, thanks to his experience managing properties.

I've heard so many stories from people about how difficult they've found it going through their parents possessions after their passing. But for me, it was a special and cherished experience. It's a unique and intimate feeling when you open a drawer and discover what your mother had decided to hold on to. Old letters, school reports and birthday cards from grandchildren. There were even special items that'd belonged to my father, like the medal he'd received for his contributions to Israel. With everything I came across, I felt the warmth that flowed from my mother's philosophy on life.

I made sure anything useful found a new home. My mother had loved to knit, and there must have been thirty of her hand knitted wool jumpers. I gave a special one to Nina, which she still wears, and most of the others to the cleaning lady and local op shops. Mum was still giving with a warm hand, even after passing.

The house had to be sold though. I asked Richard, a good friend from school and RMIT days who was now in real estate, to be the selling agent. Richard had known Mum and I'm sure, if it were up to her, she would have chosen him too. He and his husband, Chris, were incredibly helpful. Between David and Richard they pulled together a team of house cleaners, painters, gardeners and maintenance guys (with David helping keep the pool clean while Richard and Chris staged the house for sale... good people and good friends). The Auction was to be held at the end of March.

The Fall

Having recovered from the operation to remove part of my lung, I was relaxing at my home in Caulfield North while I waited to get booked in for my first round of chemo. I'd done some washing earlier in the day and found myself feeling a bit faint. Thinking it might be post op fatigue, I decided it might be best to lie down in the bedroom.

I wasn't too worried about it and opted to lie in bed a bit longer. Then, it started to rain. The washing! ... I still had my washing hanging on a rack outside. I got up, but my knees collapsed under me. I thought, *oh, I must have got up a bit too quickly.* Not thinking too much of it, I got to my feet again and made my way to the lounge room. It was only when I realised how I was clinging to furniture as I went that I noticed how dizzy I was feeling. The rain was getting louder... the washing... I had to get the washing. I stumbled from one piece of supporting furniture to the next. Through the lounge, into the kitchen. Then I fell down the three back steps. The washing... it was there... right in front of me... on the drying rack. Somehow, I managed to get to my feet and collect my precious washing from the rack. Next thing I knew, I was on the ground again, the washing bundled up in my arms. *I can't let the washing get wet.* Yes, that's right, I was lying on the ground, more concerned about my washing than the fact I'd just collapsed again. Summoning all the energy I could muster, I flung my bundle through the open kitchen door, then dragged myself up the stairs after it. As I tried getting up, I fell backwards, hitting my head quite hard.

I don't know how long I'd been lying there when I managed to lift myself a bit, but I realised straight away that my head had been bleeding, a quick look at the pool of blood on the floor confirming my fears.

The washing seemed of little consequence now. It had finally dawned on me that I needed help… I was in trouble… I needed to call my brother, Michael (actually, in hindsight what I needed to do was call an ambulance). I had a new quest. The phone… the one in the lounge room… I needed to reach my phone in the lounge room. By now, even crawling was a major struggle. I pushed one elbow forward, then dragged my body after it. Then rest and repeat. I've no idea how long it took to get from the kitchen floor to the phone, but by the time I called Michael it was after midnight.

"Hello?" came the groggy voice at the other end of the line as he answered.

"Michael?"

"Sandy? Do you know what time it is?"

"I've hurt myself Michael. I need a lift to the hospital. I've hurt my head and I can't get up."

"Okay, I'll be there soon."

"Thank you. I'll just have a lie down in the bed while I wait for you."

Michael arrived fifteen minutes later to find me happily sitting up on the bed feeling a bit brighter. "I'll just grab my handbag," I said as I picked it up and slung it over my shoulder, a big change from the woman who a short while ago had been struggling to crawl. But Michael had just seen the pool of blood on the floor… which then caused the colour to drain out of his face as he was overcome with worry and concern.

We got in the car and, as we drove off, Michael asked, "So, tell me, what happened?"

I felt quite detached as I rattled off the details, Michael looking white as a ghost as he listened. It's interesting how some things stick in your memory from those moments, like passing a large sign promoting Cabrini's emergency department being 'now open' to the public. "Oh, I never noticed that sign before." As I made the comment my voice conveyed the enthusiasm of a young child on a drive through an exotic holiday location. Perhaps Tom's 'Alice in Wonderland' nickname for me from my Bali days was appropriate in this case as well.

We walked in and, as Michael started explaining the situation to the triage nurse, I fainted in my chair. In an instant I was surrounded by medical staff who rushed me through to the emergency ward. Then, the questions started flying.

"I think she's hurt her neck," I heard one them say. My head started to spin as more medical staff appeared around me, taking great care to ensure I was positioned correctly.

I looked across at Michael and said, "I think I'm scared now." By now Michael was so distraught he seemed to have lost the capacity to speak.

Next thing I knew, a doctor had jumped on top of me and was beating my chest, just like you see in the movies. There was no defibrillator, just this guy bashing on my chest while everyone else was calling out, some asking questions, others giving responses.

"I need this... now!"

"Where's that reading I wanted?"

"She's stable!"

All the while my head was spinning and I felt detached as though in a dream.

Once they'd got my heartbeat back under control, I became a bit more lucid.

The doctor who was looking down at me recognised I was coherent enough now for him to fill me in on what was happening. "Your neck, we believe it's fractured. We can't treat that here. You'll have to go to the trauma unit at the Prince Alfred Hospital. We just need to stabilise your heartbeat a bit more first."

I looked across at the distressed look on Michael's face and said, "You might as well go. I'll be right from here."

The disassociation of feeling like I was in a dream continued as the ambulance transported me to Melbourne's main trauma unit, an incredible hive of activity at the frontline of trying to keep people alive. I was placed in a cubicle overnight, connected to a multitude of tubes and told I wasn't to move. Don't move? You'd be amazed just how hard that is as hour after hour ticks by. I used all the mindful breathing and other techniques I'd learned through meditation, but it wasn't easy.

Before long, I was taken into the radiology department for a round of x-rays, then back to the ward where I had to remain dead-still while teams of medical staff swarmed around me. It was really quite intimidating, particularly given that the Alfred is also a teaching hospital. So, the main doctors have an entourage of interns following them as they do their rounds... and I was getting special attention.

I had one doctor explain to me, "Your neck is fractured in three places."

Another one followed up, "There's a complication with your heart. We need to give you a pacemaker. It needs to happen today."

It turns out this is actually a common complication after having the TAVI operation. Did they explain this to me at the time? Perhaps, but I certainly had no recollection of it.

"Can I have it done at Cabrini?" I asked, desperately wanting to return to its familiar and less frantic environment.

"No, Sorry. The operation needs to happen *now*, and your neck complicates things. It'll have to happen here. However, you'll be pleased to know that your cardiologist you've been seeing at Cabrini has organized a specialist to perform the operation."

Knowing this made me feel so much more comfortable. Although I guess you could say it's questionable as to whether the word 'comfortable' is in any way appropriate. The cold, hard reality was that I couldn't move because my neck was fractured in three places. On top of that, I had to have a pacemaker to keep my heart beating!

Could it get any more surreal?

It was a major lesson for me in how the hospital system works. I'd been able to have pretty much every other procedure throughout the years in the comfort of Cabrini under my family's private health cover. It meant the difference between having a private or shared room and being able to choose my own doctor, two things that on their own make such a huge difference, particularly for someone who'd been through the number of procedures I'd had throughout my life. It's left me acutely aware of how fortunate I'd been to be able to maintain my private health cover over the years.

Once the pacemaker was installed and my neck brace was in place, I insisted on being transferred to a private room at Cabrini.

A week later, because I live on my own, I was moved to their rehabilitation unit for the two weeks it would take before my neck had set well enough to go home. Even then, I'd be in the neck brace for another six weeks.

The building was a stunning two storey Victorian structure. I made sure that my room featured some genuine home comforts with my own pillow, sarong, headphones and iPad.

My neck brace was a complex affair that needed to be removed each morning and replaced with a variation that could be worn in the shower. It required two nurses working carefully together to ensure my neck didn't move at all while one brace was replaced with another. This was a process they were keen to teach the other nurses. So they used my changes as a demonstration opportunity. But David just happened to be visiting and couldn't resist the opportunity to have a bit of fun acting as a narrator for the whole demo.

"Welcome to our demonstration of how to change a neck brace." He sounded like the voice of the safety demonstrations you get on aircraft before take-off.

"Am I lying in the correct position?" I asked. "Is my hair straight?"

It was really quite hilarious. We had half a dozen nurses gathered around and they were in fits of laughter.

During the whole time I was there, I had to remain as still as possible and could only sleep on my back. Fortunately, they were giving me a powerful painkiller, *Oxycodone*. This didn't just keep the pain at bay, it also helped relieve the frustration of being immobile for so long. The Netflix series, *Shameless*, helped as well… all one hundred and thirty-four episodes.

It was while I was there that Mum's house went on the market. I picked up *Domain*, the real estate section of the paper to see how its advertising looked. My eye was caught by another property that was going up for auction the following Sunday. *'Two bedroom townhouse with private courtyard in popular Elsternwick'.* Buying a new home hadn't been on my radar at the time, but this was close to where I'd grown up and looked like a perfect fit for me. The sale of Mum's house would easily put me in a position to buy, if it sold quick enough. I needed to have a look, despite the inconvenience of the neck brace.

I called David. "Hey, can you pick me up?"

"Pick you up? I thought you were going to be in there for another couple of weeks."

"I've found a house that I want to look at."

I looked a real sight as I got into David's car to do a drive by, but I was determined. Something in my gut told me this place was special. And it was. I fell in love with it. The only problem was it was going to auction that Sunday and I couldn't see a way that I'd get the finance in place in time to make a bid. Mum's house was going up for auction too, but a week later.

The only hope was that the Elsternwick house would get passed in, that no bidder would reach the reserve price. And that's exactly how it played out.

I just needed Mum's house to sell and I'd be able to make an offer.

My Sanctuary

It was March, 2020 and, just as it had in the rest of the world, COVID 19 had hit Australian shores.

Mum's house went to auction on Saturday, 21st of March. It was an extraordinary experience. I lay on the bed in what had been my room throughout youth, wearing my neck brace as I waited with Michael, Lilli and David while the auction went on. Flashbacks of studying final year high school, and the last time my father popped his head in to say goodnight ran through my head.

Fortunately, the auction was a success.

As soon as the auctioneer called out *sold*, I asked Michael, "Can we go and have a look at the townhouse in Elsternwick?" Two hours later, there was a group of us there meeting the agent. I walked in and said, "It's perfect, I love it."

"But what about the stairs?" asked Michael.

"You can get a lift installed," replied David. I could see it so clearly as the discussion rolled on.

Then, on the following Tuesday, Melbourne went into lockdown. The timing was just amazing. With confirmation of the sale of Mum's house, I was able to make an offer on the townhouse at Elsternwick. After back-and-forth negotiations, the contract was finally signed on the 4th April.

I don't know if I could've done it without David's help. What a kind and generous human being he is, always there doing the things that I would struggle with.

While all this was happening, I was about to start chemo and immunotherapy. And once again David was there, picking me up from my North Caulfield unit and taking me to each appointment. Not only did he pick me up, but on his way, he'd pick up a super-healthy berry smoothie for me to enjoy enroute to the hospital. Each time we'd laugh and share stories on the way.

It wasn't just David though. Gab was there for me too. She'd worked with me for so long helping with the cooking classes that she knew the foods I needed and how to prepare them. Living on my own, this was important to me. Even though cooking and taking care of myself was usually an easy pleasure for me, I simply didn't have the energy to spend time properly preparing food for myself.

Gab made several meals at a time so they could be reheated as needed. But she did more than that. When you're recovering from a round of chemo, you just don't have the energy to deal with housework. I love a clean home. Thanks to Gab's efforts, my unit continued to *feel* like a home.

And that brings me to a point that I'd really like to emphasise as well. Your home and your surroundings are so incredibly important for your wellbeing. It needs to be a place where you feel absolute comfort. The things that you surround yourself with in your home matter. Original artworks, plants that bring life into the home and furniture that suits your needs and taste. I'd been living in the North Caulfield unit for nearly twenty years and had created a space during that time that was a reflection of who I am. It was a space where I felt totally at ease, whether doing a morning meditation or Qi-gong session, cooking a meal, or simply lazing on the couch watching a movie. It was a space where I could feel happy enjoying my own company or entertaining friends.

I had no illusions. No matter how much I'd been looking after myself, my body was about to be hit hard, and getting my new home ready was of paramount importance.

Before you start with chemo, you need to be aware of what lies ahead. You need to be educated about what you're going to be dealing with.

First up I was looking at four rounds of chemo every twenty-one days, with the immunotherapy being delivered at the same time. This was new, cutting-edge treatment and I had trust in my oncologist, a specialist in this medical frontier. Once the twelve weeks of treatment were concluded, it would then be time for a scan to see how my chemical bombardment had affected the cancer and my body.

I'll give you a quick rundown on the treatment in case you're not familiar with the processes when someone's getting chemotherapy.

My Chemo protocol was administered in what is usually referred to as the "Day Treatment" centre in the hospital. At Cabrini this includes twenty-eight chairs in cubicles with screens for privacy, four treatment and recovery bays with beds and two isolation rooms. I opted for the privacy offered by the chairs in the cubicles. Not regular chairs though. These chairs are specifically designed for patients to sit in for long periods while they have a drip in their vein administering the drug they've been scheduled. Each patient's infusion pouch – hanging above them – is connected to a cannula feeding the chemical into their veins, one that will invariably contain something different to the patient next to them. This is therapy that's tailored to each patient from a huge range of drugs on offer.

And that cannula? Well, it's not *always* delivered by cannula. Typically, patients who are facing a full course of chemo will have a 'port' surgically put in their chest. This allows for the intravenous drip to be hooked up directly to the port, negating the need for a cannula to be inserted each time. This is especially important for those who don't have particularly robust veins. This wasn't really an option that appealed to me, and I was glad to have one less scar and no obvious permanent port on my body.

By the time both the chemo and immunotherapy have taken place, you're looking at seven hours or longer in the chair.

Before the first treatment, I had a comprehensive rundown from one of the nurses on what side-effects I might expect. With the chemo these included: shortness of breath, swelling, pain when swallowing, and potential hair loss. The immunotherapy potential could lead to skin rashes and blisters, fatigue, aching muscles, constipation, chemo-belly and more.

I was fortunate in that I could have a separate booth, away from the open room, giving me greater privacy and the opportunity to create a sense of my own space.

Prior to David arriving to take me to the hospital for my first round of treatment, I packed myself a little 'care bag'. In this I included a filtered water bottle (tap water was not a good taste for me), a small container of walnuts, Brazil nuts and fresh dates, my headphones (for listening to relaxing music or podcasts), my iPhone and iPad and my usual favourite large maroon-patterned shawl that I'd bought when I was in India and had taken with me to every hospital stay since. I'd drape it over the vinyl chair each time, removing some of the environment's sterility. It was a familiar comfort that meant a great deal to me (it's a shawl that has stories to tell).

One of the side-effects a lot of people stress about is the potential for hair loss. For some, this can be averted by making use of a 'cooling cap'. If the sight of someone sitting in one of the chairs with the drips running into their arms doesn't freak you out, the sight of them wearing a cooling cap might just do it. It's quite bulky and covers the entire scalp and has a series of big tubes feeding into it. A friend, who'd used one during treatment for breast cancer, filled me in on what it was like. She warned that it would be incredibly cold, and she was right. It's like having ice blocks on your head for several hours. Not a good feeling! But I was determined. I wanted to keep my full head of hair.

Wanting to be discreet about this latest brush with cancer, I'd told only a select few about my treatment. I figured the COVID lockdowns would help in this regard but knew that if my hair started falling out it would be a giveaway of what I was going through.

The first treatment was on the 15th of April, less than two weeks after putting the deposit on what was to become my new home in Elsternwick. I went home that evening feeling a bit of heartburn, but not thinking too much of it. Round one didn't seem to be too bad, or so I thought. The discomfort of the coldcap seemed the worst aspect of it.

The next day I felt dizzy and weak and was quite aware of acid in my stomach. My legs and neck ached and when I looked in the mirror, my tongue seemed to have gone white. By the third day it was getting hard to walk, and by the fourth day my body smelt like chemicals. I showered a few times in the day to feel fresh. Changing sheets and towels helped a bit too, along with having aromatherapy soy candles burning throughout the day.

By the time day five came around I was in the thick of the side-effects. Stomach cramps accompanied by multiple trips to the toilet, where I'd struggle to pass the odd pebble-sized stool. There was also kidney pain. I ended up staying in bed all morning. Eventually I managed to get up and prepare myself a mashed banana, spending ages trying to consume minuscule mouthfuls. All food tasted bitter. And where had my appetite gone? Eventually, I found nutrition-rich homemade smoothies or juice were the best options.

My stomach continued aching from the chemical onslaught I'd endured and there seemed to be no relief. Needing to focus on something else, I turned on the television and started watching the episodes of *Shameless* that I hadn't got to while binge-watching in rehab after my neck fracture. Thankfully there were still plenty of episodes to keep me absorbed.

After a couple of hours though, it became apparent that I really needed to deal with the gut problem. The battle of the bowel was on! I tried sitting in a warm bath for an hour, adding sea salt in the hope this would relieve the discomfort. All this effort led to just a few more pebble poos when I next tried sitting on the toilet, but any relief was a good thing.

I had to get myself together… had to get out of the house! Just getting dressed was a struggle, but I was motivated to move. David kindly picked me up and gave me a lift to check my post office box. Straight after arriving home, I collapsed on the couch, exhausted.

To try and counter the side-effects as best as I could, I was taking vitamin C, D and paracetamol, along with magnesium. I ate some of my homemade Chia Berry jam and drank a glass of water that had some gut relief formula in it.

By this time my toenails and fingertips were getting sensitive as well, a reminder that body focus is real. Even though my tastebuds were dulled and I was not hungry, I did enjoy homemade organic apple compote with some coconut ice cream (this became a soothing treat throughout these treatments) while ensuring I consumed plenty of alkalizing filtered water and coconut water.

The next day I woke up with stomach aches and cramping. I had pain in the lower back and aches around the chest. I spent copious amounts of time sitting on the toilet seeking relief that didn't seem to come easily. This was new to me, as I always had easy bowel movements from the plant-based foods that I loved to eat.

To help with sleep and appetite, I took some medically prescribed THC/CBD oil on the eighth day and slipped into a dream, then woke up to a sunny morning. I managed to sluggishly get some laundry done, watered the garden, then enjoyed a late breakfast, talked to Gab on the phone, then managed to go for a one-and-a-half-kilometre walk, with stops – acutely aware that to get through this, exercise was important.

While resting on my return, I pondered how fortunate it was that the TAVI operation had taken place *before* the tumour on my lung was found. It was hard to imagine coping with going through the impacts of the cancer treatment with my heart in its previously weakened state.

The next morning Gab came over to do some cleaning. Needing to be extremely conscious of being immune-comprised (particularly with the

COVID lockdowns in place) I took the opportunity to go for another one-and-a-half-kilometre walk. It was even more exhausting than the day before.

But there were worse things to deal with than the exhaustion. During this chemical onslaught, bowel movements become a focus... something to celebrate. 'Chemo belly' is more than uncomfortable. The gurgling and bloating in the intestines is very real. I tried slippery elm and magnesium before going to bed and ate fibre-rich foods as much as I could. The battle of the bowel was continuing.

On the eleventh day since the first intense treatment, I was starting to feel a lot better. I was able to get through my morning chores with ease and, for the first time, was able to drive myself to the shops. Still, the busy morning left me feeling tired by the time afternoon came around.

The next day saw me waking from more THC/CBD-oil induced dreams. I was able to walk a whole two kilometres this time and had a wonderful feast in the afternoon.

Then I got hit with another side-effect. My hair had started falling out... ugh! I got in touch with Nina and she washed and styled it for me, but I could see that my hair was getting thinner after finding more loose strands on the pillow. That was after I'd started the day with a nosebleed before heading into the hospital for a blood test.

Getting through this and surviving was going to require my full dedication. My body functions, which were becoming increasingly strange, became more and more a focus.

Something that's crucial when going through chemo is to have support in the form of a therapist.

I'd realised that I needed help with grief a few weeks after Mum had passed. A friend who was a on a similar spiritual wavelength recommended Claudia who had trained as a Gestalt, psychodynamic and family therapist.

SCRAMBLED TURMERIC TOFU

4-6 Serves. Keeps for 3 days in fridge

Ingredients:

- 4 Shiitake mushrooms, dried or fresh
- 250 g Tofu
- ½ tsp Turmeric, ground
- 1 tbsp Tamari OR 2 tbsp white miso paste (Spiral Foods Shiro – a sweeter choice for this recipe)
- 1/2 cup Shiitake soaking water or water, as required
- 1 tbsp Toasted sesame oil
- ½ cup Fennel, diced
- 1 tbsp Furikake Traditional Japanese seasoning (Spiral Foods)
- 1 small Carrot, shredded
- ½ cup Parsley, chopped

Method:

- If using dried shiitake: Soak shiitake mushrooms for at least
- 30 minutes in 5 cups warm water from the kettle or for even better flavour, soak overnight. Strain soaking water and keep. Discard stems and slice shiitake caps.
- If using fresh shiitake, slice.
- Mash tofu, turmeric, tamari or miso paste together.
- Add shiitake soaking water or water as needed to blend.
- Heat oil in a small wok and add fennel. Saute.
- If using fresh mushrooms, add and sauté.
- Add tofu puree and seasoning.
- If using dried shiitake, then add here. Add a little more liquid for a smoother texture.
- Add shredded carrots and chopped parsley.
- Cook uncovered for 10 minutes, stirring occasionally.
- Serve on gluten free bread or I also wrap it in an iceberg lettuce leaf or nori sheet.

Claudia integrates this training in a cognitive and spiritual approach using self-enquiry, guided imagery, mindfulness and Buddhist practices. She'd been wonderful helping me deal with the grief of losing Mum, and became critical in helping deal with the chemo and COVID.

Having the right therapist to help you through the emotional roller coaster makes an incredible difference – and it's something I highly recommend.

There were other things I was doing for my mental and spiritual wellbeing. I've mentioned my practice of doing meditation and Qi-gong in the mornings. The importance of these two spiritual practices for me can't ever be underestimated. Meditation helps clear the mind and bring you back to the moment. Qi-gong is like a moving meditation that brings tranquillity to the mind and energy to the body. It lowers stress and anxiety and helps with balance and flexibility. Just seven minutes each morning of Qi-gong is an indispensable part of my morning routine. I work on an online 30-day program that's been put together by Lee Holden. For a one-off payment I have ongoing access. With meditation, there are myriad guided meditations available online, or you may prefer to do a course somewhere near you. There's a reason meditation has been widely practised around the world for so many years. It really makes a difference to your peace of mind. My choice is the free forty days Mindfulness Daily with Tara Brach and Jack Kornfield via the Radical Compassion Institute. It's worth checking out.

Monday, May 4th, the day of my second round of chemo, started with a nosebleed, accepted and managed – and a healthy bowel movement, yay!

I packed my care bag and David picked me up. His big grin as he handed me my super smoothie was wonderful medicine in itself. I had an early meeting with my oncologist before the scheduled start of the day's chemo session.

The next day I woke to more hair on my pillow. The cooling cap obviously wasn't going to work for me. I called my hairdresser, and friend, Peter.

MY ENERGISING ALKALIZING PROTEIN SMOOTHIE

Use Blender.

Ingredients:

- 10 blueberries or raspberries
- 1 small banana
- ½ cup papaya or pear or apple
- 2 cup alkaline filtered water or almond milk (I make this recipe in *My Wholefood Community Cookbook*)
- 1 TBS Super green powder eg. Vital Greens
- 1 TBS organic brown rice protein powder

MY RAW LIVE FOOD GREEN ENERGISING SMOOTHIE

Use Blender.

Ingredients:

- 2 stalks celery
- ½ cup cucumber
- 1 cup kale
- 1 cup baby spinach leaves
- ½ lemon or lime, peeled
- 1 tsp ginger
- Sprig parsley and/ or fresh mint
- 1 golden delicious (sweet) apple
- To blend add about 2 cups Alkalized filtered water as desired.

"Hello, Peter?"

"Sandy? Hey how are you?"

"To be honest, I've been better."

I opened up to Peter and explained the situation to him. I told him that I wanted to keep it confidential, so he agreed to come over and shave away what remained of my hair. It was a difficult decision, but I just couldn't go through having it slowly falling out, waking up each morning to discover more hair on the pillow and an ever-patchier scalp. It was actually much easier to look in the mirror and see my clean scalp. I would recommend the same to anyone who's going through this. Once it's obvious your hair is going to fall out, you might as well take that big step. A wig looks far better than hair that's falling out in big clumps.

Michael came over later that day with some of his delicious apple compote (my favourite comfort food) and commented positively on my new bald look.

The next morning it felt so weird to shower for the first time with no hair. The same side-effects as I'd experienced from the first round were there, the single pebble bowel movements and so forth. But this time I also felt a burning sensation behind my breastbone and my belly felt hard and swollen.

The ensuing days became a bit of a blur; I was feeling red-faced and rundown, largely moving from bed to couch to bed. I had to more or less force-feed myself, but remained conscious of the importance of keeping up nutrition. Gab had prepared some easy-to-eat favourites, so when I went to look in my fridge there was a choice. Being organised gave me focus and strength. Projects have always been my thing, and I highly recommend that if you are going through this, then find something: journalling, meditation, keeping your home in order, watering indoor plants, drawing, puzzles, anything creative and satisfying. Doing it as best as you can, under these extreme circumstances, becomes an important ingredient in a *recipe for living* during cancer treatment.

A few days after the chemo Lilli was kind enough to pick me up to go wig shopping. In the end we found something that wasn't too far different from how my hair had been before, saving me from the need to have a beanie pulled down over my ears every time I left the house.

> **MY FAVOURITE DRINKS**
>
> - Lots of water. I prefer to use filtered alkalized water. As my tastebuds were effected, I found this chemical free water was easier to taste and drink.
> - Dandelion tea
> - Mint tea- used homegrown fresh mint leaves.
> - Hibiscus tea which is great cold too.
> - Kukicha twig tea
> - Matcha Green Tea
> - Hot water with a little grape juice or lemon juice with mint leaves.
> - Homemade green smoothies and berry smoothies.
> - Organic pear juice

By the end of the week my oesophagus felt like it was burning, and I was waking up with a bloody nose again. *What's with all these side-effects?* I kept saying to myself, *this too shall pass, this too shall pass.*

David turned up in the morning to take me over to Mum's house at Pleasant Road. It was another opportunity to relive many wonderful moments shared together, and a potent reminder of how lucky I'd been to have such a wonderful relationship, not just with Mum and Dad, but with Omi and, after Dad's passing, with Ted. Once David and I got there, we and saw that the swimming pool had a lot of leaves and dead insects in it. So what did David do? He became the pool cleaner. He made me laugh as he was skimming the debris out of the pool.

I took the opportunity to go for a walk with him later in the afternoon. A day that had started with pain and a bleeding nose had ended quite enjoyably.

In mid-May 2020, Melbourne came out of lockdown.

Mum's house still hadn't settled but almost everything was out. Then a week later, on the 20th of May, contracts for my new home in Elsternwick exchanged. Walking through the pre-purchase inspection was the most amazing feeling. Despite everything, the TAVI, the broken neck, the pacemaker, the lung cancer, the chemo, and my heartache over losing Mum, I'd managed to land the home that I could see myself settling into as my perfect space, my zen palace as I would come to call it.

A few days later I had another appointment with Claudia (once I'd dealt with the morning nosebleed). We discussed a lot that day, including the potential for enhanced primary care. Later in the day, I felt inspired to put a few thoughts down on paper.

More than my body
More than my illness
Surrender to what is
Surrender to trust
This is what my journey dished out to me

Letting go
Inhale, compassion, love
Breathe out - let it go,
Exhale, grief
I've done everything I could
Processing healing

I started to think of each moment, each day as an adventure. Not all adventures are good, but hey, it is still my life.

POLENTA

During chemo or just when I feel like eating softer foods, polenta is my go-to.

Ingredients:

- Polenta (cornmeal) — 1 cup
- Water — 3 cups
- Sea salt — ½ tsp.
- Dried herbs (eg oregano, basil) — to taste
- Extra virgin olive oil — to oil baking dish

Method:

- Pour water into a heavy based saucepan.
- Slowly add sea salt and polenta, stirring with a whisk to prevent lumping.
- Bring to boil over medium flame, stirring continually, until thickened. Add a little more water (about ½ cup) if needed. Add dried herbs as desired. Make sure to mix well until mixture is still and starts to pull away from the side as you stir. This takes about 5-10 minutes.
- Place mixture into oiled heatproof glass baking dish, spread with spatula and place in preheated oven at 150'C for 10 minutes.
- Remove from oven and cool.
- Cut desired amount for snack or meal into about 5cm squares or triangle and serve with green miso pesto or tahini miso sauce
- The remainder will keep in the fridge for 3 days.
- To serve again, cut into desired shape and pan fry in a little EV Olive Oil for a few minutes on each side.
- Serve with miso tahini sauce or green miso pesto.

(for variation I use besan (chickpea) flour instead of polenta. This recipe in My Wholefood Community Cookbook)

A day later it was time for round three. David picked me up, wearing a big grin as usual as he handed me my healthy super smoothie, and off we went.

What was happening in my body? In addition to the side-effects I'd experienced before starting to lose the taste sensation in my tongue, which had become quite dry, my hands and feet had started tingling. It would only take another day or so before the tingling became peripheral neuropathy. Have you ever tried tying a shoelace when you've lost feeling in your fingers? Or how about balancing when you've got no feeling in your toes or feet? It added yet another layer to what I was dealing with (at least I was having some decent bowel movements though).

Another side-effect you'll often hear people talk about is chemo-brain... a general fuzziness where thinking becomes difficult, and the memory doesn't function well. It's almost as though the workable parts of the brain become smaller and less capable.

In a cruel irony, I was now able to eat small amounts quite easily, but had lost all sense of taste.

I kept daily notes on my progress: what I'd eaten, how much sleep, bowel movements and the side-effects I was encountering.

Meanwhile, I had things to do. There were still the last bits and pieces to get out of the house at Pleasant Road. The white goods were donated to charity and then the gas, power and water had to be switched off. When David and I went over to take the bins out one last time, it felt like a symbolic end to that chapter of my life.

The 15th of June came around and it was time for treatment four. I packed my care bag and David picked me up, presenting me yet again with that big reassuring smile and the super smoothie. This was my last scheduled full round of treatment. The promise was that it would get easier from here. I went first to my appointment with Prof Richardson. "Well

Sandra," he said, "your blood is looking good. The immune markers, thyroid, iron, cortisol... they're all where we want them to be."

It was reassuring to know that, despite how I felt, the chemo/immuno was doing its job. I'm quite sure that it was due in no small part to the nutritional supplements, meditation, Qi-gong, acupuncture, and high quality nutritious food and drinks, albeit in small amounts that I'd taken, to help deal with the onslaught of the potent drug cocktail (not directly around the chemo/immune time but a few days after and before). It's not that I was trying to *counter* it with the vitamins, minerals and naturopathic supplements recommended for oncology patients... more that I was doing what I could to work *with* the treatment.

On June 18th the final inspection before settlement at Pleasant Road took place. The process had dragged on, but it was finally complete.

Meanwhile, the pain was getting so bad that I had to take pain meds. Even swallowing was difficult. And the constipation was like nothing I'd experienced before. I tried taking a bath in Epsom salts in the hope it would loosen the bowel. But still the best I could manage was a few small pebbles that were incredibly painful to pass. To make things worse, I was starting to have issues with my vision as well.

A few days later the constipation was easing, but bowel movements were still painful. I was more fatigued than ever, and the peripheral neuropathy was making it increasingly difficult to write notes in my journal.

Then, as if I didn't have enough to worry about, I had an infection on my upper leg from an ingrown hair. As if I wasn't in enough pain already! That's part of the problem when you're going through chemo though – the immune system is copping such a hit that infections can take hold easily.

On July 6th I was scheduled for the next round of chemo/immuno... and grateful for the fact that this round was supposedly going to be easier. But the best news came when I saw Prof Richardson and got the result of the latest CT scan.

"You're in remission," he said. "There's no sign of any cancer cells."

I'd killed off those shitty cancer cells! My body working with the health system... what a team!

The immunotherapy still had side-effects: dry mouth, taste buds still not great, appetite low and fatigue, among others. But the relief at knowing I was in remission made it so much easier to deal with. And best of all, as I was in remission, I could *stop* chemo and immunotherapy. Hallelujah!

Throughout the months of treatment, I'd spent many hours looking at photos of my soon-to-be home in Elsternwick. I created a scrap book and bought house and garden magazines. Soon the scrap book was filled with cut outs and inspirations of what I wanted for my new home.

I was starting to feel a bit better when David and I went out to IKEA and Harvey Norman looking for some of the new furniture I'd need. I was particularly keen to get a nice entertainment unit to house a large television and my sound system. We found the perfect unit that was just the right size (David had a measuring tape in his pocket to make sure that it would fit).

At this time, I had made an appointment with a highly recommended integrative medical doctor at the National Institute of Integrative Medicine. I wanted to know whether it would be worth having intravenous vitamins and minerals to help my body rebuild after dealing with the chemo, a process I started the following week.

Then, once again, Melbourne went into lockdown. Courtesy of my treatment, I was already keeping my distance from other people. Oh, what a year... both internally and externally! Yet somehow, I managed to maintain a sense of acceptance.

On Thursday, 28th July, David accompanied me to my new townhouse for an inspection. The cleaners hadn't been through yet, but I had that incredible excitement when you know a place is about to become officially yours. With the advice and help of Michael, I organised the funds, ready to transfer them so settlement could take place. But then there were issues. The seller didn't have the paperwork fully in place. It ended up delayed until the following afternoon. At 2pm, the townhouse in Elsternwick was officially mine!

With David's help, I could then get the tradies in to do what was needed before being able to move in. Despite lockdown, the tradies were still able to get on with their work as no one was living there (albeit with only one of them there at a time).

Having climbed the seventeen stairs to the upper level during the inspection, I was grateful for having made the decision to install an elevator that would go from the living room straight to my bedroom. There were new carpets that had to be laid (courtesy of my friend, Tony), updated electrics and plumbing to go in, and painting to be done. The courtyard and garden also required attention. The courtyard had been one of the big attractions when I first looked at the place. The main area downstairs is open-plan living, dining and kitchen, all with a wall of plate glass looking onto the courtyard. I always loved surrounding myself with plants, and could now envision this becoming my perfect little north-facing courtyard garden oasis – one that could be seen from every window. A few simple pieces of landscaping would lay the groundwork to build on. A Bali day bed advertised online reminded me of one I had while living in Bali. It would go well with the Balinese pots I'd kept from my old import business.

By mid-August my hair had started to grow back, but not on my legs or arms. What was weird though, was that before chemo, I had only a few grey hairs. Now it was growing back fully grey! I resolved to tell people I'd simply stopped colouring my greys away and decided to go short grey hair during COVID.

My legs still ached, my hands and my feet were still tingling, I was still getting constipated, and I was still fatigued. However, I was eating better and able to do more before the fatigue would set in.

In the end, it took a few months to get my new home ready for moving in. Meanwhile I had asked my friend Richard, the real estate agent who'd helped sell mum's house, to recommend a managing agent for renting out my unit.

Then, the big day came when the removalist truck arrived at my home of twenty years in North Caulfield, loading up my possessions to transport them to my new home.

As I opened the front door of my next home, the sunlight flooded in through the floor to ceiling windows – and I was brought to tears when I noticed the light was casting a rainbow onto the floor.

It was an immense joy being able to guide the removalists as they placed the furniture. I unpacked the boxes over the ensuing days, with much appreciated help from Gab. My new townhouse went through a magical transformation into a home filled with art, furniture, books and the odd piece of memorabilia that spoke to who I am and the life that I'd lived so far.

In the centre of the main room downstairs, I'd placed the teak dining table and chairs that Michael had handmade for my parents over forty years earlier, still in as-new condition and looking just as stylish as the day he'd finished creating it. The history of my family that this table has borne witness to makes it by far my most prized piece of furniture.

Thanks to David's suggestion and follow-through with advice, the elevator was without doubt one of the best decisions I'd made… and great for moving my clothes and possessions to the upstairs bedrooms. The new kitchen was adequate for my needs, but too small for me to consider running cooking classes. That was fine with me. I'd been running cooking classes for over thirty-five years. Now, I had a cookbook out there, along with dozens of online cooking videos. My primary job now was to look after this body that had worked with my doctors to beat cancer yet again.

What a year it had been! I may have gone into it a brunette and come out the other end with a full head of grey hair, but I was alive and filled with joy.

Without the *recipes for living* I'd developed over the years, both nutritionally and spiritually, I don't see how I could've processed and got through it all with equanimity.

Something to Write About

It's the word every cancer patient wants to hear when they go into an appointment with their oncologist—remission.

And when Professor Richardson had told me in my previous appointment that there were no signs of cancer cells, that I was in remission, it was a testament to so many things:

- Professor Richardson's treatment regime.
- A sound understanding of nutrition and supplements.
- Spiritual practices.
- Exercise regime.
- Chinese herbalist regime.
- My underlying health.
- The love and support of those who helped me.

While I certainly put Professor Richardson's treatment at the top of the list, I believe it was a combination of all those approaches combined, the holistic approach, that ultimately led to my ending up in remission.

It was 2022 and I was looking forward to pushing forward and beginning new life chapters after the COVID lockdowns were behind us.

I'd had thoughts about writing a memoir for quite some time. And now, having confirmation that I was in remission, it seemed like I had a good story to tell. The 2022 Byron Writers' Festival was approaching so, hoping it might energise me, I asked Fay if I could stay with her again.

One of the speakers on the Friday was Debbie Lee, who at the time had a senior position with global publisher, IngramSpark, at their Australian operation, based in Melbourne. She was going to be speaking about self-publishing, which made her session a must to attend. Having been through the process of self-publishing with my cookbook, I was aware that I'd more than likely need the self-publishing pathway again. So, I wanted to do as much research as I could.

I attended Debbie's session and was impressed by her depth of knowledge. I made a point of catching up with her after the session had finished. You know those people who are so easy to talk to you feel an instant rapport, like you've known them for ages? Meeting Debbie was very much like that. It took no time at all to realise that we had a few things in common: living in Melbourne and being Jewish topping the list. Not only that, but it turned out she was someone who also got involved in her community.

"Wow, so you've already done a cookbook?" asked Debbie.

"Yes, and I want to write my memoir. I really want to share my story. I know it can help others who are going through what I've been through."

"Well, it seems like you've got one hell of a story to tell."

"Yes, but I need help. I had a design company helping me out with the cookbook, but this is different."

"You need to meet my friend, Graham. He's got an author services company. He's really good. We did a joint workshop yesterday on self-publishing that was fully booked out."

We talked some more and then this middle-aged smiling guy with a cap wandered out of the bookshop. Debbie ran up to grab hold of him. "I've just been talking to someone I want you to meet. You'll love her."

A moment later, Debbie was introducing us. It was another one of those cases of instant rapport. Graham told me about the writers' groups he facilitated, about the vegan cookbook he'd photographed and produced with one of his friends, and about the broad range of books that his recently formed business was producing.

I had no doubt that this was one of those moments when the universe brings people together. "I want you to be my writing mentor," I said to him.

"I don't know if I'm qualified for that, but I can certainly introduce you to someone who is," he replied.

"I've just spent the last five minutes talking to you and I know that you're the right person. I need you to help me with this."

"Okay," he said, "how about if we do a few Zoom sessions together. If you feel good about where it's heading, then we'll go ahead with it."

Little did I know that these two people I'd just met were also destined to become my close friends.

Our first Zoom session took place a few weeks later. I had three short sections I'd written up and we spoke about voice and structure, exploring what the book should open with. Graham was quite strong on the idea that it should begin with the discovery of the lump on my neck. "You need to throw the reader into the heart of the action. Then you've got them," he said. "If you start from the very beginning, with family introductions and the like, you risk losing them before the real story even starts." What he had to say made sense. And, as you can see, that suggestion from the very first Zoom session stuck.

He spoke about things like using dialogue to drive the story wherever practical. "It doesn't matter if the conversations aren't word-for-word verbatim of what was actually said at the time; the important thing is that the general gist of what's being said is accurate. By using dialogue, you put the reader in the moment."

Graham went through some of the work I'd already produced for the memoir and set about restructuring the sentences and developing a more consistent voice.

I knew intrinsically his involvement was going to make a crucial difference. I placed trust in my instincts once more and certainly have no regrets.

It's Back

It would be so easy to slip into complacency when you've been told you're in remission.

After all I'd been through, you'd think I would've known better, especially considering how the chemo/immunotherapy had led to some profound changes for me. Every time I looked in the mirror, the mop of grey hair framing my face was a reminder.

There's a regime of regular tests you need to follow up with. So, letting you know it's 'all clear' is really just 'all clear at this moment... as far as we can tell'.

I'd been chemical free for six months... six months spent getting my garden established and enjoying my new home. Then, toward the end of November 2022, I paid a visit to Canberra. The Hemp, Health and Innovation Expo was on, and while I was in town I decided to check out what was on display at the National Gallery and to pay Parliament House a visit.

As the day wore on, I found myself continually having to stop for a rest. Breathing while I walked became a struggle. After resting, I'd walk twenty metres and have to stop again.

Something was wrong.

My body was struggling.

As soon as I'd returned to Melbourne I got on the phone and made an appointment with my respiratory specialist. Fluid was accumulating in the lining of the lung. To drain it out, I'd need a pleural infusion.

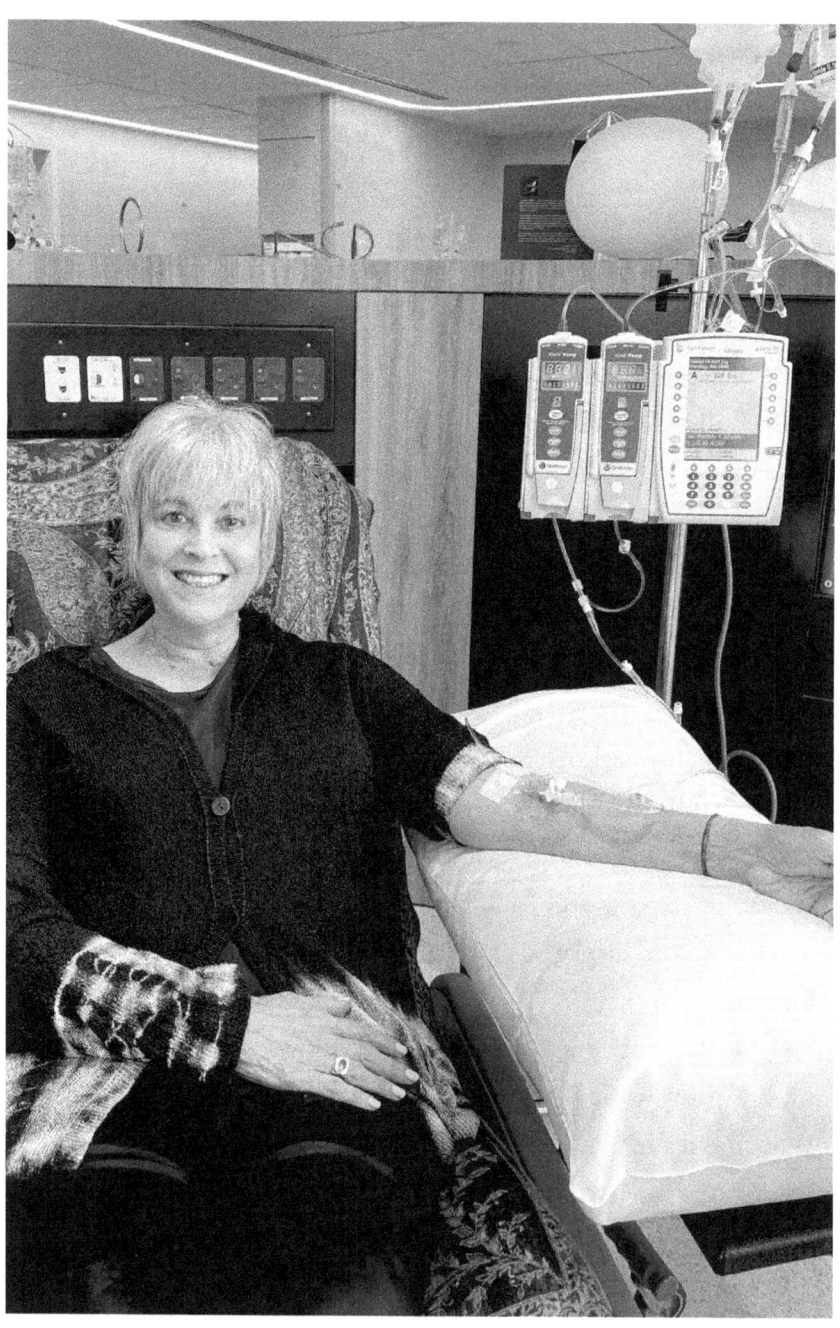

It helps to keep smiling

During this process I leaned forward while the doctor applied a local anaesthetic to my back, just above my right rib cage. Then, via a small incision, he inserted a tube through a space in between the ribs in my back. I watched as the pinkish fluid drained away and accumulated in a bottle at the end of the tube. It took forty-five minutes, all while I sat leaning forward onto a soft pillow. That one and a half litres of fluid was then sent to the pathology lab.

Once the procedure was over, they allowed me to rest for half an hour.

The doctors recommended someone be with me for the next twenty-four hours. So, Gab picked me up and kindly stayed with me overnight, displaying again what a blessing she is in my life.

I knew what the pathology lab was going to find. I could feel it, like I'd developed another sense.

When the tests came back they revealed that my worst fears were well founded.

The 'Big C' was back!

It was in the lining of my lungs.

My new cancer treatments, every four weeks this time, would once again require a combination of chemo and immunotherapy. But there was worse news in what my oncologist had to say.

"I'm sorry to say this, but you'll be on chemo and immunotherapy for the rest of your life."

What the…? Surely not!

At least they weren't setting out to place a limitation on how long they thought that life might be. To be quite honest, I really don't think it helps when patients are given some sort of estimate on their potential longevity.

And I was determined to head into my treatment with the most positive frame of mind I could muster. Once again, I chose to only tell a select few what was happening.

At least this time I felt better prepared. If my immune system was going to cop a hiding every few weeks, I was going to do what I could to help it, and the rest of my body, be as well-equipped as possible to deal with it. Self-care was my priority. I resolved that I would take some degree of pleasure in using my years of accumulated knowledge to take care of myself in the best way possible.

And I wasn't going to be content just throwing the chemo at it either. I contacted my traditional Chinese medical practitioner and had a regime prepared by him as well that combined acupuncture and Chinese herbs. I'd been seeing Professor Jerry Zeng for twenty years and had recently found Ehud Tal, a doctor of traditional Chinese medicine, herbal medicine, acupuncture and physical therapy

The treatment at the hospital was always going to be on a Monday. So, I decided that in the preceding week, I'd make a trip to Melbourne's National Institute of Integrative Medicine (NIIM) to have an infusion of vitamins and other supplements to make sure my body was ready for the coming chemical onslaught. This included vitamin C, B dose forte, B12, zinc and magnesium.

I contacted my exercise physiologist, Ryan Free, a specialist in exercises for people whose immune systems are going through challenges like cancer and the side-effects of chemo. Chemo leaves you feeling incredibly tired and listless. It's crucial to keep exercising. But knowing what level is appropriate for the phase of treatment you're going through requires that specialist knowledge.

Was it as though I was preparing to go in to battle against the cancer?

No, certainly not. But by this stage I'd become acutely aware that you don't fight cancer. Instead, you accept that the cancer is there and work with your body to make it a place where the cancer is unable to thrive. It's a process you need to approach with a positive frame of mind and an array of tools to support the treatment. Hence the importance of approaching it from a spiritual perspective as well.

Right next to where I do my morning Qi-gong is a small table that hosts one of my most cherished books. It was given to me by a wise and dear friend, David Bardas (a different David to the one I met at Gwinganna), who has sadly passed on since then. Titled *Buddhist Offerings 365 days*, the book contains three-hundred and sixty-five pages, each with a photograph and a single line of Buddhist wisdom.

The fact that I read this daily, do my Qi-gong and my meditation while looking out onto my garden is an important component in my daily routine… a component that became more essential than ever as I prepared to start my treatments. And, regarding the garden, you don't need a big garden for it to bring magic into your life. My courtyard isn't much more than three metres by fifteen metres, and more than half of it is paved. But it takes me to another place. Its lush plants and ornaments leave me with the feeling that I could just as likely be in Bali as in Melbourne. Even if you have only enough room for a few pot plants, they'll still make a huge difference to your state of mind and general wellbeing.

In fact, the whole of the space you live in is important. While going through treatment, your home becomes a bigger part of your life than at other times and it's important to feel as comfortable as you can. As I said before, my home is a museum of my life with artefacts that all have a story to tell.

I've also been incredibly fortunate to have had Gab come into my life all those years ago… one of the most important friendships I've been blessed with. If, like me, you don't have a life partner, it makes a big impact on how you handle your treatments if you have someone who can be there to help with daily needs like housework and cooking. You only need one person with a big heart to help.

Part of the routine I'd adopted in my previous rounds of cancer treatment was that, in the week leading up to treatment day, I'd ensure the sheets, towels and house were clean and that the fridge contained a selection of snacks, soups, juices and whatever other health supportive snacks and treats might help (a favourite of mine is organic coconut ice cream). One thing I can assure you of is that you don't feel like doing a load of washing in the days following each session. And, to be able to deal with the loss of appetite, it's a big relief to be able to open your fridge and find supportive, nutritional foods already there. You're certainly not likely to feel like cooking when your taste buds are changing and you lose your sense of smell.

For me, order helps both my mind and emotional wellbeing... and visual aesthetics are also important to me. As such, I knew that caring for my pot plants, both in and outdoor, would give me pleasure in the weeks after treatment when I would mostly be unable to leave the house and would need to rest a great deal of the time.

As I prepared for that treatment, most days began with me waking up having difficulty breathing, punctuated by moments walking about where I needed to catch my breath. I'd need to sit and do some deep breathing (meditation practices help with techniques). My lungs became so surrounded with fluid that my belly became swollen.

To deal with it, I went in for another pleural effusion.

Then, the day of the first round of cancer treatment approached.

This would be my first time at Cabrini Brighton, a newly-built large, special purpose room in the hospital just for oncology patients, As it turned out, I was the first one to walk into the day treatment centre that early morning on the 21st of December, 2022. I settled in with my usual comfort pack. It was not as private as it had been in Cabrini Malvern where I was I able to have my own cubicle. I watched on as the other twenty chairs filled over the following few hours... twenty people with twenty different stories. Some had visitors who seemed focused on talking about their own issues. I observed (but largely switched off) as I set my mind to nourishing my inner world. I just wanted peace and quiet and, ironically, this was in a way provided by listening to music on my Bose headphones which drowned out all the noise of the room.

As my chemical cocktail flowed from its little bag, down through the translucent plastic tube and into the cannular feeding my vein, I contemplated how it felt like a fascinating experiment involving my body, learning through direct experience about what my body can do, what it can absorb while continuing to thrive despite the assault from the drugs treating the cancer in the lining of my lungs.

I went home in the afternoon, already wiped out with the physical reality of the chemicals in my body and in emotional shock. I was in this again!

I tried to cry, thinking it may be cathartic, but I just couldn't. I was in a daze, processing what was happening.

Once home, I could wander around and lie down on either of my two couches or my bed. For a scenery change I could use the bed in the guestroom as well.

I woke the next morning conscious that the taste in my mouth was the taste of chemicals, all of it courtesy of the cancer (I found sipping on organic peppermint tea helps and the *Nutribiotic Mouthwash*, formulated with grapefruit seed extract, aloe vera, and zinc is a big help too).

After six hours of drug-assisted sleep. I was wide awake. I chose Temazepam that night instead of Melatonin. I never would have imagined in my youth that I'd one day be weighing up the pros and cons of different sleeping tablets. Melatonin was usually my first choice. It's a natural compound that supports a hormone made in the body that regulates the sleep-wake cycles. However, due to the onslaught of chemotherapy and immunotherapy chemicals, along with the corticosteroid medications, I needed something stronger like Temazepam.

Dexamethasone, a strong corticosteroid, was one of the support medications I was having to take which I'd started the day before treatment. Two per day starting a day before infusion, then two on the day and two the day after. The steroids created a sense of urgency, compelling me to get up to get going, with flashes of high energy from the moment I woke up. It was also a mood lifter, but after a few days I wanted to be off them. They screwed around with my gut and made my bowels congested.

When I woke up the next day and looked out my bedroom window at the falling rain, I smiled at how gorgeous it looked splashing on the window pane.

Get up Sandy!

The corticosteroids were pumping and a host of morning rituals awaited. I made my way downstairs, flipped the page on my book filled with pieces of Buddhist wisdom. The day's quote was from Jack Kornfield *'Everything that appears is singing one song, which is the song of emptiness and fullness. We experience the world of phenomena and consciousness, of light and dark, playing themselves out in a dance without separation.'* It resonated, leaving me sitting with the words for several minutes.

It was a good time to get out of my head and into my body. I did my seven-minute Qi-gong exercise followed by a brief meditation.

Such a beautiful way to start the day, energising my body and supporting mind and spirit... all in less than thirty minutes. Then it was onto the other morning rituals, starting with my super-charging liquid cocktail of supplements.

Like before, I had medications that needed to be taken with food and I was naturally aware that this should include a little fibre and a bit of a protein boost. So, I forced myself to eat a toasted slice of Healthy Bake Organic Hemp bread or Naturis Brown Rice Bread, topped with almond butter and my home made chia berry jam.

I'd started to make chai every morning by this stage to satisfy the need for flavours that I could still taste while taking such a broad array of chemicals. This felt particularly important as I thought back to my experience in 2020 where my sense of taste all but vanished three weeks after chemo started. I wanted to savour flavours as much as I could in the interim.

I sat with my cup of chai tea and just watched the rain falling in my courtyard garden. It was a few days before Christmas... summertime in Melbourne. And summer that year had seemed to be all about unpredictable weather patterns. I wasn't bothered by it as I sat in my cosy retreat, surrounded by comforts and remedies.

I've never liked the idea of taking my iPhone into the toilet, particularly as usually my bowel movements typically just flow from me as I relax and let go. But the chemicals had put a stop to my flow—as I knew they would. Knowing I'd need sit for much longer, I decided that, under the circumstances, it would be the appropriate place to write some notes on my phone's *Day One* journal app. I documented my emotional, mental and physical state with the hope I'd be able to share those words with others. It may amuse you to know that the notes for the words on this very page were written while sitting on my toilet.

Past experience had taught me bowel movements would be a major focus throughout treatment. How you have to deal with it requires a range of many things... perhaps Coloxyl, perhaps Nutrition Care Gut Relief, perhaps a home made berry smoothie with extra psyllium, perhaps it's simply more water?

This was set to become a personal mission for me.

And on that morning my bowel was in protracted protest. I had little choice but to patiently wait on my 'throne' and write more notes.

I sat there and wrote about how much I enjoyed the recipes I'd prepared beforehand, like my chia jam mixed into coconut yogurt, especially in the days after treatment. Having a non-dairy berry smoothie or fresh juice (I loved celery, apple and cucumber with a bit of mint prepared in my cold pressed juicer) is a staple for me. My burning mouth appreciated the taste and texture.

I stared out the window again as the rain played with the lime-green leaves of the robinia tree.

Day turned to night, and I watched some television then eased myself into another six hours sleep with relative calm and ease.

My eyes opened on the next day. *Another day in paradise* I thought as I slowly readied myself for the day's activities... thinking ahead of the morning rituals: gut drink, medications and nutritional supplements, Qi-gong, meditation, walk in the garden.

Somehow, I got myself to transition from thinking about those things to doing them. Then it was time to make a list for the day's upcoming shopping trip with Gab, as well as preparing for a family gathering at a local cafe for my great niece Lyla's thirteenth birthday.

When Michael stopped by to pick me up for the party, I couldn't help but think about how much I treasured our moments in time spent together.

Although tired, I had to rise to the occasion. Rallying my energy reserves. I smiled, chatted and ultimately achieved my aim, managing to take my very essence with me into the cafe that played host to Lyla's birthday celebrations.

The day's activities continued after the party, the gaps between them filled with deep breaths and sighs... and the regular need to sit down. I felt present and in the moment, despite my body having been flooded with chemicals designed to kill the cancer cells... along with the other chemicals designed to support my immune system. I could feel them doing their thing. I was certain of that, especially in my confused and stubbornly stuck gut. While there were a host of remedies I could use for that particular issue, I felt it best to be patient as I waited for the measures I'd already taken to work.

Gab picked me up and we drove around my various required shopping stops: Sunnybrook Health, Impulse Flowers, Malvern Post Office (to pick up my mail) and the Blue Fin for some brown rice vegetarian nori rolls.

We got home with time to spare before my gardener, Lachlan, arrived to sand and weatherproof my outdoor seating, preparation for me to sit outside under the robinia tree on those warm summer days. While my treatment

HOMEMADE BERRY CHIA JAM

This is a high fibre tasty sweet treat.

Ingredients:
- Organic frozen berries 2 cups
- Organic chia seeds 4 tbs
- Organic liquid sweetener 3 tbs either maple or rice syrup
- Water ¼ cup
- Organic vanilla extract 2 tsp
- Sterilised glass jars

Method:
- In order to sterilise jars, they need to be submerged in (covered by) boiling water for 10 minutes.
- Place frozen berries in a saucepan with ¼ cup water. Melt over a low heat, stirring and gently pressing berries to a chunky puree consistency.
- While berries are softening add in chia seeds, vanilla and 3 TBS of your desired liquid sweetener and stir to combine. Add extra sweetener if required.
- Remove from heat and allow to cool in saucepan for about 10 minutes.
- Transfer to a clean, sterile jars and refrigerate until cooled and set. The jam will thicken as it cools.
- Keeps well for two weeks.

If you don't want any sugar, then you can sweeten the jam with stevia instead.

meant I needed to be vigilant about avoiding too much sun, I still loved being outdoors just as much as ever before.

It was amazing how much I could still do the day after treatment, I recommend having a 'to do' list that can get you going rather than feeling bad about yourself.

As the days continued to tick over, I found myself remembering wise words that my mother had shared with me in in past times. I used to write down her pearls of wisdom on Post-it notes, many of which I still have in a box on my desk.

- *No disappointment... things don't have to be 'wrong'.*
- *Frustration does not make you happy*
- *You are not a victim.*
- *Be yourself*
- *This too shall pass*

There's some from my stepfather, Ted, as well.

- *Learn to enjoy living with yourself.*
- *Look at yourself in the mirror, smile and say hello!*
- *As he spoke Hebrew he often said 'Im ein ani li mi li' which is one of the wisest sayings in Hebrew. It means, 'if I will not care for myself, who will?'*

I woke up at 5.45 am on New Year's Eve, four days after my last successful bowel movement. At least I'd managed to get a decent eight hours of sleep. It was grey skies outside, humid and foggy. Early morning bird songs added a gentle touch of magic to the scenario.

In the interest of assisting my bowels I'd kept eating my chia jam & almond butter on buckwheat toast, vegetarian poke bowls and berry smoothies. The day before I'd tried a psyllium husk drink as well. I'd been drinking ample amounts of water, eating coconut yogurt and some brown rice sushi. After four days I felt stumped. What was the solution? Is a bowel movement really too much to ask for? Best to just relax

I settled once more into my retreat, surrounded by all that I have.

I went through my morning rituals then became conscious once again of how loud and obvious my breathing was.

I lay down in the hope of coaxing a bowel movement, massaging my belly in a clockwise circular motion, a technique I had learned at a macrobiotic retreat in the nineties. I pressed gently on the colon and bowel tract, round and round for several minutes. Ah, yes... I could feel something. There was dense matter in there... but I could feel movements within the mass.

It was happening!

Time for some throne sitting.

Breathe, relax, smile.

At last... an easy but firm discharge!

"Hooray!" yes... I actually said 'hooray' out loud.

After the incredible relief of my first bowel movement in over four days, I set out to take on another first since treatment. Being such a mild morning, I ventured outside and went for a walk around the block. It was 6.15 am and I felt pleased with what I'd achieved in the first half hour of the day.

Being New Year's Eve, I spent the evening reflecting on recent events and writing about them in my journal.

Feeling a bit more relaxed when I woke up on New Year's day, I played the video of the Sydney fireworks I'd left recording the night before and celebrated 2023 with some brown rice nori rolls. I'd refreshed these by panfrying them in a little black sesame oil. This is a good tip, putting sushi in the fridge dries out the rice but panfrying the leftovers makes them delicious. My chai tea was less tasty than usual though, as my taste buds were suffering. Still, I was taking care and being kind to myself.

A few days later my breathing had slowed, like it was telling me my lungs didn't have enough space. I'd stayed at home since New Year, feeling out of breath whenever I used the stairs and I needed to lie down more often. I felt my body around my lungs and could sense a swelling.

I called my oncologist and explained the symptoms.

"That's not good," he said. "You need to go to emergency at Cabrini. I'll let them know you're coming."

After heading to the hospital in an Uber and then checking in with the triage nurses, I was taken to my own room at emergency where I was seen

SOFT MILLET WITH CAULIFLOWER

Hulled millet is easy to digest and a little sweeter than other wholegrains.

Ingredients:

- 1 cup leftover cooked hulled millet (See *My Wholefood Community Cookbook* or YouTube channel for best method to cook hulled millet)
- 5 cups water- alkalised filtered
- ½ cup finely chopped cauliflower
- Pinch sea salt
- Dried herbs or seasoning

Method:

- Place leftover cooked hulled millet, cauliflower, sea salt and water in saucepan
- Put lid on saucepan and place over a high flame
- Bring to a boil and reduce the flame to medium-low
- Let the ingredients cook over medium-low heat for 10-15 minutes
- When finished cooking, remove the lid, mash the ingredients and spoon into serving bowl
- Sprinkle with dried herbs or seasoning

to by a comforting doctor and the nursing staff. Lying on the bed, attached to blood pressure monitors, all I could do was relax into the experience and wait... and wait... and get a little impatient... and then wait... and wait. Eventually, after about five hours, I was taken to have another pleural effusion.

There was just the one room where this complex procedure could be carried out. But, despite there being other bookings for that day, the doctors managed to slot me in during the afternoon and I was on my way home with Gab,,, just in time for dinner.

It led me to reflect on how, throughout all my challenges, I've always thrived by supporting myself with well thought out and learned lifestyle choices. I don't panic and think about how to deal with situations in the best and easiest way possible, *the path of least resistance*. The philosophy behind this has served me well since my visit to the Sedona vortex.

Also, plant-based nutritional foods have proven to me beyond doubt that they are what I need and that they are what works best for me.

It's not about weight loss, it's about maintaining my compromised immune system and my mental stability.

During my time spent in Bali, travelling in the USA and India, where I spent time at ashrams and health retreats, as well as while I've been at home, I've read great spiritual and nutrition books. The tools and skills that I've learned from these books all come into play when facing mortality and dealing with life's more difficult times.

And I've found this inner work is invariably rewarded when confronted with a crisis, like the need for the pleural effusion that day. I found myself wondering how well I might have coped without having nurtured my mind and body so conscientiously throughout the years.

Among the people I'd chosen at that stage to tell about the new round of chemo was Graham, who was mentoring me for this memoir. We'd had a few Zoom sessions by that stage, and I was comfortable with where we were heading. But now, my desire to get my memoir done had become more urgent than ever.

I'd discovered the impact of this new treatment regime was going to be different from the first. So much was starting to be impacted this time that hadn't been such a problem before. Chemo-brain, it's a word that gets tossed about quite a bit and its definition is quite broad, covering everything from difficulty remembering things to a general fogginess that makes it difficult to think in general. As well as dealing with that,

QUICK COMFORT SWEET POTATO MASH

It's easy to steam or boil sweet potato to make a mash. So easy and tasty to eat it with homemade green miso pesto.

GREEN MISO PESTO

Topping for pasta, noodles and stir-fries.

Ingredients:

- 150g   spinach leaves
- 1½ Cup   fresh basil leaves
- 50g   fresh walnuts, cashews or seeds (you can use pine nuts)
- 2 Small   garlic cloves, chopped
- 2 Tbsp   lemon juice
- 2 Tbsp   miso paste (I like using white shiro miso here, but for a stronger, saltier flavour you can use darker genmai or mugi miso)
- 2 Tbsp   extra virgin olive oil

Method:

- Wash greens and drain
- Roast nuts in a low, pre-heated oven for 8-10 minutes. remove and allow to cool.
- Place half the spinach and all basil leaves in a food processor and add the remaining ingredients (except for the olive oil). Blend until the mixture is evenly chopped.
- Add the remaining spinach and oil and pulse on and off for a coarse puree consistency. Add a little water if required.
- Serve as desired.

when I sat down at my computer to try and put some words down, I found that my eyesight had been impacted too. There were other side effects that had hit harder than before as well. Once again, the peripheral neuropathy in my hands made it difficult to do simple tasks like putting on shoes. But the big problem with the chemo-brain and failing eyesight was that it prevented me from working as much as I would have liked on my memoir.

I called Graham. "It's back," I said. We had a conversation where he expressed his surprise and sadness that I'd had to return to the day cancer treatment centre.

"Well, I'm happy to continue with the Zoom sessions whenever you're ready," he said.

"I can't do it though, Graham. I can't write. And I'm worried that I'm running out of time. I'm going to need you to do it for me."

"So, you want me to act as your ghostwriter?"

"Well, yes. I guess that's what you'd call it. It still needs to be my story, as told by me. But I need you to write it."

"Gee, Sandy. I don't know. I'm not really qualified to do that."

"That's what you said about the mentoring... and you've been terrific. I got so much out of the sessions we've done so far. You're the only one who can do this for me."

It took a bit of convincing, but Graham eventually agreed to take it on the extended role.

I should say that I do understand that it's not the norm to be so upfront about having someone ghostwrite your memoir. But I figured in this instance it's important as Graham and his efforts have effectively become a part of the story. What I've since learned is that your ghostwriter is someone that you ultimately have to share your most personal details with if they're to have a good and thorough understanding of your life story. You have to share details with them that your own family aren't aware of. It's a degree of trust that is unique in that they are given license to tell your story but with an understanding of the nuances of discretion required to allow the story to be told in a manner that is respectful to the sensitivities of others within that story. You need to ensure that they

To satisfy the need for a sweet taste.

STEWED ORGANIC FRUIT WITH ORGANIC COCONUT YOGHURT

It's easy to steam or boil sweet potato to make a mash. So easy Kuzu is a Japanese starch which has anti-inflammatory health benefits eg strengthen the stomach and intestines. See more info in My Wholefood Community Cookbook or via google.

Ingredients:
- 2 ½ Cups filtered water or pear or apple juice
- 1 Cup pear sliced
- 1 Cup apple, slice
- ½ Cup organic currents, raisins or chopped dried dates or a mix of all.
- Pinch sea salt
- 2 Tbsp kuzu, diluted first in ½ cup water
- Organic coconut yoghurt as topping

Method:
- Peel fruit if preferred then slice.
- Place the dried fruit and water or juice in a saucepan.
- Add a pinch of sea salt, bring to boil, then reduce the flame to medium-low
- Simmer 5-10 minutes
- Add the fruit slices, cover and simmer about 3-4 minutes
- Turn the flame to low and add the diluted kuzu, stirring constantly to avoid lumping
- Simmer until the kuzu forms a thick clear sauce
- Serve as is or with organic coconut yoghurt.

Variations - Sometimes I use other fruit such as blueberries, raspberries, strawberries.

understand who you are as a human being to the extent that they are able to write something from your viewpoint. That means there can't be any secrets.

On the morning of the second round, David arrived to pick me up. As per usual, he arrived with a super healthy berry smoothie for me. It reminded me of how he did this every time he picked me up to take me to my chemo treatments in 2020.

I certainly didn't plan to start this ritual again but at least it feels familiar and full of supportive nourishment. Although his smile is probably even more nourishing than the smoothie itself. I will be forever grateful to David for all he's done during these toughest of times in dealing with my cancer and other issues in my life. His witty presence while driving me to the hospital ensured that I arrived each time with a positive attitude and a smile on my face. It's a reminder that this kind of caring and positive friendship is without doubt one of the key ingredients in any worthwhile recipe for living.

Returning to Cabrini Malvern. I went to see my oncologist. Then, went upstairs to the fourth floor oncology unit and the day treatment centre with its many people sitting in their chairs preparing for or already receiving their chemical cocktails. My chair had a great view over Melbourne City and the bay. I draped my special travelling shawl over the chair then organised my headphones, iPad, iPhone, berry smoothie and snacks of nuts and dates so I had easy access to them all. Then I surrendered to the chair and let the nurses do their thing.

The next morning, I moved slowly and tentatively through my Qi-gong, meditation and other morning rituals, including my favourite pastime of watering the garden. As I watched the water glisten on the leaves of my plants, I thought again about the challenges of living on my own as I kept news of my treatment discreet.

> For dehydration and for cooling tastebuds, make ice cubes to suck on or to add to water as needed.
>
> ## CUCUMBER ICE CUBES
>
> - 2 cucumbers peeled and seeded.
> - Blend with 2 cups water.
> - Pour into ice cube trays and freeze.

With the few friends and family, who were in the know, all I hoped for from them was to at some stage do or say something kind, to be thoughtful. You'd be amazed at how much random acts of kindness mean so much when faced with the heavy burden of a cancer diagnosis.

Send a card, send flowers, bring a punnet of blueberries... anything at all can make a difference.

One of my friends cooked a recipe of mine and sent a photo. This meant so much to me. It's become a very happy and fond memory that came at a time when happy, memorable moments were in relatively short supply.

The next day was a better day, albeit quite hot outside. Inside though, it was cool and pleasant.

The following days became a blur of sleeping and lying about in my wondrous retreat on couches and beds in the bedrooms. I just went with it, feeling there was little other option. The most I was willing take at night was my medically prescribed THC/CBD oil and melatonin in the days that followed.

By the sixth night, the fatigue had shifted and lightened its impact. So much so that the next day I could walk with my shopping trolley to the supermarket and health food shop near my home. And, knowing that it would dry fast on the hot Melbourne summer's day, I even managed to do some laundry. Ah, the delicious aroma of fresh sheets became so powerful after five nights of putrid chemical odours pouring out of my body… out of every crevice… permeating the air throughout my home. Candles, incense and natural body lotions… I used them all as they nourished me and evoked thoughts that took me beyond awareness only of the treatment I'd received on the Monday.

When developing recipes for living with cancer, aromas are crucial. Especially while the sense of smell is reduced but still functional.

A week after the treatment, a THC/CBD oil-fed afternoon brought me to a sense of inner peace. I was in my paradise.

It made me acutely conscious of how happy I was with my lifestyle moving through this stage of my life. At the age of sixty-six, I was facing the fact that cancer existed in my body. And yet it wasn't always consuming my thoughts. My body had cancer, but I felt my mind and spirit did not. It was something that kept me enthusiastic and enjoying every day. I was feeling more equanimity in my life… a sense of calmness and composure as I balanced all the aspects of dealing with the medical challenges of chemotherapy, coupled with the accompanying immunotherapy, and all that these brought to my physical state. I accepted the fatigue, the swelling around my belly, the loss of words somewhere in the chemo haze, the need to rest. I accepted it and let myself just be.

I recalled how, in a time not long before then, a yoga teacher friend of mine had said goodbye to all his social media. He'd done so in a beautiful manner, letting his followers know that he was going into a period of retreat, of rest and privacy. I reflected on that and completely understood where he was coming from and why. The recollection helped and comforted me as I embraced my solitude.

I've come to realise over the years that, even though I'm outgoing and socially confident, having loved my career, public speaking, travelling, and generally enjoyed being out and about, I'm actually more of an introvert than most people realise. After stepping out into the world, I've always relished slipping back into my own space and retreating for a while. It

This is a favourite soup that is easy to make and certainly tasty and nutritious to eat during the chemo process.

RED LENTIL BEETROOT SOUP

Serves 4–6 big bowls

Keeps refrigerated for up to 3 days. Good to keep some in the freezer for the times when you don't feel like cooking.

Ingredients:

- 1 tbsp Sesame oil
- 1 large Onion, medium diced
- 1 cup Red lentils
- 2 medium Carrots, chopped
- 2 large Beetroot, peeled and chopped
- 5 cups Water
- 8 cm Wakame sea vegetable, dried
- 3 Bay leaves
- 3 tbsp Miso paste (I use Spiral Food Organic Genmai)
- To taste Black pepper, ground
- Garnish Parsley, chopped
- 1–2 tsp Plum vinegar (I use Spiral Foods Plum Vinegar – Ume Su)

Method:

- Soak wakame in enough water to cover until soft (approx. 10 minutes), remove stem and chop. Retain soaking water to add to soup.
- Wash and drain red lentils.
- Heat oil in a large soup pot and sauté onion for 5 minutes, stirring with wooden spoon.
- Add lentils, carrots, beetroots, water, chopped wakame and bay leaves then bring slowly to boil.
- Reduce heat (use a flame diffuser if you have one) and simmer for 40 to 45 minutes, or until lentils and vegetables are softened. Turn off heat.

- Remove bay leaves and discard.
- Puree in a blender or food processor then return to pot.
- You can leave it a bit chunky if you like. (I often use my stick blender and I'm careful with not scratching good saucepans.)
- Dissolve miso paste in ½ cup water then mix into soup. You can also add a little miso paste to individual soup bowls if desired.
- If the soup is too thick for you, add more water.
- When serving, sprinkle with black pepper and garnish with chopped parsley and a dash of plum vinegar (Ume Su).

allows for a return to inner peace again after being engaged with so many others, hearing their stories and the issues they're dealing with, and seeing so much of the injustice in the world.

It takes time to let go of what I have heard and seen. Perhaps this is because of a tendency to psychoanalyse as I endeavour to understand the world and where the people who I cross paths with are coming from. Whenever I go through such an experience, it makes me yearn for home, a space where I feel more comfortable than being in a room or restaurant full of loud people, all wanting to be heard but not keen on listening.

My inner life allows me to put my thoughts into words, to think and to let go. I've often put my thoughts on paper, a practice that has become a rich resource for this memoir.

All the spiritual experiences and teachings I've accumulated over so many years kicked into gear as I settled into my renewed chemo regime. Meditation, mindfulness and nutritional knowledge have developed into the strong and robust pillars of my life. I had succeeded in creating a home that truly was (and still is) my sanctuary. The whole of the downstairs area looks out onto my beloved plants and contains all my favourite things. Everywhere I look there are artworks, books, collectibles and other items, all holding a meaningful place in memories of my travels and times spent living immersed in other cultures. It seems so natural to me that I've landed where I am now, in my perfect museum of life. It's there, everywhere that I look, while writing this and reclining on my lounge room couch, taking in occasional glimpses of the *Australian Open Tennis*, there were wonderful items all around me: a sign on my shelf from The Museum of Sex in New York City, a collage of two hands by a wonderful artist going by the name of Salvo who I met at an urban and fine art studio in Melbourne called the Blender Studio, my mother's beautiful Venetian glass bowl, and looking outside at the tall Robinia tree with its luminous lime green leaves.

A few days later I took my shopping trolley from the garage and prepared for the walk to the nearby shops to buy supplies of must-have organic coconut ice cream, organic salad mix and a bulk package of toilet paper. After all, there's nothing quite like being prepared, and I'd been starting to feel like I was up to it.

However, once I'd showered and dressed, it became apparent that it wasn't going to happen that day. I simply didn't have enough air coming into my lungs to walk that distance. It felt like it was flooded with excess fluid again. I saw it as a sign. Any exertion led to shortness of breath and feeling drained of energy.

I chose to lie down for a while before making the decision to drive. Fortunately, I found a parking spot that was close, courtesy of my disability parking permit, another one of those new necessities as an ingredient in my *recipes for living*. I initially didn't think that I'd need the permit but the reality was that I couldn't walk far and I ended up grateful to have one.

With the shopping done I felt relieved that I'd made the decision to drive. I got home and took some of my THC/CBD drops, ensuring I rested well as I lay on my bed throughout that Sunday afternoon.

Once again I looked out at the lime-green of my Robinia leaves over the grey sky, enjoying the warmth of the afternoon. I had a busy week ahead as Graham was going to be flying down to spend the week trawling through my diaries and recording interviews that probed details of my life. Details that I struggled to remember. Details that would find their way into this book so my private life would become public knowledge.

As part of the preparations Gab came over with some food shopping and helped with some housework. The gardener came over and blew away the dead leaves and did what he could to freshen up the garden. It seemed like every day when I looked at my garden I found myself thinking of a Chinese proverb that Peter and I saw on a plaque in a New Delhi garden, I think it might have been at the Imperial Hotel, *'If you want to be happy for a day, get drunk. If you want to be happy for a month, get married. If you want to be happy for life, become a gardener'.* It felt so pertinent as I gazed across my courtyard full of delights.

Cancer or no cancer, life goes on, including some of the more difficult and confronting tasks. Mum and Ted's estates were still in the process of being finalised, and now, their property (other than the family home which had already been sold), was officially in the hands of my brother Michael and myself.

Because of David's extensive experience in property management, I called him seeking advice on the current lease contract for the property. I connected David with my lawyer and again felt grateful that he'd come into my life. He's the gift that just keeps giving.

But that wasn't the only contract I had to deal with. There was also the one between me and Graham, ensuring we were both protected and had a fair arrangement.

Having sold almost all the copies of my cookbook's initial print run, I decided it was time to make it available as 'print on demand' where individual copies of the book are printed as people order it through online booksellers around the globe. That's fortunately an area where Graham has a lot of experience. So, I arranged for him to go through the details of the file preparation with Russel from Hive Design, who had designed the book and felt blessed to have acquired a network of people who, between them, could solve so many issues.

Next on my 'to do' list was the need for a new dishwasher. David and I went to an appliance store, found the one that suited me and made the purchase. I love quick decisions!

Chemo Conversations

"I remember it so well... what were we talking about?" That's a pretty good way of summing up what chemo-brain can do to you. I was feeling quite lost. And I was getting concerned about Graham's progress on the memoir. I wanted to feel sure that it'd be finished with plenty of time for me to enjoy taking it out to the world.

"How's it going?" I'd ask him.

"It's good... I'm just trying to sort out the timelines..."

I soon realised it was going to require more than just regularly emailing and talking on Zoom. He was going to have to spend some time with me, in Melbourne, to become immersed in my lifestyle... to have access to all the artefacts of my life.

"I think you need to come down and spend a week with me in Melbourne. I'll pay for the airfares and you can stay at my place."

"Do you think that's really necessary?" he replied. "We're managing to work our way through in the Zoom sessions..."

"I think it's important. There's so much more we'll be able to get through if you come down and get away from all your other distractions." And, can I tell you? Graham had plenty of other creative projects on the go that were keeping him from getting through the memoir at the pace I'd hoped for. But they were also distractions that contributed to what made him the right person for the job in the first place. All of them were related to creativity of one kind or another. Distractions like the writers and arts festival that he'd founded and continued to run at the time in Maitland. And in his author services business, he found it hard to say no to those who needed a helping hand. He's a man who believes deeply in community.

"Okay," he finally said. "I think you're right. It *will* make a big difference."

"There's also a memoir that I've just read that I think would be worth your while looking at, *Between Two Kingdoms: A Life Interrupted*. It's by Suleika Jaouad, a journalist living with cancer. I can really relate to her story and I think it'll make a big difference if you have a read of it. The whole style of how she's written it... I'd love my book to have a similar feel." The New York Times best seller documents Suleika's odyssey through illness, healing, and self-discovery. Its title, *Between Two Kingdoms* is a reference to a concept Susan Sontag put forward: that we have dual citizenship in the kingdom of the sick and in the kingdom of the well.

"Okay, I'll download a copy and check it out." I wasn't sure at the time how serious he was about having a look, but sure enough, he did buy a copy which he all but finished reading by the time he reached Melbourne.

And so it was that in late January 2023, Graham arrived at my doorstep with his backpack and computer bag for the first of what would become many trips to my home in Elsternwick, Melbourne.

"You were right about Suleika's book," he said as he entered. "I'm inspired by it. The way that she's used a narrative approach and frequently allows snippets of dialogue to bring the reader into the story. It's pretty much the direction I'd wanted to take in the first place, but it's so well executed."

As he entered into my world it made an immediate impact on his understanding of my life. The art, the garden, the sense of order. It all contributed to my home being a sanctuary.

Over the course of these trips, Graham would meet some of my dearest friends, like Jenny, Peter K, David and Gab. He ate with me in some of my favourite restaurants and cafes and he became familiar with the uniqueness of the area I live in and my daily routines. But most important of all was going through the 'boxes' and the long explorations of memories they led to.

Working through the boxes holding my memories

I probably should explain here that, during the 90's, I was inspired by a practice of Andy Warhol's that I'd read about. At the end of every year, he would place items that held special memories of that year into a box that he'd then place in storage on a shelf. It was like creating an annual time capsule. He saw them as a means of instilling a sense of order in a chaotic world. I actually saw some of them on one of my visits to New York and again in Melbourne. I felt so inspired that I decided to take on the practice for myself, and that decision was about to pay a big dividend.

I'd lie on my black velvet couch in the living room while Graham collected the boxes from the garage. Then we'd work our way through the contents, with Graham recording our conversations as we went. Many of the boxes had diaries among the contents and, whenever Graham came across one of these, he'd methodically photograph each page to go through in detail later, questioning me as he came across particular points of interest. It allowed him to visit a place inside my thoughts and memories I'd never shared with anyone before. Not my closest friends, not any of my partners over the years, not even my mother.

It would've made quite a sight when we were sitting there, very much like the stereotypical image of the therapist with their client lying on the couch. These sessions would typically last for two or three hours, with both of us exhausted by the end. It was especially difficult for me. Living on my own, I was unaccustomed to spending so much time immersed in such in-depth conversation. And the chemo-brain made such endeavours far more tiring than they'd normally be.

But the memories the process triggered were at times astounding!

And it wasn't just from discovering the gems from the past hidden within those boxes. It was from the ensuing discussions as well, some of which lasted several hours.

Sometimes it might have started from seeing a restaurant menu I'd kept, or a ticket from an exhibition or stage show.

Graham also bore witness to my morning rituals, meditation, Qi-gong, exercise, and the time I'd spend tending to my garden (plus the myriad medications and supplements I took each morning).

And it became an introduction for him to Jewish culture. Something that, despite having had many Jewish friends over the years, he'd never really experienced before coming to my home in Elsternwick – where Jewish culture is all around you.

As Graham spent more time at my home, forensically exploring my past, the timeline of my life started to drift into better focus, for me as well as for him.

I shared other aspects of my life with him during those stays: my love of tennis (one of his stays was during the Australian Open. So we'd finish each day watching the main match of the day), my love of cooking and my art collection... a reflection of so much of my inner self.

There were afternoons and evenings spent working through the decades of photo albums, another process that triggered one memory after another, taking me back to those moments and also helping to further clarify parts of the timeline that had still been unclear. Likewise with my book collection. And speaking of books, there was another book that I really wanted Graham to read. One day, while we were out for lunch in Elsternwick, I took him to the Avenue Bookshop and bought him a copy of Viktor Frankl's *Man's Seach for Meaning*. Once he'd read it a few days later, he understood why it was so important to me (more on that later).

Graham's stays were a unique experience for both of us. I was sharing incredibly intimate details of my life with a trust that went beyond what is normally reserved for special partners. Many of those details are too intimate and personal to appear in this book. But for Graham to be able to write the book from *my* perspective, he had to have an appreciation of that most private side of myself, so much of which I've never shared before.

Our 'chemo conversations', as we came to call them, led to the scope of the book evolving. For example, on his first trip down there was a conversation that revolved around the content of one of my diaries.

"Reading through this diary from your trip to India in '82, it seems like you and Peter had quite a turbulent relationship," he said.

"Actually, I think I'd rather not mention Peter. There were things that didn't go well in that relationship, so I think it's better left out altogether. I don't think he'd be happy about it. In fact, I think maybe it's better not to spell out any details about my relationships. That's not what the book's about."

"Well," replied Graham, "I think you might want to revisit that. If you want readers to connect with you, they need to see you as a full person. Relationships that do or don't work are a fundamental part of being human. I personally think it's important that you have them in there, even if the names are changed. Perhaps it's worth talking to Peter and seeing how he feels about it?"

"No, I'm really not comfortable with it."

"Well, how about for the time being it stays in there but with another name as a placeholder? Then we can make a final decision later."

"Okay, but rather than a name, just refer to him as 'P'."

And so it was that for the next six months Peter's name was represented as P___.

This changed as we delved further into my life and relationships. As that story started to unfold, I began to see that yes, it was important to include these episodes. Why the change of heart? There were several reasons. The whole process of going through my life was allowing me to see some events in a different light, somewhat detached from the emotions of the time. I was starting to see my life from a more holistic perspective.

Over time, Graham interviewed many of my friends and colleagues both in person and on Zoom. Then one day he asked, "How about if I talk to Peter on Zoom? I still think it's really important to include him."

By this stage I was warming to the idea of including him, and Graham had already talked to Ian and Jim, two of the other important relationships in my life and ones that I'd had no issue with featuring in the story, both having had such a huge impact on my direction during the times I was with them. "I'll give him a call and we'll see."

I called him then and there. And his response?

"Yeah, I'd be happy to talk to Graham."

When Graham spoke to him on Zoom, they got on well. They talked at length about the relationship with its ups and downs, and how both of us had felt sadness and heartache when it never quite worked out. But the conversation went further. They also spoke about how happy we were that we'd managed to maintain a lifetime friendship. Peter is actually one of the most likely friends to call from time to time just to see how I'm travelling… something that I greatly appreciate.

Peter was also happy for his name to appear in the book and for the warts and all tale of our time together to be shared.

There were other important introductions while Graham was staying with me. Like Tom, who I'd got to know in Bali, and who knows how to turn any story into a humorous adventure. He came to visit one day while Graham was in Melbourne and re-told in hilarious detail the story of an intrepid sailing troupe that went on an epic journey to Komodo Island. And there was Geoffrey, who, on the spur of the moment we spoke to together one afternoon on Zoom while he was holidaying with his family in Bali.

Graham was there when Ryan, my exercise physiologist and personal trainer, came over, guiding me through an exercise regime that was tailored specifically for my needs. He explained to Graham in detail why each exercise was included and the importance of people going through cancer treatment doing daily exercises where possible.

It's truly wonderful that so many aspects of this memoir writing process have ultimately proved to be therapeutic. And importantly, the time spent with Graham has led to our professional relationship developing into a very special and unique friendship. The most difficult times during his multiple stays at my home in Elsternwick have been when I've come downstairs the day after his departure to realise that he's gone.

You may be wondering, is it Graham's words or mine that you're reading right now? Well, throughout the book, Graham has worked hard to take the details from our conversations, my diaries, his conversations with my friends and his own observations, then translate them into a contextually coherent storyline. I've then gone through and made notes on what I felt didn't fit with my 'voice' so Graham could fine tune the narrative into his refined version of my 'voice' before passing each section on to the editor, Brian.

The whole process has certainly yielded results. The raw honesty within the content of this book is testament to the importance of having flown him down on those occasions throughout 2023 and 2024 for our chemo-conversations. For me, they also became a significant ingredient in my *recipes for living* and a wonderous way of reflecting on my life.

Why not take a Holiday?

I sat down in Professor Richardson's office. "I've got good news," he said. "Your results are looking really good. The tumour's almost gone... there's not much fluid left at all."

"So, I'm managing to beat it again?"

"It would seem so. We're still going to have to continue chemo and immunotherapy into the future, albeit at lower doses. These results are extraordinary. Whatever it is you've been doing, keep doing it. There's no doubt in my mind that it's made a difference."

Once again, I had what appeared to be a vindication for everything I'd dedicated my life to... and my oncologist had just acknowledged it as well. It was now abundantly clear that my approach to nutrition and both physical and spiritual well-being had been working to help the treatments do their job. I'm not trying to suggest that it was my approach on its own that was responsible for the good results. Like when I'd gone into remission the first time, it was a combination of everything, with the treatment Professor Richardson had prescribed topping the list.

I found myself needing to seek qualification on one key point though. "So, when you say 'into the future' what exactly does that mean?"

"It means that you'll need to continue with this lighter course for the rest of your life."

I nodded my head in response as the words *rest of your life* sank in.

He'd told me before I'd started this renewed treatment that it would be ongoing, but it was still difficult to accept those words.

The lighter chemical load made a difference. One of the three ingredients in my previous chemical cocktail, carboplatin, was now off the menu, leaving just Pemetrexed and the immunotherapy, Pembrolizumab. And Carboplatin? Well, that was the main culprit for some of the nastier side effects.

It *did* make a difference, a big one. When I got home from my new, lighter treatment I called a few close friends and family members to share my good news.

While I still needed to regularly stop and rest, I was feeling more like my old self. There were also parts of my morning routine that remained a testament to the fact that I was living with cancer.

Aside from always showering after my meditation (which I'd now started to do while still in bed), attending to skin care and putting on my day clothes (I'm not a 'hanging around in night clothes and dressing gown' kind of gal), I'd then go downstairs, raise the blinds in the living room to reveal the courtyard garden and do my seven minutes of Qi-gong.

You may have got the feeling by now that these morning rituals are, in my experience, an essential ingredient to a positive mental and health-supportive *recipe for living*, particularly when dealing with health challenges.

What are your morning routines and rituals? Do they support you in being present and aware of life's precious moments? Do they help you in setting your positive intentions for the day and beyond? I know this is true for me. The more I practise and experience these routines, the less reactionary I've become to situations outside of myself that I can't control... the outside forces and issues in the world. This helps me process, cope and maintain equanimity. I'm in the 'post work' side of life and, as I mentioned earlier, I don't feel the need to engage in daily news stories (although I do keep abreast of what is happening overall), this makes it easier to feel grateful while living with cancer.

I'd follow these rituals up by beginning on the updated morning supplements and medications. I mixed Nutrition Care Gut Relief with Turkey Tail, Reishi Powders and Wonderfoods Vitamin C Powder (I've always preferred powders to tablets for supplements). Then added to that a few drops of Bioceuticals Zinc Drops and Selenium into Water. After that I'd take a Bioceutical Ultrabiotic 60 supplement.

With the first of the day's supplements out of the way, I moved on to the medications, starting with the ones that had to be taken *before* eating.

After a light breakfast I had other medications to take that required a full stomach. In all, there were four separate medications to take each morning.

Later in the day I'd have some Vital Greens powder in water, take a CoQ10 supplement and most days, a B12 lozenge and folic acid. (another recommendation for those on chemo and immuno).

During my next oncology appointment with Professor Richardson, I mentioned that Michael and Lilli were planning a trip to Israel. "I wish I could go too," I said... of course I did! I've always wanted to go too.

"I can't see why not," he replied.

"Really? You think I can go overseas?"

"Sure you can. What's the point in keeping yourself alive if you can't actually *live* a bit. And Israel's got a good health system in place. If you have any issues while you're over there, you'll have good support." I could barely believe what I was hearing. "You'll need a break from the chemo when you go though." Even better!

I called Michael and said, "You know the trip you and Lilli have booked? Can I come too? The doctor says I'm good to travel."

Michael and Lilli were thrilled that we could all go together. It would be a chance to catch up with our cousins in Israel.

This was the best news I'd heard in years. A month later I had the final round of chemo and immuno before I was scheduled to fly out. While my energy levels were low for the following two days, I found myself lost in thoughts of how the treatment left me feeling high but in a haze, as the chemicals worked their way through my body.

I discussed the upcoming trip with Claudia. "You'll need to look after your nervous system," she said. "Remember, self-preservation is a gift. You're going into a volatile environment. You're going to have to be very mindful of remaining in the present. Don't let other people's anxieties impact on you." I imagined myself moving around inside a bubble that would push away any of those anxieties she mentioned. With Claudia's help, I trained my being, my mind. I used conscious relaxation as I shifted my perception to focus on the true nature of the people I encountered. The mind doesn't need to succumb to the violence of the times. It can shift into a genuinely healthy way of living. I even worked out a simple routine that helped me achieve this:

- Consciously relax.
- Come back to your senses.
- Engage an attitude of friendliness.
- Smile.
- Breathe.

This was going to be a crucial ingredient for me to include in my *recipe for living* while travelling again.

Arriving at the airport was so different to when I'd last travelled. While I was given the green light to travel by my oncologist, I was still very weak and suffered a lack of physical stamina. But I'd found out that I could ask for special assistance due to my medical condition. From the moment I checked in, a wheelchair was waiting for me.

I was booked to fly from Melbourne to Tel Aviv via Hong Kong on Cathay Pacific. The flight was delayed on the tarmac for three hours after we'd already boarded, then we all had to deboard with the option to stay overnight at the airport hotel or, as I insisted, go home for the night. Waking up in the morning in my own bed, but with my suitcase nearby, it took a while to remember that I had to get back to the airport to start the journey again.

This time I was to fly domestic to Sydney to catch the Cathay flight to Hong Kong. Everything had been delayed by a day. After landing in Sydney, I was transported in a special van to the international terminal... where the Cathay Pacific staff informed me that I'd have a twenty-hour stopover in Hong Kong for a different flight to Tel Aviv.

I was not impressed, and I let them know.

Four staff spent the next ten minutes furiously focused on their computer screens as they tracked down a flight that entailed less delays. They ended up finding me a seat on an Emirates flight that had a short stopover in Dubai before going on to Tel Aviv.

I settled into my seat after boarding and put on the headphones to listen to the plane's on-board music options, smiling as Julie Andrews sang about the hills being alive with the sounds of music.

How good was this? I was on an international flight again... heading to the *Promised Land* (a title that seemed so pertinent under the circumstances). It was something I hadn't dreamed would be possible when I'd first restarted chemo.

Once we were airborne, I listened to some Coldplay, the band that would be the soundtrack of the flight for me.

And the wheelchair special assistance service? That really made a difference. There's so much walking you need to do in an airport terminal. And when the flight boards, it's the people who are disabled or in wheelchairs who board first. It also affords special attention on landing and going through customs and baggage collection. I highly recommend requesting the special assistance when you book if you need to travel while undergoing chemotherapy. For me, the whole trip wouldn't have been viable without it.

Fourteen hours from Sydney to Dubai, three hours in Dubai airport and four hours later I was in Tel Aviv. I had to pinch myself. It was like walking through a dream hearing the welcome *Shalom* at the airport then arriving at the hotel with the sun shining over the blue Mediterranean Sea. My dream had come true, this was reality.

I luxuriated in the scents, the sounds, and the hustle and bustle as I soon as I left the airport in Tel Aviv. The shops, the beach, the people sitting in cafes talking with great gusto about politics—it all motivated me to keep moving. My breathing was short and I required regular rests. Walking would always be a greater effort than it had been before; after all, a lobe *had* been removed from one of my lungs.

Although I was there with Michael and Lilli, what they wanted to do with their days and what I chose to do often differed, which was absolutely fine. One outing we did go on together was when we went with a cousin to Jerusalem. I just loved being at the Machane Yehuda Market (shuk), taking in all the top quality, fresh produce while working our way through the bustling throng of people. We indulged heartily in the local cuisine, washed down with fabulous coffee and fresh juices. I was in my happy place.

But just the fact that I was able to be there, in Israel, was enough in many ways. I developed a bit of a routine of going for a morning walk, then sitting by the pool for a while and then lunch. Some afternoons I would look down at the Mediterranean from my room on the twenty-second floor for an hour or two. Or perhaps I'd just lie back on the bed and watch a movie. I was on holiday, and I didn't 'need' to do anything in particular other than enjoy just 'being'.

Breakfasts at the hotel were a daily treat. Sitting on the patio overlooking the beach, eating a fresh and delicious Israeli breakfast full of middle eastern and mediterranean delights. I loved the fresh hummus, tahina, salads, fresh-baked gluten-free breads, fresh pomegranate juice. Michael and Lilli joined me most days and I even met a friend from Sydney one morning in the restaurant/cafe. I felt a lightness of being; it was like I was receiving a huge reward for what I'd been through.

A major highlight of this trip to Israel was paying a visit to the *ANU Museum of the Jewish People* located in Tel Aviv University. This cutting-edge museum and cultural centre was a special experience for me. A well-curated story of the Jewish People, strengthening Jewish identity and perpetuating Jewish heritage worldwide. It celebrates the multiculturalism of Jewish diversity and its inclusive, pluralistic approach.

Also on my must-see list was the *Peres Centre for Peace and Innovation*. It was mind blowing to see all the impressive innovations that Israel has offered to the world, from medical, to agricultural to technology. Founded by the late President of Israel, Shimon Peres in 1996, the virtual reality experience was a revelation. Did you know that Israeli scientists developed cherry tomatoes into a tasty, long-lasting and nutritious food? That the USB memory stick was invented by an Israeli high-tech guy? Or that Israel is one of the global pioneers in the use of medical cannabis? The first mobile or cell phone was developed in Israel by Motorola's research and development department in 1973. So many important contributions to the world from such a small population base.

I'd spent three weeks in this special place, with family, enjoying the delicious foods, the bustling cafes and restaurants, and immersing myself in hotel life which was a new-found pleasure. Walking slowly along the beach and enjoying the youthful energy of Tel Aviv, a city that's celebrated as the vegan capital of the world (it has around four-hundred vegan and vegan-friendly kitchens catering to all the veggie lovers there). It was perfect for me but, after three weeks, it was time to go home and return to my 'rest of my life treatment'. How wonderful it was though to know I could travel again despite the therapy.

In the foyer of the Viceroy, Santa Monica, with an inspiration looking over my shoulder

One More Bite of the Big Apple

In October 2023, one of my great fears was realised when my treatment regime was complicated by contracting COVID. This had been one of my great fears since the pandemic first started. Now, I had to deal with it. My breathing became more restricted and it felt like there were knives in my throat. But the calming environment around me, my zen sanctuary, kept me going (along with some THC/CBD oil).

It meant postponing a round of treatment and, after several weeks, I was feeling as though this extra level of ill health associated with COVID might be my new 'forever' normal.

To make matters worse, I got shingles down the back of my right leg. And I'd also managed to fracture a couple of ribs. I was a mess! As much as the THC/CBD helped I needed *Endone* for a couple of days as well. I kept calm by reminding myself over and again that *'this too shall pass'*.

It took quite a few weeks before I recovered (aided by my usual supplements and plant-based food regime) and had Graham come down again. While he was here, walking me through my past, I found myself thinking about my old friend George from the Comedy Club days in Sydney, and his famous line that his show was based around, 'I'm tuff...'. I smiled at the thought of what I'd just been through and how easily that line could have been applied to me.

After Graham left, I was preparing for my next chemo round. Part of the prep the previous day was to take Dexamethasone. This drug that I had to take the day before, the day of and the day after treatment had some interesting side effects of its own. It gave me energy, it caused bloating that made me look and feel like I was pregnant, and it made me *high*! All just part of the routine.

But then when my January appointment with the oncologist rolled around, I got some great news. "I think we can let you take a drug holiday... another break from the treatment," he said. "There's no signs of the cancer there at all. You're essentially in remission again. You're cancer-free. We can let you take time off for good behaviour."

This was the best news! Freed from chemo, I found my body and mind were becoming stronger. I was more willing to take on challenges. I booked in to stay at Gwinganna again, hoping it would help to revitalise me further (while there I sadly had a fall early in the stay which tarnished the experience somewhat).

But more importantly, I planned for one more trip to the States. One more opportunity to meet up with the friends I'd made over there (although this time, I was going all out, flying business class and booking into top hotels. If not now, when?). On the 2nd of May, 2024 I was at the airport waiting for my date with the Qantas Dreamliner that would take me across the Pacific one more time.

Sitting in the airport lounge, I found myself enjoying a flirt with a young Italian guy who prepared a Campari and soda for me. It never would have gone anywhere... my treatments left me with zero libido and my grey hair made me so conscious of just how much older than him I was. But the flirting game? That's always been fun, and I ended up with another Insta friend as a result.

Fifteen hours later, I was heading through customs in LA. I made my way to the Viceroy hotel, across the road from the beach in Santa Monica.

Oh, how Santa Monica and Venice had changed. Some things had remained the same, like the Urth Caffé, famous for its delicious wholefood offerings. Walking around, I also noticed an Australian-run café at Venice Beach,

Bluestone Lane, part of what has become a successful chain in the States. Oh, and the accents... far more variation in accents than what I remembered from previous trips, including a lot more Australians. I would no longer be the novelty that I once was. As I walked the streets exploring, I came across an interesting shopfront called the *Rose Collective*, I asked a guy who was leaving, "What are they selling there?"

"Cannabis products," he replied as he dragged on his vape.

A few minutes later I was walking out with a beautifully packaged box of ten gummies.

What I found sad though, was for the first time in that great city I'd visited so often, I didn't feel particularly safe walking the streets. People seemed to be angrier and more threatening in a way I'd not encountered there before. Was it just that I felt more vulnerable now? No, definitely not. I'd have been sensitive to it if that were the case. It was hard to discern the reason for the change. Was it drugs, could it be a lasting impact from the COVID lockdowns? Who knows? The reality was there had been a change in general for the worse and it was palpable.

On the second day I caught up with Oren for dinner at an upmarket (and noisy) Japanese restaurant in West Hollywood. A few days later I was on a flight to New York City so I could take one more bite out of the Big Apple.

For the first time, I was booking myself into hotel rooms instead of staying in apartments that I'd lined up through my connections. Needing the comfort of a proper hotel room and a cool location, I booked myself into a glamorous and spacious hotel in Soho. And, being on the thirty-ninth floor, my room featured magnificent views. Even while luxuriating in the bathtub, I looked out at the Empire State Building and, from my bed, the east village and Brooklyn Bridge.

The New York City vibes were just the medicine I needed. There's so much to see when you go on walkabouts or ride the subways.

I had never been to a service like this Friday night Jewish service that Ruth took me to before. Lighting candles for Shabbat with prayers, music, delicious food and a wonderful community. It was held at Brooklyn's Gotham Depot Moto, a motorcycle parking area that also hosts events. An amazing and unforgettable experience. The service featured beautiful music of the Sephardic Jews of North Africa and the Ottoman lands. History, tradition, community, art, delicious food and music... all that I love. It was a perfect experience for me.

I went to MOMA, where I soaked up the works of Joan Jonas, Matisse, Picasso and Miro. On the subway later that day I sat next to a guy on the train reciting his Hindu prayers out loud with no one paying him any attention. I smiled at the thought that yes, I was in New York where there's so much that people simply take in their stride.

There were plenty of old friends and connections to catch up with while I was there. Like my old friends from Bali days, Valery and Ruth. Valery launched his latest book of poetry while I was there, featuring artwork by Ruth (I have a few of her beautiful collages in my art collection at home).

Valery Oisteanu is a Soviet-born Romanian and American poet, art critic, essayist, photographer and performance artist. Influenced by the Dada and Surrealist movements, He is the author of more than a dozen books of poetry, short fiction, and essays.

Valery and Ruth also joined me when I went to see John Batiste, the musician husband of Suleika Jaouad, when he performed at a gig in New Jersey. I'd always enjoyed his music, and his connection to the author of *Between Two Kingdoms* made it feel even more special to be able to see him live.

Months earlier in Melbourne, I'd talked to Anna, who I'd worked with organising the AIMA conference years earlier. She now worked as Professor Avni Sali's Executive Assistant at NIIM, where I'd been going for my pre-chemo vitamin and mineral infusions, and we'd stayed in touch throughout the ensuing years. On the day when I'd finished my most recent appointment I'd gone upstairs to her office. "I'm off to New York!" I told her excitedly.

"Oh? I've got a brother living in New York," she said. "He's a photographer... living and working out of the Chelsea."

"Really? I've always wanted to go there."

The hotel had become famous for the artists and bohemians who had lived there... and the artworks they had donated to the hotel over the years in lieu of rent. One of those artists (who arrived there in late 1967, just

"Love Letters" by Lexi Tsien

before Leonard Cohen wrote his famous song about the Chelsea), was the Australian icon Brett Whiteley.

Anna's brother, Tony Notarberardino, a well known photographer, had lived there on the sixth floor since 1994. He, along with a handful of other artists, had refused to move out when the building was bought and renovated. One of those artist's was Australian Vali Myers. Anna's brother has become a keeper of her works and now lives in what was her apartment

I took Valery and Ruth with me to meet him in the Chelsea and discovered they shared many of the same friends (which I guess shouldn't have come as a great surprise). It felt good to be able to travel around the world and still end up bringing like minded people together.

Another person I caught up with was the other Tony, my special lover who I'd caught up with on every trip to New York since we'd first met. As we sat in a Japanese restaurant together and talked at length as old friends, I opened up about the extent of my health issues. I ended up telling him, "I'm so sorry, there won't be any sex this time." He understood, and we had a lovely time together.

While there I also took advantage of having one more opportunity to see the type of shows that New York does so well. *Michael Jackson the Musical, Hell's Kitchen, Water for Elephants* and *Message in a Bottle*... all of them were brilliant!

Without doubt though, one of the most profound moments while I was in New York was when I reached 53rd Street and was struck by the power of Robert Indiana's *Hope!* sculpture. It dawned on me that this whole trip was about hope, and it was hope that had made it possible for me recover from stage 4A lung cancer... to get myself to the point where I could travel across the globe again. That hope was further supported when I returned home from New York and was told that, seeing there was still no sign of the cancer, I was still in remission, with no need for further treatment.

Hope – it's an ingredient at the very heart of any *recipe for living*. The recipes simply can't work without it.

A Last Word

Throughout everything, as I've set out to find the ultimate *recipe for living*... reading through the notes and documents, looking at so many photographs and having the insightful, in-depth discussions with Graham (while I mostly lay on my soft black velvet couch), I now see the key ingredients that are fundamental: relationships, purpose and meaning.

It's important to appreciate that when I'm talking about relationships, I'm meaning it in its broader context, far beyond notions of romantic partnering (not that these don't have their own importance).

I feel blessed to have loved many times. I've had some important romantic relationships throughout my life. There was Ian, a good man who was my first real experience of romantic love and real intimacy. There was Peter, with whom I came to know and understand myself better as the result of our tumultuous relationship. And, naturally, there was Jim, who inspired and influenced me in sharing knowledge about using foods in cooking and foods as medicine (there are a few more romances, but they will remain private). Each of these hold special memories and in each case, an important relationship has been maintained, but its nature has changed over time. A lover has become a friend.

Friendships are one of life's greatest gifts. Friendships are relationships that bring joy and fulfillment into your life. A sharing of minds on levels that create a connection. Some friendships form between people with obvious similarities, while others form over less obvious connections. Throughout this book, I've introduced you to some of the more important friendships I've

The Dubs crew.....Lilli, Max. Jacqui, me, Michael, Lyla, Joel, Marlon

enjoyed in my life. There are those that have been lifelong, and those who have come into my life in more recent times.

There have been the lovers who have briefly swept through my life, many of whom touched a part of my soul, if only for a moment.

A person you meet for just five minutes, five hours or five days can have a profound impact on your life.

Beyond friends there are the professional relationships that develop. Among the most important of these are the relationships I've developed with those involved in the health and wellness movement.

I've had some incredible professional relationships with some of the most extraordinary chefs and leading lights in the world of wellness and nutrition, many of whom have also been friends. I sought out inspirational mentors that add to my chosen life experiences. I've also been blessed with the professional relationships I've enjoyed with the medical professionals who have helped me throughout the years. Then there are some of the foundation relationships…

family. For me, the most important of these has been the relationship I shared with the undoubted love of my life, my mother. Although it's some years now since she passed, I still feel her giving with a warm hand each and every day, as I do my father and stepfather. Meanwhile, Michael, Lilli, their offspring, Marlon and Joel, Marlon's wife, Jacqui, and Marlon and Jacqui's offspring, Max and Lyla are a constant part of my life. We continue to always celebrate our special occasions together and maintain traditions together with family dinners on high Jewish holidays (I still revel in lighting candles on Friday nights, as my Omi and mother have done, to reflect on the week gone past, to bring in light and bless those in my life).

But the most important relationship of all is the one that each of us has with ourselves. You can't hope to have healthy relationships with others if you don't have a relationship with yourself that is built on love, honesty and respect.

To have a healthy relationship with yourself, your life also needs to have purpose and meaning. Do you remember when I mentioned Viktor Frankl's book, *Man's Seach for Meaning* a few chapters back? He wrote it years after having been in the concentration camps during the Holocaust. He'd watched as many people he knew or had met in the camps withered away and passed. He also witnessed those who survived, and he observed something the survivors had in common. Their lives had meaning, a reason to hold on to hope when there was so little else to hold on to. For himself, that purpose was the book that he was working on when he'd entered the camps. His entire manuscript was lost, but remained with him in his head. The desire to rewrite this manuscript so he could publish his book gave his life meaning, something to hold onto. For others, it was the need to connect with a special family member. As long as people had a goal and hope of some kind, it gave their life a meaning and a reason to hold on. He watched many who had no such purpose lose all hope and ultimately pass away.

After the war, Frankl took the observations he'd made while interned in the camps and developed a whole new branch of psychology, *logotherapy*, which is built around the need for life to have meaning.

For me, my pursuit of knowledge about nutrition and wellbeing, along with my desire to share it, has flooded my life with meaning and purpose in so many ways. And it's not just knowledge about wholefoods and how to prepare them, it's also about being in touch with yourself spiritually and physically. About understanding your mind and body and how they are linked. As I've grown in my own understanding, I have always sought to share it, through cooking classes, my cooking video and cookbook, through speaking at conferences and delivering presentations. And now, I've endeavoured to bring it all together in my *Recipes for Living*, a book that aims to accomplish multiple ends. To not just tell my life's story, but to share some of the wisdom that has allowed me to live well into my sixties—despite dealing with the challenges throughout my life that have been the consequence of my earliest brush with cancer. I have learned during this life to live with cancer and make the most of whatever situations I've had to face.

Had I not been diagnosed with cancer at twenty, I may not have followed the path I have and developed the meaning that has become so apparent in my life. There's no point speculating on what may have been under different circumstances. What's important is that I feel happy about the life I've lived and the way I've lived it.

I sincerely hope that everyone who reads this book has been inspired by some of the ingredients for my *recipes for living* in a way that helps them and that it helps each and every reader to embrace meaning in their own life and to appreciate the richness of their relationship with themselves and those around them.

Epilogue

In early June, it was time to visit the oncologist again – and I was concerned. Was it just the extra effort I'd put my body through with the travel? After so many years spent living with cancer and carefully managing my relationship with the disease, I felt sure... it was back again.

The CT scans and blood tests showed I was still all clear.

"I'm concerned," I told him. "I've been getting short of breath – so much more than I'm used to."

"You need to remember, there's a significant proportion of your lung that's been removed," he said. "There's also a good deal of scar tissue in your lungs. That scar tissue itself takes up space. Your lung capacity will never be what it used to be."

I wasn't convinced. But I took what he'd said onboard. It meant adjusting to a new normal, taking more rests and not exerting myself so much.

I've come to know my body and have developed a keen sense of how it reacts when cancer is present.

By mid-August I started feeling out of breath more often. My instincts led me to revisit a respiratory specialist I'd been seeing over the past few years. He conducted the appropriate tests and on my follow-up appointment told me some of the cancer cells had escaped and were taking up more of the space in my lungs. The big C was back again. It was fortuitous that I'd investigated and that this specialist was connected professionally with my oncologist, whose office happened to be next door. He made an appointment for me with

Professor Richardson and, when I went in, I was met with absolute empathy and sympathy by Madeleine, Professor Richardson's personal assistant, whom I'd come to know well by then. It made me feel cared for in the face of this latest diagnosis.

I felt somewhat detached from reality as I sat in Professor Richardson's office and he went through the results, not really listening while he spoke the words that I really hadn't wanted to hear but knew were coming, "You're going to have to go back into chemo and immunotherapy."

A few days later I was sitting in the chair with a cannula in my arm... much the same routine as before.

But it panned out differently this time.

After the first few rounds of treatment, I could tell—it wasn't working.

On Monday, October 28th, 2024, I went to my usual pre-therapy appointment with the Professor.

The news wasn't good.

He confirmed what, in my heart, I already knew, that I wasn't responding to the treatment as I had before. Not only that, but the tumour was now solid and pushing down above my liver. It had also developed more in the pleura of the lung.

You can't possibly know how you'll react to a situation like that until you're faced with it. I don't know how long I sat there absorbing it before responding. It could've been a split second or it could have been a pause of several seconds.

"I don't want to know how long you think I have." I said.

"Of course." After an uncomfortable pause he continued. "There's a clinical trial that's being run, on a new treatment. There's already been a trial in the States and there's one that we're launching here. If you're interested, I can recommend you as one of the participants. There's no placebo control group, just people in the late stages. We want to see if this treatment can help."

I nodded in approval as I took in what he was saying. He presented me with the list of potential side-effects and the conditions for taking part.

One more ray of hope.

A few days later, more bad news... it turned out I didn't qualify to join the trial. "There's other options," Professor Richardson assured me. "There's other trials being run as well; we'll get you into one of them."

But even worse news was to come. The tests showed that I had a perforated bowel that required emergency surgery. It was another week before I was able to leave hospital.

The surgeon who performed that surgery, Doctor Joseph Kong, had this to say, "The day I met Sandra in the hospital, she was a vibrant and resolute woman, surprisingly upbeat despite the severe pelvic infection revealed by her scan, a consequence of a perforated colon. Difficult choices lay ahead; the risks of surgery loomed large, given her precarious condition. Without the operation, though, it seemed unlikely she would recover and would ultimately succumb to the infection. We decided to go ahead with the surgery, navigating the challenges posed by her past major surgery years earlier. To my relief, I successfully removed the infection, and I was profoundly grateful when Sandra sailed through her recovery without complications. Her remarkable ability to heal so swiftly continues to astonish me. Sandra, like many others, brings a smile to my face and reminds me of the joy these moments contribute to my career"

The next trial that I had applied for accepted me. One of the protocols is that I've had to stop taking some of my supplements, especially THC/CBD, which has had its own impact. Then, two weeks into the trial my hair unexpectedly fell out again."

So, dear reader, as you read this, you may be wondering... has the trial been successful? Whatever the results are for me personally, if the results lead to other people making it through in the future, I view that in itself as a success.

It's meaningful to me that my experience can be a useful addition to medical science, as it had been with the treatment I received for Hodgkin lymphoma when I was twenty and the later discovery of the radiation treatment's effect on future health issues.

And I am well-prepared for the inevitable. I've finalised my will and have left clear instructions as to my wants and wishes... finishing this memoir is a high priority.

There's one last thought that I'll leave you with. The Sunday after receiving the unwelcome news, November 3rd, 2024, I celebrated my sixty-eighth birthday.

There's been so much in my life to be grateful for.

I've had loving parents who are still looking after me.

I have an immense, rich inner life and really *do* love who I am as a person and what I do, especially when I consider all the wonderful people in my life.

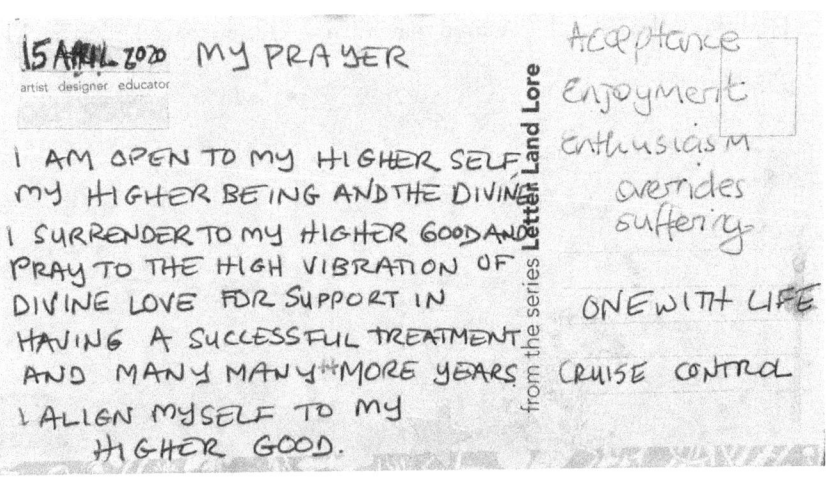

This is a prayer that I wrote down in 2020 and that sits next to my bed so I can recite it each day

And you know what? I still think of myself as a healthy person. Despite living with my health issues, I'm calm, accepting and at peace. Within my life, I've found meaning and purpose. My lifestyle and choices have always been authentically me. Managing discomfort does nevertheless take effort, awareness and understanding and I'm proud of my experiences and knowledge in being able to nurture and look after myself.

I have much appreciation for those who have shown me friendship, genuine interest in my experience and have enjoyed some of my stories… and especially those who have nourished me with simple acts of kindness and natural thoughtfulness in these past years of health challenges (you know who you are).

In one of my favourite quotes from the Dalai Lama (it's my 'go to') he says, "Every day, think as you wake up: today, I'm fortunate to be alive. I have a precious human life. I'm not going to waste it. We can never obtain peace in our outer world until we make peace with ourselves. The goal is not to be better than another man, but your previous self."

I'm so very pleased and honoured that you have chosen to read my story, My *recipes for living*.

L'Chaim *(to life)*.
Sandra Dubs.

Acknowledgements

A big thank you to the Melbourne team of medical, integrative and holistic health practitioners, both past and currently, who support me with real care and also consideration of my needs. These wonderful humans are essential ingredients in my life. Bless you all.

- Professor David Penington
- Dr Jenny Senior OAM -Breast Surgeon
- Dr Nicholas Houseman- Plastic and Reconstructive Surgeon
- Professor Dion Stub- Cardiologist
- A/Professor Alex Voskoboinik -Cardiologist
- Professor Gary Richardson OAM - Academic Medical Oncologist
- Dr Prachi Bhave - Medical Oncologist
- Dr Shehara Mendis -Medical Oncologist
- Dr Joseph Kong -Colorectal Surgeon
- Professor Ian Brighthope
- Professor Avni Sali AM-National Institute of Integrative Medicine (NIIM)
- NIIM Nurses at IV Therapy Clinic and Hyperbaric Oxygen Therapy Clinic
- Dr Peter Holsman – Integrative GP
- Dr Christopher Bagot- GP
- Dr Korina Galatis- GP
- Dr Jerry Zhang – Traditional Chinese Medical Practitioner
- Mr Ehud Tal- Traditional Chinese Medical Practitioner
- Mr Ryan Free- Exercise Physiologist
- Claudia Guersenzvaig – Holistic Psychologist
- Kuniko Yamamoto – Shiatsu Practitioner
- Carla Wrenn - Integrative Naturopath, Nutritionist & Herbalist
- Dina Cherfi - Senior Clinical Research Coordinator (Oncology)

A Word From the Scribe

It's interesting how some of the most important events in your life are the ones that are the most unexpected.

I never could have imagined, when I attended the Byron Bay Writers Festival to deliver a self-publishing workshop with Debbie Lee, that I'd end up spending the following two years ghostwriting a memoir. Having written mostly children's fantasy and dystopian science fiction, memoir writing had simply never been on my radar.

But it seemed fate had intended for me to follow this path, whether I liked or not.

I remember so clearly when I first met Sandy at the Byron festival. I'd just emerged from the bookshop tent with a new novel, freshly signed by the local author. Debbie was standing in the middle of the paddock chatting to a woman I'd never met before. She called out, "Graham, there's someone I want you to meet..."

Five minutes later, Sandy was asking me to act as her mentor while she wrote her memoir.

I tried telling her that I wasn't qualified, that I could recommend someone. She insisted.

I relented.

Despite my apprehensions, during our first Zoom session, I was on comfortable ground. By then, I had a good deal of experience facilitating writers groups and felt at ease with suggesting ways other writers could more succinctly communicate their thoughts.

Sandy had sent through what were initially a collection of short stories.

One of her stories spoke of how she made mud pies while her mother and grandmother were inside cooking traditional family meals. She wrote, and spoke, about her memories of the aromas filling the kitchen. At one point, this was where the memoir was set to begin. But the more I came to know Sandy's story, the more I started to believe the book should start with a bang… literally. The story of how a car crash led to the discovery of her first brush with cancer was just too good an opening to walk past. It was a story that took you straight into the core of what has been the driving force that changed the direction Sandy's life would then follow. The mud pies have still ended up at the front of the book, but as a vignette that gives the reader a small hint of the cultural world the book is largely set in.

Then, in early 2023, came word that Sandy's cancer was back. She was undergoing chemo again and her head was just too foggy for her to continue writing the book herself.

She told me that, instead of mentoring her, she wanted me to be her ghostwriter.

I tried telling her that I wasn't qualified, that I could recommend someone. She insisted. I relented. And I'm so glad that I did.

Writing *Recipes for Living* has been an extraordinary journey (I had strict instructions from Sandy not to use the word 'journey' in the memoir. But hey, this is my bit now… and if I want to use the word 'journey', I will). I think what's surprised me the most is just how many similarities it turns out memoir writing has with fiction. It's a genre that is character driven… a genre where it's important to let dialogue move the narrative forward where possible. Instead of putting myself inside the head of a fictional character, I was putting myself inside the head of a real person, someone I would grow to know better as the process went along. I actually found that aspect of the process far easier than I expected.

The hard part initially was trying to piece together what was a complex and fragmented timeline. Memories are interesting. The brain isn't particularly fastidious with how it catalogues and stores them (a neurosurgeon might argue the point with me on that one, whatever...). Memories get jumbled, especially the complex ones. Trying to untangle Sandy's timeline brought back memories of trying to untangle fishing lines as a kid (even though I'm allergic to fish, fishing was an integral part of being a kid... I never caught anything anyway. Just spent countless hours untangling the line after pitiful attempts at casting it).

It was more than twelve months before the timeline took on some semblance of clarity. Then much of it started to fall into place more easily. Part of what had made it difficult up until then was that Sandy had simply crammed so much into her life, much of it involving complex relationships that didn't quite make sense until the timeline was fully unravelled.

Much of that sorting was facilitated by friends of Sandy's whom we both spoke to along the way. Jenny solved many of the mysteries for me about Sandy's early years living away from home. Geoffery provided clarity about events while Sandy was living in Middle Park.

Throughout all this, I was also slowly getting to know her better. And the more I got to know her, the more I'd find myself reworking earlier sections of the story. Although much of it remained remarkably similar to its first incarnation.

Probably the most difficult task as a ghostwriter is deciding what to let fall by the wayside. The book is already more substantial that I'd imagined it would be. And, if everything Sandy wanted included had ended up within these pages, it would have required multiple volumes.

The difficult balancing act throughout has been to maintain an equal priority on what Sandy has felt is important to include and what I've felt the reader will connect with. Sometimes this has led to divergences in the mutual understanding of where the narrative should flow. And that flow has been of great importance to me while chronicling a life that has followed a few simultaneous threads while encountering major upheavals and sometimes sudden changes in direction.

I find it quite extraordinary that someone who has been through some of the health challenges Sandy has faced has managed to reach such great heights in her chosen field. Her story is a testament to the holistic path of wellness and nutrition she has devoted so much of her life to understanding.

Most importantly though, I'm hopeful you've found a message of hope within these pages. I'm hopeful you've found inspiration, and maybe a recipe or two you'd like to try for yourself. I'm hopeful it has at times stirred emotions of joy and, at times sadness. But most of all, I hope you've enjoyed reading a story of a life well lived under difficult circumstances... a life that it's been my great privilege to have a role in taking to the public.

www.ingramcontent.com/pod-product-compliance
Lightning Source LLC
Chambersburg PA
CBHW072145070526
44585CB00015B/1007